The Next Three Traits

The Psychology of Tension

By: Glenn Gasner

Table of Contents

The Basics of Tension

The Seven Tension Spectrums

Selection Factors (Triggers)

Conclusions

Post Script, Endnotes, References

Dedication

This book is dedicated to everyone who took a personality profiling walk with me, to everyone who answered my endless machine-gun style questions on a night that was supposed to be casual, to everyone who sat on camera for hours answering questions and baring their honest souls, to the 257,335 of you who finished the PersonalityExpert.com personality test and the 169,438 of you who took the eChemistry.com personality test to give me lots of data to work with. This book is dedicated to everyone who let me live in their houses and ask them questions all day long about why they made the choices they did, and to the friends who let me interrupt our flowing conversations to write down the exact words they'd just used. This book only exists because so many of you were patient enough to tell me what the world looks like through your eyes, especially when I asked things so obvious that it was hard to put into words.

Introduction:
Tension Is About The Observer

If two humans look at an object, the person who sees that it's red is experiencing one default world, while the person who sees that it's gray is experiencing a different default world. Both would only know that the other is seeing something different if one verbalized a part that was "obvious." Even then, a colorblind-for-life person and a color-sensitive person would have their own, different definitions of the words "red" and "gray."

Likewise, a person who is flushed with tension when a friend is hurting, when they lose a game, when there's no flavor in their drink, or when they repeat an autopilot motion is experiencing one default world, while a person who feels no tension in those same moments is experiencing a different default world.

The Limbic System acts as a subjective sense organ which detects reasons for pleasure, pain, tension, and satisfaction. There are three families and seven classes of triggers for those feelings. Humans vary in how much emotional drugging is triggered, how easily, and by which inputs. But, just like color sensitivity, tension-sensitivity feels like objective recognition of the exterior world. People don't know they're having an individual experience unless they ask other people to describe parts of reality that are already obvious.

This book shows what it's like to feel the maximum tension and no tension at all from common triggers. What would it feel like if you stopped feeling tension around the things that currently trigger you? What would it feel like if you got flushed with tension around the things that don't trigger you? Immersing in both ends of each spectrum will leave you with deeper insight into what others are experiencing when they act in dramatic ways (because they're feeling tension that you don't), or calm, detached ways (because they're not feeling tension you feel).

The end goal of this book is for you to have as clear of a concept of your emotional sense organ as you already have of visual, audio, tactile, smell, and taste sense organs. Then, with that information, the goal is for you to manage that system better so that you feel less pain tension, and feel more pleasure tension (excitement and enthusiasm).

The book is called The Next Three Traits because it ties the information up in a quick three-letter shorthand (RCS, SCR, CSR, RSC, SRC, or CRS) that makes it easier to discuss and compare different people's individual tension stackings. A person's three letter Limbic profile can stand alone as its own personality type ("I'm SCR"), knowing that it's only the tension parts of someone's psychology. Or, it can be added as the next three traits to Myers-Briggs® (ENTJ RSC), Enneagram (CSR-8)[A], Five Factor Model®, Love Languages®, Astrology ("I'm an SCR Taurus"), or any other classification system. This adds scientific rigor to those systems and helps separate Limbic influences from the other aspects of personality that each system is already measuring.

A   This is much more detailed Instinctual Subtypes, to the point where what was formerly the "subtypes" might actually be the main type.

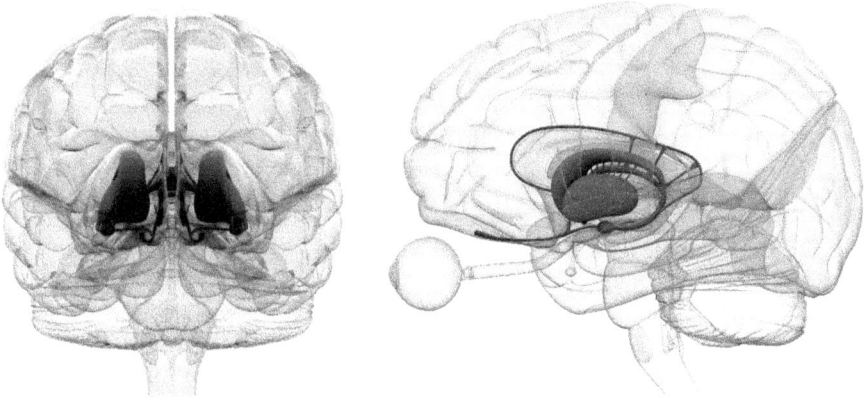

The Limbic System
is an Emotional Sense Organ

Your eyes have three separate, basic sensors which each only detect red, blue, or green. Your tongue has separate sensors which each only detect sweet, sour, bitter, salty, or umami. Your skin has multiple sensors which detect pressure, heat, pain, and location. Your consciousness experiences all of these combined at once. You can't choose to see just the red input data even though a purely-red input stream happens in your current hardware, right now. You also can't choose to exclude bitter from a taste, even though it already happens as an individual input stream.

Your Limbic System[B] detects inputs called "selection factors." It returns signals of **pain**, **pleasure**, **tension**, and **satisfaction**. Emotions are so striking, and vary so significantly between observers, that the absence of emotional components is a fifth classification: **neutrality**. Neutrality is the emotional equivalent of the color black, which seems just as much like a color as red, but is actually the absence of color signal inputs.

The building blocks of consciousness are simple and mechanical. Input streams can be active or inactive. Sensors can be at extremes

---

B   There are competing definitions of "Limbic System" right now. The definition used in this book includes at least the Amygdala, Hypothalamus, and Basal Ganglia (including the Nucleus Accumbens) and the structures connecting them.

of signal strength or in the middle. Signals can be recognized or unrecognized. Specialized areas, like recognition of faces, can be active or inactive. Each of these functions can be drugged to feel positive, negative, tense, satisfying, or not drugged to feel anything. By the end of this book you'll see how drugging each of those in the different ways, ***especially with tension***, results in different understandings of external reality.

When a quality of an object doesn't depend on the observer, like the weight or density, that quality is called "objective." When a quality of an object depends on the system measuring the object, that measure is called **"subjective,"** *because it is a reaction happening inside the observer*. Pleasure, pain, tension, and satisfaction are reactions happening inside the observer and vary significantly between observers, making the Limbic System a subjective sense organ.

The Tension / Anxiety Spectrum

Tension is the feeling that something could and should change. It is the feeling that something is missing, or that something extra is present and should be removed.

The opposite of tension is neutrality. Neutrality feels like acceptance. Something simply is how it is. There are many inputs around you right now that you weren't individually noticing because they don't feel good, bad, satisfying, or like they should change. Neutral inputs don't draw attention. They feel like they already are what they are going to be. So, the nuance to thinking of neutrality as "acceptance" is that inputs which are truly "accepted" usually aren't even considered. Most of the time it doesn't feel like there would be any benefit to focusing on them.

Pleasure or pain _without_ tension (So _neutral_ pleasures, and _neutral_ pains) feels like fixed, momentary recognition of the good and bad parts of reality which already are what they're going to be. Neutral pleasure and pain don't take the additional step of wanting the good or bad thing to be better. It is noticing that something is pleasurable or painful and letting it be just as it is.

Tension happens alongside pleasure as much as it happens alongside pain. Tense pleasure is excitement because something better is coming. Tense pain is anxiousness wanting the negativity of something to be reduced.

The first step in deconstructing emotions is recognizing tension separately as its own concept, rather than necessarily tying it to pain. Tension is desire. People feel as much excited, joyful desire as they feel painful, repulsed desire. This book will go through quite detailed isolation of the positive and negative experiences of each tension. As a first step, the important thing is to start with the idea that tension is the hunger for something to be different. It is the thought that anything could be improved, whether it's a good thing getting better, or a bad thing getting better.

Tension can be momentary or persistent, depending on whether it's triggered by something in the moment, or held in place by the memory of tension triggers. This distinction becomes important later.

Momentary tension happens over and over, all day long. It drives small actions. It is what makes you respond to someone else's sentence. It is what makes you adjust how you're sitting. It is a feeling that something is incomplete, and a hunger to get to completion. Momentary tension is relieved when the anticipated resolution happens. Part of what makes tension momentary is that it's quickly forgotten and isn't revisited later.

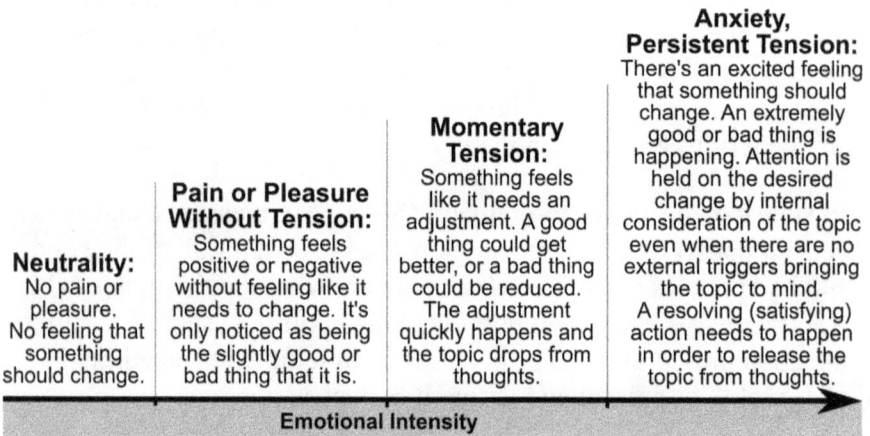

Neutrality:	**Pain or Pleasure Without Tension:**	**Momentary Tension:**	**Anxiety, Persistent Tension:**
No pain or pleasure. No feeling that something should change.	Something feels positive or negative without feeling like it needs to change. It's only noticed as being the slightly good or bad thing that it is.	Something feels like it needs an adjustment. A good thing could get better, or a bad thing could be reduced. The adjustment quickly happens and the topic drops from thoughts.	There's an excited feeling that something should change. An extremely good or bad thing is happening. Attention is held on the desired change by internal consideration of the topic even when there are no external triggers bringing the topic to mind. A resolving (satisfying) action needs to happen in order to release the topic from thoughts.

Emotional Intensity →

Tension becomes **anxiety** when it doesn't resolve even when the external trigger isn't present. **Persistent tension (anxiety)** is tension which is stuck, waiting, generating more and more hunger while resolution keeps not happening.

Most people don't think of anxiety happening alongside pleasure. Not only do they happen together, but most people want to feel that combination. Anxious pleasure is the feeling of love, hope, excitement, enthusiasm, positive hunger, positive craving. The feeling of anxiety and pleasure together motivates predictions of how pleasurable something will be and feels some of that exaggerated goodness now in anticipation of the striking goodness to come. This anticipated pleasure will keep returning to thoughts

6

on its own, even in the absence of external triggers. Positive anxiety is a pleasurable lack. It is anticipation of life getting better.

Hopefully that helps with the first step of separating any previous connection between tension/anxiety and only negativity. Tension is a focusing on a desired action that would make things better. It's a detachment from accepting present reality and a waiting for a change. Pleasurable tensions consider how getting closer to a loved thing, experiencing more of a good thing, purifying, owning, consuming, or loving a good thing will make life even better.

At the other extreme, **when <u>anxiety</u> happens alongside <u>the feeling of pain</u>**, it is heartbreak, loss, sadness, devastation, fear, hopelessness, anger, jealousy, righteousness, hunger, or betrayal. Something is bad and the observer detaches from simply accepting that negativity into a hunger for it to be adjusted so it's not so negative anymore.

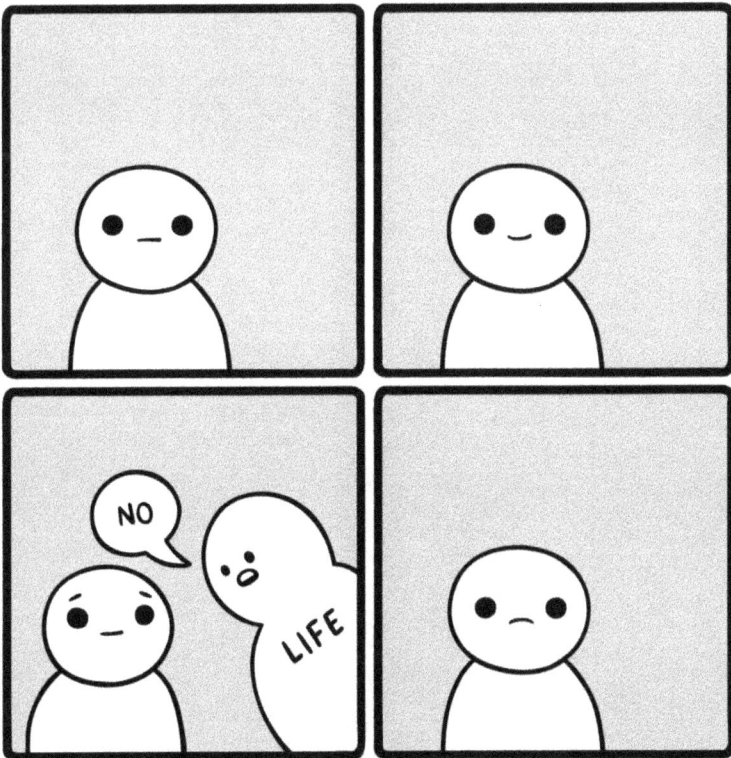

© *J. L. Westover – MrLovenstein.com*[4]

Satisfaction halts tension and anxiety. A change was desired in the moment before satisfaction. In the moment after satisfaction, a lack of tension is what would be felt if the observer noticed the feeling. Things might be good or bad, but they are what they are. A satisfied observer may still not like the outcome, or may love the outcome, but they've stopped imagining other options. They're in a state of acceptance rather than a state of resistance or hunger. They have switched back into observation mode: seeing something for what it is. They've switched out of expectation mode: imagining how it could be different, and how it would feel if that difference happened. A satisfied observer moves on to other things because there's no tension holding attention on changes anymore. They're back to feeling either neutrality, or pain or pleasure without tension.

3 Families of Tension

"To everyone out there suffering from anxiety:
You are not alone. There's someone behind you."[6]

Tension comes in three general families: **Social**, **Relational**, and **Comfort**.

Social tensions cause the feelings of others and the harmony and actions of the group to feel triggering for the need for change. **Relational** tensions cause the sexual features of others, and the familiarity and extremeness of experiences to feel triggering for the need for change. **Comfort** tensions cause sensations, physical and emotional dangers, identity, ranking, consumption, and acquisition to feel triggering for the need for change.

Just like most humans can see multiple colors and taste multiple taste qualities, ***most humans can and do feel all of these***. But which tension is most easily and least easily triggered varies from observer to observer. And which tension is triggered in each moment changes depending on the situation. It may initially seem like isolating which tension is being felt is a meaningless detail, but it quickly becomes obvious why it's important when different people feel different tensions in the same moment, especially from the same input. While observing the same inputs, one observer might be flushed with Social tension, while another is flushed with Comfort tension, while a third is flushed with Relational tension, while a fourth feels no tension. Since they're feeling different tensions, they'll be considering the changes that would make things "better" using different value scales which satisfy their own, individual flavors of tension.

These <u>three general families</u> are groupings of <u>seven distinct classes</u> of tension.

<u>Comfort Tensions (C)</u>

C_B: **Body** – Sensory, Mental, and Physical Health and Safety
C_I: **Identity** – Individuality, Self, and Ranking
C_R: **Resources** – Consumption and Acquisition

<u>Relational Tensions (R)</u>

R_S: **Sexual** – Arousal and Attraction
R_A: **Experiences (Adventures)** – Purpose and Meaning

<u>Social Tensions (S)</u>

S_C: **Community** – Harmony and Direction
S_F: **Friendship** – Similarity and Emotional Merging

When an input is considered while feeling Comfort tension, it's considered for how the sensory qualities, ranking, individuality, consumption, or acquisition of it could be improved. When something is considered while feeling Relational tension, it's considered for how sexual arousal or the novelty and extremeness of the adventure could be increased. When it's considered while feeling Social tension, it's considered for how other people's tensions can be relieved, and what can be changed for the good of the group.

People inaccurately think that each tension spectrum goes from "do I **ever** consider how this could change," to "do I **never** think about how this could change?" The actual spectrum is "do I more often notice this part of life as it is and practically work with the reality of the goods and bads," to "do I more often invest in how this part of life could be improved and hunger for those adjustments?" The actual spectrum is from the feeling of neutrality (acceptance) about that topic to the fixated hunger for change about that topic. Each person is somewhat more invested in the changes that could improve sensations, identity, resources, sexual arousal, experiences, community, or friendships, while more accepting of the balanced reality of another.

7 Classes of Tension

"People with anxiety don't have a train of thought.
We have 7 trains on 4 tracks that narrowly avoid each other,
and all the conductors are screaming."[8]

The next 14 chapters crank the intensity of each of the seven tensions up to the maximum and then down to zero to show the spectrum of each option. ***Each human's Limbic profile is not just one type, but a reading on each of the seven scales.*** In order to isolate and differentiate those seven spectrums, the other six competing tensions are about to be stripped away. This is analogous to tasting the five pure tastes in the absence of combinations, or looking at the three primary colors in the absence of combinations. Each is oversimplified. Real life can and does have multiple tensions happening at once. But seeing the pure options in isolation helps break down each moment's tensions into their basic components. That becomes critical later when it comes to intelligently hearing other people and managing your own tensions.

Here is the general framework of the next 14 chapters:

C_B **(Body-based Tension)**: What is life like for people who are frequently fixated, thinking change is required, when they experience touch, smell, sight, and sound sensations? What is life like for people who experience touch, smell, sight, and sound sensations as neutral parts of the fixed background of reality?

R_S **(Sex-based Tension)**: What is life like for people who are frequently fixated, thinking change is required, when they notice sexual features? What is life like for people who experience most sex related inputs as neutral parts of the fixed background of reality?

C_I **(Identity-based Tension)**: What is life like for people who are frequently fixated, thinking change is required, when inputs relate to self, individuality, ranking, and attention? What is life like for people who experience self, individuality, ranking, and attention as neutral parts of the fixed background of reality?

S_F **(Friendship-based Tension)**: What is life like for people who are frequently fixated, thinking change is required, when a friend is feeling emotions? What is life like for people who more often experience other people's emotions as neutral parts of the fixed background of reality?

C_R **(Resource-based Tension)**: What is life like for people who are frequently fixated, thinking change is required, when food, entertainment, effort, items, money, resources, acquisition, or consumption are involved? What is life like for people who mostly experience food, entertainment, effort, items, money, resources, acquisition, and consumption as neutral parts of the fixed background of reality?

S_C **(Community-based Tension)**: What is life like for people who are frequently fixated, thinking change is required, when they notice humans working together, conflicting, succeeding, or failing? What is life like for people who almost always experience humans working together, conflicting, succeeding, and failing as being a neutral part of the fixed background of reality?

R_A **(Adventure-based Tension)**: What is life like for people who are frequently fixated, thinking change is required, when they consider new, extreme experiences? What is life like for people who almost always experience new, extreme experiences as neutral parts of the fixed background of reality?

Read The Book About You First

If this is your first introduction to these concepts, it's preferable to begin by reading the discussion of *your* dominant tension. Give yourself some time to notice and increase the love you feel in your own psychology before coming back and immersing in the experiences the people near you are having.

It is a dramatic mindset shift for most people to focus on just one tension. This step is hard. But isolating and identifying the tensions you're feeling in any moment is the first step toward managing that tension more intelligently. In the second half of each chapter, immersing in the life experience of the people who rarely or never feel your tension helps clarify the path toward a less frequently anxious life.

So, which of these topics calls to you the most?

Frequent, strong **sexual arousal**, page **16**.

Frequent, strong tension about **individuality, ranking**, and **self**, p **58**. This includes if you feel tension about being grouped in with others since *you are unique and unclassifiable*. If you can't choose among the options listed here because you're equally all of the options, then start with this one, on page 58.

Frequent, strong tension about the **harmony** and **direction** of the **group**, page **105**.

Frequent, strong tension about **smells, sounds, visuals** and **tactile sensations,** and **physical** and **mental wellbeing,** page **151**.

Frequent, strong tension about **meaning, purpose, fully experiencing life,** and **trying new experiences,** page **188**.

Frequent, strong tension about the **hurt feelings of friends,** and **how those friends prioritize friendship,** page **228**.

Frequent, strong tension about **money, taste, fun, effort, acquisition** and **consumption,** page **269**.

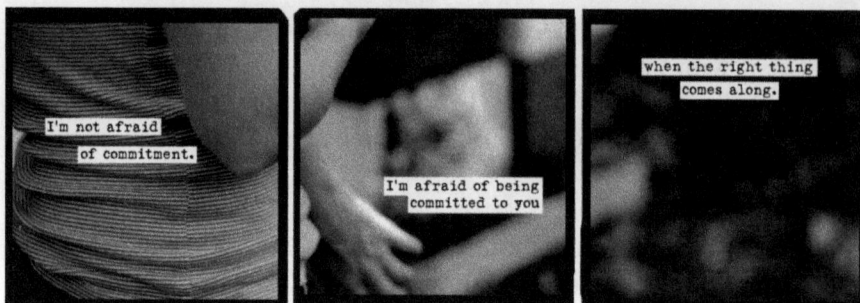

R_S: The Sexual Tension Spectrum

"Tis better to have loved and lost
Than never to have loved at all."[10]

Sexual Relational (R$_S$) tension adds a focusing need for escalation or repair, paired with relieving sexual satisfaction to the noticing of sexual inputs. Each person is somewhere on the spectrum from being frequently triggered with very strong tension about sex (being flushed with fixating arousal by sexy inputs, heartbreak over missed sexual opportunities, and hunger for adjustments to unsexy qualities), to being infrequently triggered with weak or no tension about sex (observing sexy and unsexy things for what they are without fixating hunger for escalation and satisfaction).

Terminology & Abbreviations

Sexual **neutrality** happens when observing a sexual target with no features which match the observer's sexual arousal triggers. No pleasure is triggered, no pain is triggered, no tension is triggered, and no satisfaction is triggered. No sexual emotions are triggered even if the observer focuses on the unarousing target and tries to think of sex. Most people feel sexual neutrality when considering cows, birds, fish, and ugly humans. Those things exist, but don't bring the topic of sex to mind, and especially don't trigger a focusing hunger for orgasms. When starting from a neutral mind, it feels like a change of topic to then start considering sexual arousal, sex, and orgasms.

The Sexual Pleasure Spectrum

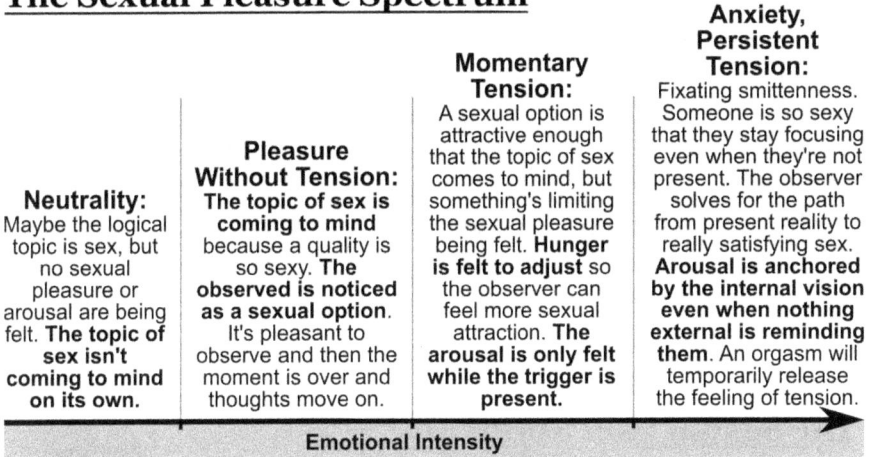

Neutrality:	Pleasure Without Tension:	Momentary Tension:	Anxiety, Persistent Tension:
Maybe the logical topic is sex, but no sexual pleasure or arousal are being felt. **The topic of sex isn't coming to mind on its own.**	**The topic of sex is coming to mind** because a quality is so sexy. **The observed is noticed as a sexual option.** It's pleasant to observe and then the moment is over and thoughts move on.	A sexual option is attractive enough that the topic of sex comes to mind, but something's limiting the sexual pleasure being felt. **Hunger is felt to adjust** so the observer can feel more sexual attraction. **The arousal is only felt while the trigger is present.**	Fixating smittenness. Someone is so sexy that they stay focusing even when they're not present. The observer solves for the path from present reality to really satisfying sex. **Arousal is anchored by the internal vision even when nothing external is reminding them.** An orgasm will temporarily release the feeling of tension.

Emotional Intensity →

Sexual **pleasure with<u>out</u> tension** is recognition of momentary sexiness. The topic of sex is coming to mind because something has triggered the feeling of sexual pleasure. It feels like noticing that a quality is sexy, but in a fixed, momentary, practical way. The sexuality of the moment feels complete. The trigger may be quite sharply attractive, but the observer isn't flushed with hunger for more. Encountering the sexy input made the moment better, but it's just part of the normal world. The moment passes and thoughts move on. It's not just objective, emotionless recognition. Pleasure is being felt too. But it's a complete, satisfied pleasure.

Sexual **pleasure <u>with</u> tension** feels like the noticing of a sharply sexy feature, but in a lacking way. There's potential for more sexual pleasure here and the observer notices how things could adjust to deliver that greater pleasure. But it's not just logical recognition. It's excited hunger, anticipating pleasure for the goodness that would be felt if the imagined adjustment happened.

- **Momentary positive tension** (externally triggered tension) is hunger for escalation that only exists while the trigger is present. Attention is focused and desire is felt for small adjustments. Satisfaction comes from observing a little longer, getting a little closer, or having eye contact returned. Doing so leaves the observer satisfied and thoughts move on.

- **Anxiety, persistent positive tension** (internally maintained tension) is hunger for sexual escalation which persists even when the external trigger is removed. It is sexual smittenness. It is sexual fantasy. The sexual features of a partner feel magical. Focus shifts internally to predict the sexual outcome that would be even more pleasurable. Internal attention solves for the path from the present moment to that escalated sexual intensity. Both partners will be flushed with sexual excitement, overcome with attraction, repeatedly satisfied, and life will be shockingly happy. Other topics are hard to consider because this mind is hungry for sex.

The Sexual Pain Spectrum

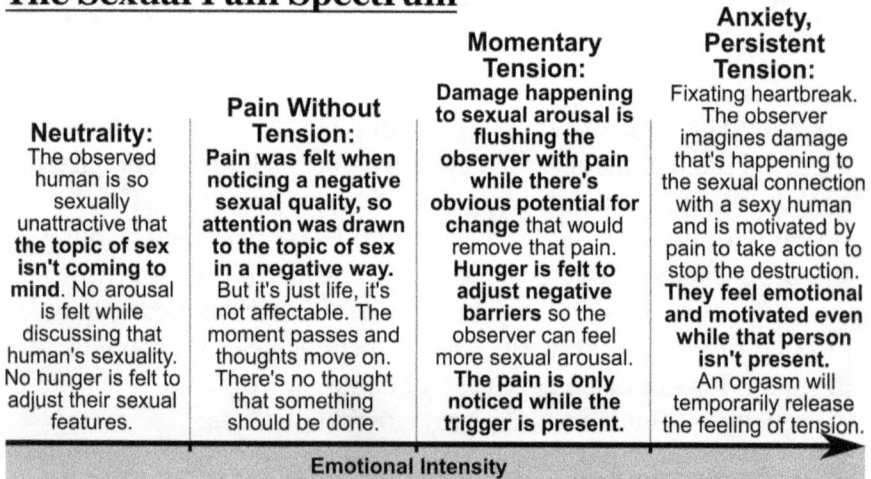

Neutrality:	Pain Without Tension:	Momentary Tension:	Anxiety, Persistent Tension:
The observed human is so sexually unattractive that **the topic of sex isn't coming to mind**. No arousal is felt while discussing that human's sexuality. No hunger is felt to adjust their sexual features.	Pain was felt when noticing a negative sexual quality, so attention was drawn to the topic of sex in a negative way. But it's just life, it's not affectable. The moment passes and thoughts move on. There's no thought that something should be done.	Damage happening to sexual arousal is flushing the observer with pain while there's obvious potential for change that would remove that pain. Hunger is felt to adjust negative barriers so the observer can feel more sexual arousal. The pain is only noticed while the trigger is present.	Fixating heartbreak. The observer imagines damage that's happening to the sexual connection with a sexy human and is motivated by pain to take action to stop the destruction. They feel emotional and motivated even while that person isn't present. An orgasm will temporarily release the feeling of tension.

→ **Emotional Intensity**

Sexual **pain without tension** is the feeling of noticing the realistic sexual negativity of an imperfect world. It's what you feel when you look at clinical photos of unattractive naked humans. The thought of sex is coming to mind, but in a negative way that feels fixed. It's recognition of sexual unattractiveness, but in a way that feels observing and accepting. It is objective recognition of a normal part of external reality. Thoughts easily move to the next topic because there's nothing more to consider about this input.

Sexual **pain with tension** feels like the noticing of an unsexy feature or sexual disruption, but in a lacking way that wants that negative feature to change. It's hungry recognition of missed sexual potential. An obstacle is keeping sexual pleasure from happening.

But it's not just logical. The observer feels sexually excited. They feel aroused and hungry for an adjustment so the pain can stop.

- **Momentary negative tension** (externally triggered tension) is hunger for escalation that only exists while the trigger is present. What's keeping pain happening is the continued presence of a sexual obstacle, or the continued observation of the unsexy feature. If they'd cover that body part, or stop talking in that voice, then they'd be attractive again. The feeling isn't intense enough to require sex for satisfaction. Removal or adjustment of the unsexy input, maybe even by looking away, releases attention to focus on other things again.

- **Anxiety, persistent negative tension** (internally maintained tension) is painful hunger for sexual escalation which persists even when the external trigger is removed. It is heartbreak. It feels like something is going wrong that's decreasing sexual potential at the same time that sex is necessary. Focus shifts internally to predict the better scenario that would've brought euphoric sexual satisfaction and solves for the path from the present moment to that escalated sexual intensity. It feels like a mistake that a sexual connection ended, or a pleasurable opportunity for sex was missed. Something should be done to reconnect, or vigilance should happen so that the next opportunity results in sex instead. It can be concern that won't go away that an existing partner needs to adjust to become sexier. An impediment to sexual arousal needs to be resolved because the pain is so sharp and lingers for so long.

Sexual **satisfaction** is relief which comes with orgasms (sometimes for the observer, sometimes for the observed), through completion of sexual fantasies (which aren't always orgasms), through verifying that the sex-related qualities of the observed were a mistake (they're asexual, they have unsexy qualities that weren't obvious at first, or sexual arousal wasn't actually threatened), or through verifying returned sexual attraction. Sexual arousal was felt, and then the great thing happened which fulfilled the sexual hope, or confirmation was found that the sexual hope was never really an option.

The shorthand for people who are triggered with Sex-based Relational tension and anxiety more often and strongly than the other options is that they're "**R$_S$-first**." When a reference is made to "an R$_S$," or "R$_S$s," it's identifying the discussed person or people as being R$_S$-first.

The shorthand for people who are triggered more strongly and frequently by all six other tension options is that people are "**R$_S$-last**." Someone who is R$_S$-last can still get very hungry for sex when looking at someone with sexy features, but that hunger for sex is more often momentary, and the sexual tension felt can be more easily interrupted by Social tension about their partner's feelings or what's proper, or Comfort tension about sensations, ranking, safety, fairness, or respect.

We're now going to immerse in the life experience people have when they're most frequently and strongly struck by Sexual Relational tension to see what it's like to live at the highest end of the spectrum. Then we'll immerse in the life experience of people who feel the six other tensions more strongly and frequently to see what it's like to live at the lowest end of the Sexual Relational spectrum.

© Randall Munroe – xkcd.com[11]

R$_S$-First: Frequently Triggered Strong R$_S$ Tension

Being R$_S$-first means feeling emotions before logic has had a chance to evaluate an input. R$_S$-firsts are stabbed with sharp pain when they see their exes shortly after breaking up. **The observers' bodies aren't getting touched, and yet they're flushed with pain as if the damage to their sexual connection were physical damage happening to themselves.** Is the pain a response to logic? No. R$_S$-

firsts don't logically assess the mate value of that partner, the value of the existing relationship, and the probability of better matches and then make a logical choice to feel pain. They can't logically choose to feel pain on command from other logical negatives which don't trigger that feeling. The pain happens automatically and simultaneously with the observation of positive sexual value in their now-disconnected partner. Logic is used after the feeling to imagine the healed version of the relationship and predict relief if sex happened again. Missed sexual opportunities feel deeply meaningful and tragic because so much sexual tension is felt when noticing someone who is attractive. That was the most meaningful moment of the month and nothing happened. Boo!

> "I'd choose you. In a hundred lifetimes, in a hundred worlds,
> in any version of reality, I'd find you and I'd choose you."[12]

R_Ss are then flushed with intoxicating pleasure when they make eye contact with a cutie. All focus is immediately drawn to the sexual attractiveness of the partner. Is the pleasure felt a response to logic? No. R_S-firsts don't logically assess the match quality, the mating value, and the function of a partnerships and then make a logical choice to feel desire while observing the sexual features and returned sexual interest of this sexual option. They can't logically decide that someone unattractive generate that euphoria and fixation instead and then feel it there. Logic is used, powered by the euphoric feeling happening, to imagine what a good match this person might be and how pleasurable sex might be which would justify the sexual euphoria which that person inspires. This is one of the life moments that really matters, and this sexual connection has to happen. Nothing else can get full attention until the sexual connection is secure.

The third feeling which really cements these in is that R_S-first observers can tolerate much bigger problems in other areas without getting triggered with excitement or concern about them. A friend is cranky right now, but not enough pain is triggered to make it feel like the friendship needs mending. Other humans are misunderstanding each other, but that's just what it's like for humans to interact. Sensory comforts aren't ideal, but they are what life is. Self isn't impressively excellent at the moment, but there's nothing to do about it right now. Resources are generic and sufficient. These topics aren't coming to mind because they're within the ranges of pain and pleasure where they don't draw attention (because this observer isn't triggered with tension about them at these levels). They're not perfect, but that's just how life is.

> *"As for lovers, well, they'll come and go too. And baby, I hate to say it, most of them - actually pretty much all of them are going to break your heart. But you can't give up because if you give up, you'll never find your soulmate. You'll never find that half who makes you whole"*[13]

Approaching the highest end of the R_S spectrum, observers are drugged with much more sexual arousal and heartbreak while observing more humans. But it doesn't feel individual and it doesn't feel internal. It feels like objective recognition that the world is full of breathtaking hotties. At the highest setting, about one in 20 sexual options are breathtakingly attractive. The observer is intoxicated, fixated, and the observed angels are obviously captivating. There is no way to consider the shocking perfection of their features and not be overwhelmed with desire for sex.

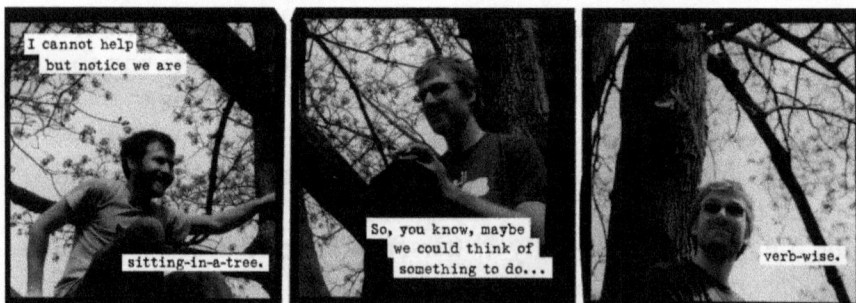

© *e horne and j comeau – asofterworld.com*[14]

Half of what makes sexual attraction feel objective is that so many humans, words, and actions inspire no arousal, even for R_S-firsts. No sexual attraction is felt to the majority of humans who pass by. No heartbreak is felt because sex won't happen with them. Since every other part of life is ignorably acceptable, the moments when a sharply attractive cutie comes into view feel important and meaningful. R_Ss don't want to think about sexual attraction again, but a critical life moment has come up on its own which requires action or regret.

Tension escalates as the opportunity starts to slip away. Is the cutie not interested in return? Is a sexually neutral option getting in the way? Was this a shot at true love that's being missed? Maybe a sexual competitor interrupts the moment. Maybe sex started, but neither person had an orgasm. This was supposed to be a pinnacle moment, and instead it's incomplete. The situation will keep cycling in thoughts so that the resolving action can be determined.

"Every little thing she does is magic
Everything she do just turns me on."[15]

Tension events alternate with being released again when R_Ss get satisfaction, which is usually an orgasm. Each day is a tug-of-war between neutral availability of focus for any thought and fixated sexual arousal or heartbreak. The emotional problems in life happen when a sexual opportunity appears but doesn't end in satisfaction.

The core of R_S-first is ***being consumed by the feeling of sexual arousal***. But it feels like the other human is what's valuable. It feels like they are sexual perfection and every pathway to being closer to sex with them is a pathway toward happiness. If you dropped all judgment and distraction and really let yourself feel the pleasure of pure sexual arousal, not clouded by any other feeling, who would you focus on? What body shapes turn you on the most? What facial features and expressions trigger the most sexual arousal for you? What words and actions could get you the most aroused? Can you focus on the face, body, words, motions, and scenario that would make you feel the most aroused, and feel some of that pleasure now?

Then feel the tension about that optimal sex being interrupted by a roommate entering the room. The roommate would have a feeling of tension as a component. They feel like a problem, something that needs to be changed. Sexual arousal could be restored if only this interruption would go away.

It's important to distinguish between the feelings of sexual attraction and any logic developed about sex and sexual attraction. R_S tension is the sexually unsettled feeling which fixates attention, which logic has to repeatedly interpret and manage. An observer might truly, logically want to feel aroused by their spouse, but sexual excitement just isn't happening. They might truly, logically not want to be aroused by their friend's spouse, but they can't help being frozen with hunger for sex. The feelings and the logic are different things which can align or be in conflict. R_S only refers to the feelings part. Regardless of any logic, are you fixated with sexual hunger, or not? If your partner is starting out neutral, are you the motivating force that gets them wound up so sex can happen?

> *"The best feeling in the world is the feeling of being freshly smitten.*
> *It's so joyful and energizing and loving. When I feel that,*
> *I feel SO ALIVE! If being with one person for the rest of my life*
> *means not getting to pursue that rush when the opportunity arises,*
> *then I don't want to be with just one person for the rest of my life."*[16]

Later on, these emotions interrupt peaceful, calm moments that don't have external triggers. Pain happens again, triggered by the memory of an ex, triggered by the missed sexual opportunity earlier in the day. No decision was made to think about either. In fact, most logic had decided it was a great idea to break up, or realizes a stranger was unlikely to be a good sexual match. But the pain is so sharp that attention is fixated on the sexual attractiveness of someone who isn't present. The memory of the sexy features of that ex, or that stranger are sharply arousing. The observer is alone. The actual exterior moment is quiet. But the observer is flushed with sexual arousal imagining the sex that could happen. They either need to contact that cutie or have an orgasm some other way if they want their mind back to think of other things.

Since tension could be triggered at any moment, R_Ss preemptively take actions to maintain their sexual attractiveness, options, and sexual escalation skills (flirtation). Even when situations aren't sexual, an R_S-first knows the situation might turn sexual, and that it will be striking if it does, so they keep making choices to protect themselves from tension that will linger in pain if a sexy moment fizzles. The way to be present and available for the rest of life is to have sexual satisfaction easily available so arousal can be satisfied quickly each time it comes up. In a perfect world, R_Ss would be in a solid romantic relationship with a horny, breathtaking hottie so they'd have access to really satisfying sex right away, every time their hunger was triggered. In the real world, there's lots of masturbating in bathrooms. Even after they marry a hottie.

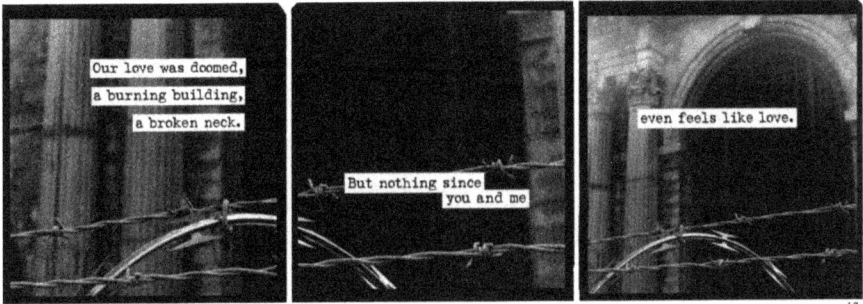

Our love was doomed, a burning building, a broken neck.

But nothing since you and me

even feels like love.

© e horne and j comeau – asofterworld.com[17]

A love for sexual arousal creates a surprising option for an enemy, and that is a sexual partner who isn't also prioritizing sexual arousal. A sexual partner who lets sexual arousal suffer for the benefit of fat, parents, social norms, self-worship, or hypochondria is attacking something beautiful and purely good. It's really not hard to prioritize love, and a partner with a soul would do that. The exterior world is still full of partners who can bring satisfaction, while a now-unattractive partner is intentionally choosing to wreck the part of life that matters.

A love for sexual arousal creates another surprising personality quirk, and that's a desire for just flirting, no sex, when not-enough sexual arousal is felt by the observer. It's sometimes still worth flirting up to the point of getting the other person aroused even if the observer doesn't want sex, because seeing the other person's arousal and attraction will feel so good. Actually having sex with an unattractive person wouldn't be sexy at all. So, feeling the attraction grow, but not turn into sex, is the most sexual arousal that some situations have to offer.

R_S-firsts think that the sexual attraction they feel is helpful. They're motivated to find sexier partners and to have more sexually attracted relationships. They make better decisions about food, jobs, friends, groups, health, and experiences, because they prioritize how these impact the sexual arousal that they and their partners will feel. They have what other people have, plus striking happiness from really great sex.

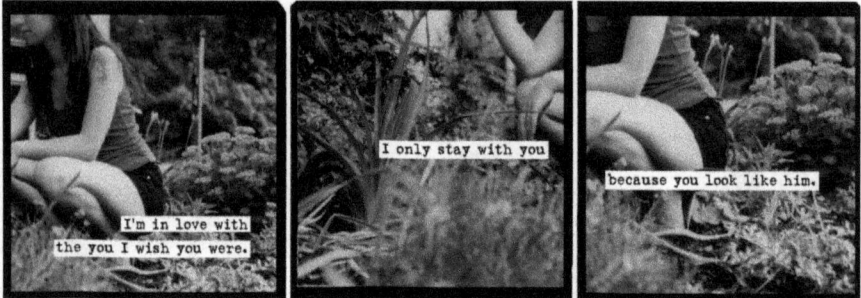

I only stay with you

because you look like him.

I'm in love with the you I wish you were.

© e horne and j comeau – asofterworld.com[19]

Meanwhile, R_S-lasts only seem to have disadvantages. Most obviously, people who don't seek and maintain sexual attractiveness are missing out on so much happiness. Some part of their soul seems muted since they're so dismissive of the most thrilling part of being alive. Lower R_S friends could be **_very_** sexually attractive if they tried. Or they have really sexy bodies that they're not using for sex. R_S-lasts settle for unaroused relationships and unarousing partners when they have much more passionate options. R_S-firsts may not have perfect lives, but they've got the foundation. They've maintained their sexual value and are skilled at engaging sexual options. An R_S's life is optimized for actual reality.

> *"When death takes my hand, I will hold you with the other and promise to find you in every lifetime"* [20]

R_Ss vary quite a bit in what and who sparks their sexual arousal and heartbreak. Different shapes and sizes of different body parts seem breathtakingly arousing to different R_Ss. Some get more stimulation from the partner's arousal and orgasm. Some are more focused on touching, kissing, words, or actions. R_Ss are accustomed to being told that they're overly focused on sex, by broken asexuals who live joyless lives.

18

R$_S$s think repeatedly feeling horny and heartbroken is just what life is. They think they're trying for a totally realistic, but admittedly high-level of sexual attraction with admittedly high frequency of sex. But they determined that something is "realistic" by imagining something better than what they already encountered, or the best thing they ever encountered, while minimizing inextricable trade offs that come with those positives. The result is an underlying, recurring ache, an unfillable anxiety, a dissatisfaction with reality, because the "realistic" goal they need to feel satisfied is just beyond what's possible.

R$_S$-Last: Living without Tension about Sex-Based Pleasures and Pains

> *"I associate those crazy feelings of passion with something that is so bad for me in the long run that I feel repulsed, because I don't want it. I'm totally okay with not having that, because it seems like that level of intensity needs a crazier person on the other end to stay engaged. I'm happy that I had it, and I'm happy to never have that again. But it makes it awkward when I'm trying to woo a potential partner when I explain that I'm fine if I never feel crazy for them. I don't associate passion with positive things. Because the negative things are way too much and I know I need more stability. I need to make choices that increase stability. Allowing myself to be consumed by someone else doesn't increase stability. I would like that level, but I am intellectually concerned that the people who I am likely to get that from would be bad for me."[21]*

At the lowest point on the R$_S$ spectrum the observer isn't automatically flushed with excitement and lack by the topic of sex. Building up to that feeling is a more intentional process. There's a distinct feeling of arousal and fixation that doesn't happen. So they think about sex the same way everyone does who isn't flushed with alertness. They can still appreciate it, but aren't hungry for it. They can sexually escalate, or they can turn to the side and refocus onto another topic. Most R$_S$-lasts can still get very sexually aroused, but it happens with more guided intention by the observer, and only when their more-easily-triggered tensions are already so secure that those other tensions won't spike and draw focus. Also, even when sexuality is aroused, it can be more easily interrupted. There isn't as strong of an underlying feeling of tension silencing other focus options and fixating attention with only hunger for sexual satisfaction.

When sex isn't required to satisfy a sexual hunger, it can help satisfy other hungers. Part of the value of sex the way it makes the observer feel safe, valued, fairly treated, seen, and like they're part of a merged team. Sex is great when it makes the partner feel good. Orgasms still relax the whole body and quiet other concerns. Sometimes sex is part of the fair trade that's happening for other benefits in the relationship. Sex can be an intense way to reconnect with a partner in moments when there are doubts about the health and safety of the relationship, or to measure the partner's current investment.

What's missing is the idolization of the partner, but also the critical feelings about the way the partner could improve their sexual attractiveness. The partner is a balanced human with positives and negatives. The partner is objectively seen for what they are, rather than imagined for what they could be if they made some adjustments to be sexier. Sexual attractiveness isn't overvalued because it only triggers pleasure and pain and not fixating concern about destruction of what's valuable.

Instead, an R_S-last observer is idolizing themselves, money, sensations, health, safety, the connectedness of the friendship, or the goodness of their group. They're distracted in a different mindset, so sex is considered more for how it can help satisfy a hunger they're feeling elsewhere, if it's considered at all. An R_S-last is still critical of their partner, but they'd like adjustments in how the partner handles money, respects them, pays attention to them, adjusts based on their feedback, makes them feel safe, merges, agrees, or invests in the greater good. They notice those things because they're more easily triggered to feel tension in those areas. Smaller problems in those other areas trigger a greater feeling of alert fixation that feels like a change should happen.

The sexual aspects of a partner might still feel magical when they have focus, but other parts of life are happening that focus moments in other directions most of the time. The center of the moment feels more about what's impressive, what's healthy, what's monetarily valuable, how aligned and merged the friendship is, or how harmonious the group is. That's happening because those things feel lacking in the moment. Something happened and the observer is triggered, maybe only momentarily, to hunger for some adjustment and to make sure that adjustment happens. Fewer moments are spent idolizing the sexuality of the partner, because the balanced reality of both people's bodies stays obvious. There's less flushing of the drugged hunger that makes the partner's sexual flaws temporarily invisible.

Since reality triggers less sexual disappointment, and fantasies trigger less sexual arousal, R_S-lasts stay present in actual reality and choose relationship partners among the actually-available option. They aren't also dating a sexually idealized fantasy partner in their minds. They might love their partner more for how safe and loved they feel, than for the sexiness of that partner's body. They might love how easy it is to love this other person's soul because their struggles are so relatable, rather than for the shape of their body. They might appreciate that this other person is always on their side, or keeps them on their toes. There are so many bad matches and crazy people out there. So many humans bring so many headaches through such awful decisions. Having a teammate who is remotely sane can be a real blessing sometimes. R_S-lasts are also realistic about their own sexiness. They're not perfect either. If they want more in that area from a partner, then they need to be prepared to sacrifice something else that matters.

An R_S-last isn't as fixated on finding a partner who is sexually fixated in return as well, because that returned sexual intensity is valued for how it affects their more-dominant motivators. An R_S-last will get more satisfaction from having a partner who is impressed, or impressive, who is also excited about resources, who is also deeply concerned about safety and health, who is deeply concerned about the harmony and progress of the group, or who is fixated with concern when the observer is concerned. R_S-lasts still get flushed with tense attraction, but it's to things the partner does or says about other topics than sex. So, when it comes to sex, there's a calm practicality in noticing that both partners have better and worse features, but this soul is valued so much for other qualities that they're the one to have sex with. There's a calm practicality in knowing that the partner is having sex more because of non-sexual reasons than because the observer is so breathtakingly sexy. It's really okay if the partner isn't hungry for sex with the observer. The friendship, respect, and shared values are still secure. The sexual part ebbs and flows along with everything else. R_S-lasts have a more holistic view of relationships, and their appreciation during sex might be true gratitude that they got a partner who looked out for their needs today while also cleaning the house without being asked.

In addition to feeling less R_S tension, some R_S-lasts find fewer humans or fewer features to be sexually attractive, or they find those features to be less strikingly attractive. Every time a person passes through your input field and you don't consider sex with them, that person felt sexually neutral to you. Sexual neutrality isn't sexual rejection. It's not a consideration of sex and a decision against it. It's not any thought at all. Sexual neutrality is a lack of sexual attraction or heartbreak which would bring the topic of sex to mind. Someone might still be pleasurably attractive if you're asked to focus on that aspect of them, but seeing them and interacting with them wasn't enough to trigger you to consider them sexually. In the most extreme cases, sexual neutrality is a lack of the feeling of sexual arousal and heartbreak even when someone brings up the topic of sex. Sex is logically possible with the person in question, but no sexual desire is triggered even when the observer tries to appreciate the observed as sexually as possible.

The vast majority of people (67%) are having sex twice a month or less. 60% of people have ongoing sexual desire problems, and another 25% have them intermittently. Only 15% of humans think they're lacking sexual desire "rarely" or "never."[22]

As R_S-triggers reduce in number and drug intensity (moving down the R_S spectrum) fewer observed sexual partners trigger the observer to feel sexual arousal and sexual heartbreak. More observed sexual options feel fixed as being sexually neutral, so their sexuality isn't even considered, rather than noticed and imagined with modifications that would make them more sexually arousing. Most people, even R_S-firsts, feel sexually neutral about most people. In fact, getting people to accurately assess their own levels of sexual attraction is difficult because most people don't realize how many people they exclude from sexual questions.

At the lowest point on the R_S spectrum all humans feel sexually neutral. One partner option might be more attractive than another, but none of the options inspire a fixating sexual arousal that makes the observer fixate with hunger for sex with them right now, especially a hunger that can only be satisfied if orgasms happen. But, from the inside, it feels like objective recognition that humans aren't very sexy, and that sexual options are plentiful and mostly pretty similar. Everyone feels how R_S-lasts feel when they're in a room of only somewhat-sexy options. Once a sexual relationship is established, it feels like sexual disconnections are easy to avoid by doing things the obvious way, and not tragic if they happen. Body shapes and a partner's sexual attraction aren't more striking than other daily concerns. Some sexual options still look better and worse than others, but they're not fixating in attractiveness, just passively noticeable in attractiveness. Sexual features feel momentary and unchangeable. They stay passively noticed as external, rather than moving into internal fantasies of escalation. If a desired partner isn't interested in return, it feels like an unchangeable reality. Tension isn't added. The recognition is practical, present, and momentary. No alternate sexual scenario is imagined, so no hunger is felt for it.

> *"I've never felt what most people would describe as horny,*
> *and if I ever do feel any slight inkling of that it's very, very small"[23]*

Being R_S-**last** means having higher Comfort and Socialness. So R_S-lasts aren't lacking in emotion, and they're not lacking in tension. They're just flushed with different flavors of love, craving, appreciation, distress, and satisfaction when it comes to relationships and sex. In fact, R_S-lasts often feel like they feel more complete love for their partners, more full love, because they're so deeply smitten in so many ways, rather than just sexual ways. And even the sex part they can still feel deeply attracted and deeply appreciative, they're just not also distracted with visions of what could be sexier. They recognize the realistic beauty of what's in front of them, accepting that everything has balancing goods and bads in reality, rather than creating a version in their heads that's slightly better so that their partner or sexual situation can feel insufficient. R$_S$-lasts feel certainty that their partner was the best possible option among their choices because they chose from the options in reality, while R$_S$-firsts have an unsettled wonder if they could've done "better" because they're comparing reality to an imagined version that isn't actually an option in reality.

© *Jim Benton – JimBenton.com*[24]

Most R_S-lasts still can feel pleasure from observing some body shapes and feel sexual pain from observing others. Most still really prefer certain sexually distinctive features on their partner. But the experience of appreciating sexual features is different when those features don't automatically trigger hunger for change and escalation. There was a moment of sexual pleasure or pain, that's just reality, and then the moment ended. The thought ends there. The observer can still look to the side and discuss a different topic. Sexually pleasurable inputs don't fixate the observer with hunger for an orgasm. The rest of reality isn't silenced. The observer's focus isn't distracted away from the moment with an internal sexual fantasy. Instead it seems weird that we're still talking about that moment when it was over long ago.

Most of the time, the option of being obsessed with fixation about the sexiness of a stranger isn't even considered until someone else is freaking out. Yes, a body shape is nice. I guess I could get excited about it if the conditions were right. No, I don't need kisses with that person now that you've pointed it out. If you could feel the process of turning yourself down in tension, you'd feel a silencing of the urgency felt when noticing that something is sexually attractive or unattractive. As a result, there's a natural acceptance that the sex which is available to you is everything that's available. When sex time comes, the sex that's available will be there. That simple reality reframes thought away from sex and onto whatever topic you'd like to focus on instead.

> *It's always seemed ridiculous to me that people want to be around someone because they're pretty. It's like picking your breakfast cereal based on color instead of taste.*"[25]

At the lowest point on the sexual spectrum, sexual features don't catch attention on their own. Of course the better options are better and the worse options are worse. But each is what it is. There's no thought that positive features could be combined, or that negative features could be removed, or that good things could be even more extreme. All the adults in the room can easily tune out the sexes of the people in the room while the meaningful task gets attention. It feels like surrounding people just aren't attractive enough to trigger that level of fixation. The actual experience of being at the extreme minimum is that it feels weird to even consider people sexually because the options are so not-sexual. The topic of sex doesn't seem to fit because nothing about the moment feels sexual. It's like considering which cow has the sexiest genitals.

> This guy said, "Look at that girl. She's got a nice butt!"
> I said, "Yeah, I bet she's excellent at sitting down!"[26]

Now imagine that you're at a restaurant and someone starts choking. The TV in the background shows live scenes of riots nearby, moving your direction. Your car ran out of gas. A creepy person is staring at you. Your tooth is suddenly sharply painful. For all humans, sex isn't the topic of the moment while other meaningful life events are happening. R_S-last observers have more Comfort and Social triggers connected to more drug intensity with more sensitive triggers. So, smaller disruptions in other areas become sharply fixating much more often. No choice is being made to ignore sex. It's just not a sexual moment, because it's obviously a critical Social or Comfort moment (which happens to be a lot of moments).

Choosing a mate is different when their sexual features aren't intoxicating, especially if other qualities of the options are made positively and negatively triggering. Someone being forced to choose among neutral (cow) options wouldn't have feelings of sexual arousal and heartbreak to help with the choice (to distract the choice away from logic), or to make them feel especially lucky if they got certain options. R_S-lasts see mate options for who they really are, because their mind isn't hijacked by the sexual fantasies, or afraid of that sexual attraction might fade, because attractiveness just is what it is, it's an external reality which is observed. The trade offs for a more attractive partner don't get minimized. Meanwhile, those same humans, and same bodies, more easily trigger self-protective feelings, sensory-protective feelings, resource-protective feelings, friendship-protecting feelings, and group-harmony-protecting feelings. Penises are penises. Vaginas are vaginas. If you're managing a life where you're easily triggered by Social and Comfort concerns, it's worth disqualifying choices that will trigger your recurring pain tension, and prioritizing partners who will help resolve those tensions. If you want to care about sex then choose the best looking gorilla from whatever makes it through your Social and Comfort filters.

"Based on what people have told me over the years, physical attractiveness, although important initially, is never the most important factor that causes someone to talk to one romantic option rather than another. What strikes one person as attractive will seem unattractive to someone else. No one way of appearing will seem attractive to everyone. Not only that, what is attractive, or unattractive, to a particular person at a particular time may seem quite the opposite at another time and place. Not uncommonly someone goes unnoticed until he/she begins to talk, and then abruptly seems very attractive. I think that experience is more the rule than the exception. Often the circumstances in which people meet color their attractiveness. Someone might be attracted to a man or woman who seems to be at the focus of a conversation, or who is in a position of power in a business or some other institution, or who is demonstrating a skill or talent, or who seems to be poised in the face of an argument, and so on. [These people may] seem more attractive than they would be in some other setting. When I ask a patient why their spouse appeared attractive to them at first, not uncommonly they respond by saying, 'he/she liked me!'"[27]

Instead, deviate slightly from reality in Social and Comfort directions. Imagine finding a soul so similar that the two of you are natural extensions of each other who work together flawlessly as a team. Imagine them being such a good person, with such wholesome values that you are never repelled and often cringe together at what other people are saying. Imagine someone who makes you feel safe and comfortable, who naturally manages smells, sounds, sights, and tactile sensations to make them great. Imagine someone impressive, who is impressed with you in return. Meanwhile, you're both in normal human bodies that aren't particularly sexy.

Reality isn't fairy tales or porn. Humans look like humans. If you pick a person based on physical appearance, that person is way less likely to be compatible with the rest of your personality. It quickly becomes difficult to have sex with someone who keeps making you upset. If you focus on the problems with sexual attraction, you only find more problems.

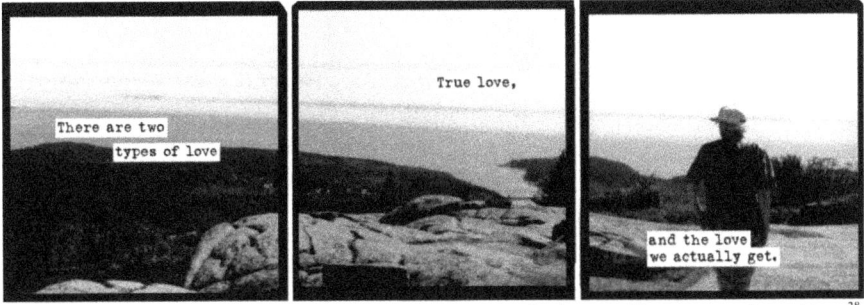

© *e horne and j comeau – asofterworld.com*[28]

R$_S$-lasts choose from the mate options they actually know, who would choose them back, with none of the options being intoxicating because they all come with balancing drawbacks. An R$_S$-last is observing reality without creating something different inside, which is what it feels like to accept reality as it is. They choose and then don't revisit the question again. The topic is complete.

> *"When there's sexual tension, the things you care about aren't getting done. Instead life is wasted with mindless biology of what we're programmed to do with our bodies that doesn't actually matter. When I focus on that I ignore my own needs, and then crash because I haven't gotten my own me time. Then the crash turns into conflict. I resent my partner, because the things which make a contribution in the world are being put on hold. I don't like that cycle. It's addictive behavior rather than intelligence. So, in future relationships it was healthiest to have that passion spread over my whole life, instead of used up in just sex. When I increase kissing in my life I decrease productivity, and I'd rather have the productivity."*[29]

R$_S$-lasts have tried to get happiness from being with someone really sexy, and it wasn't worth it. The joy was temporary while their long-term happiness suffered. Sex has moments of function and pleasure. Sexual attraction doesn't have a deeper meaning. The meaning of life has to do with friends, family, sensory pleasures, health, food, entertainment, good deals, and loving yourself. Sex is pleasant too, when it happens, but it's definitely less important than the rest of that.

> *"The #1 thing people who were satisfied with their marriages*
> *had in common was that they never bought into*
> *the dangerous fantasy - the myth - of Happily Ever After.*
> *Sometimes you will be miserable.*
> *This is the reality of long-term intimacy. Carry on."* [30]

From the perspective of R_S-lasts, R_Ss only seem to have disadvantages. Why is the immediate framing of new inputs in terms of sexual attraction and orgasms? Why can't the framing just be love for sunsets, love for people, love for food and fun, and caring about things because they're fulfilling? R_Ss invest their time and emotions in relationships that are obvious mismatches from the start, repeatedly hurting the feelings of whoever their next victim/target is. They're so focused on finding their imaginary "true love" that they overlook the actual best real-world matches because that person wasn't born into a symmetrical-enough body or has a lower sexual appetite. R_Ss seek very high sexiness from partners while having sub-optimal real-world bodies themselves. R_Ss think romantic options are sexually aroused when they're actually feeling Social or Comfort based attraction. R_Ss overestimate how sexy a new partner will be in bed and how much the other person values sex. R_Ss passionately disregard reality, enthusiastically find ways to be unhappy with what exists, and make bad decisions among existing options. They seem to be unaware of real-world sex, while thinking they're experts in real-world sex. R_Ss bully other people into having sex, into leaving acceptable-but-not-especially-sexual relationships, into sacrificing to look sexier, because the R_S is immersed in an individual exaggeration of the value of sexual arousal. In critical moments, R_Ss sacrifice friends, memberships, the good will of others, resources, image, health, and safety because they're distracted with having sex that won't be very good. What R_Ss are actually experts at is generating hurt feelings, broken families, STDs, and unwanted pregnancies. Why would anyone want that life?

> *"Of course it's possible to love a human being,*
> *if you don't know them too well."* [31]

There is no disappointment to feel with real-world sex or the attractiveness of real-world sexual partners. Sexual excitement comes and goes for everyone, and often isn't present at all. The way sex happens is fine. The frequency of sex is fine. There's no need for more, less, better, or different. It's still worth making sure that sex gets maintenance, but that maintenance can happen without tension and relief, without fixated daydreams, and without judging what's happening as good or bad. R_S-lasts are realistic about what they've got, what they get from it, what their options are, and what it costs. Part of what makes sex valuable is that it doesn't need extra attention in order to do its function. R_S-lasts live in the sexual satisfaction that R_S-firsts can't find, because R_S-lasts live in reality, undistracted by visions of not-reality.

> *"I don't believe in true love. But I do believe in something*
> *even more miraculous and beautiful. Which is that two people*
> *who were not created explicitly for each other can still find a way*
> *to share a lifetime of joy and grief and wonder and hope.*
> *We spend all this time in our culture talking about falling in love.*
> *We should talk more about being in love, and growing in love,*
> *and how the decades of that can really be amazing."[32]*

Cross Overs

"Yeah, well **my** first husband left me for a tennis ball."

© *Teresa Burns Parkhurst[33]*

Most R_S-lasts can be overwhelmed with sexual attraction to the point where it silences other focus options because they are about to kiss a breathtaking hottie. Most R_S-lasts can be overwhelmed with heartbreak when a very sexy partner leaves for someone else. But sexual fixations happen with WAY fewer people, WAY less frequently, and satisfaction comes much faster just by realizing that what happened is the fixed reality.

> *"The best part of a romantic relationship is the very beginning, when you haven't met yet and you're still single."*[34]

Many times a day R_S-firsts interact with sexual options without considering the sexual arousal of the moment because those sex options don't have arousal triggers. R_S-firsts can be distracted by other topics, even while interacting with someone they would otherwise find attractive, but have true neutral lack of consideration of sex in that moment. Even for an R_S-first, it feels like awkward, tedious work to generate a sexual fantasy about someone they feel no attraction to.

R_S Conclusions

If I could only bring three things to a desert island,

all three would be you.

And I'd make you all kiss.

© *e horne and j comeau – asofterworld.com*[35]

The addition of R_S means sex isn't just functional anymore. Other people's words, actions, bodies, and sexual excitement are loved, exciting, beautiful, and desirable, triggering excitement, joy, concern, disappointment, pain, and relief. R_S tension and relief aren't necessary for a person to form a partnership, have sex, and reproduce. But sexual tension and relief add focus and incentive to seek out healthy-looking partners with sexually exaggerated features and have more sex with them. It adds incentives to protect and amplify the observer's own sexual qualities.

> *"I still hold onto a small, childish hope that there's someone out there in this crazy world so completely, utterly meant for me that even the stars will sigh, at last, in relief at our meeting."*[36]

R_S-firsts have more enthusiastic sex with more attractive partners because they invest so much time and energy in seeking out, building, and maintaining sexual excitement. A consistent focus on sex quality and quantity helps them seize opportunities to have orgasms. They're constantly sacrificing for the benefit of the sexual attraction they'll feel. But they're the least satisfied with sex because daily tension reminds them to focus on what's wrong and imagine and feel desire for better.

i'm not very attracted to you

never have been really...

are you talking about gravity?!

yeah... just not feeling it

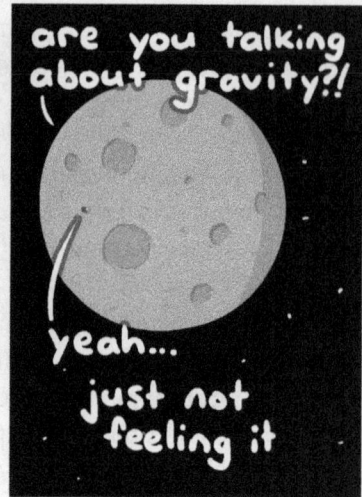

Easily Confused for the R$_S$ Spectrum

*"Love is a form of prejudice. You love what you need.
You love what makes you feel good. You love what is convenient."*[38]

This chapter compares R$_S$ to the six other motivators one-by-one. It holds the topic constant (sex) and looks at it from each of the seven perspectives so you can hear that it's the framing of the topic that gives away the observer's motivators, not the topic itself. Each observer's experience of other people's sexual features is different when they're feeling different kinds of tension and seeking different kinds of relief from sex. This is the chapter to come back to when determining the relative influence of R$_S$ versus any other motivator for a person. But, also, for the people who think the last chapter got R$_S$ a little "wrong," this is where you find out that you're actually dominated by a different motivator than R$_S$, and your "right" definition of sexual arousal comes from valuing a different emotion.

*One person's "she belongs in a psych ward,"
is another person's "she's all I ever wanted."*[39]

Valuing Sexual Attractiveness, Sex, and Orgasms While Feeling Sex-Based Relationalness (R$_S$):

An observer who dominantly gets flushed with sexual attraction is more likely to think that other people are also thinking about sexual attraction. Meanwhile, other people aren't horny because they rarely get triggered with the feeling of being horny. Other people aren't noticing sexual features on surrounding bodies because they're rarely or never triggered with sharp, fixating excitement about the shape of body parts, or the sexual arousal of other people. Instead, not-R$_S$s are in a totally different mindset where sex isn't relevant.

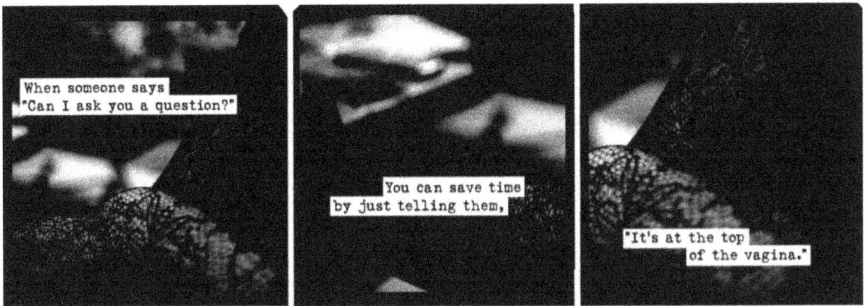

When someone says "Can I ask you a question?"

You can save time by just telling them,

"It's at the top of the vagina."

Others are listening to the R$_S$ to be polite, to support their friend's emotions, hoping to be entertained, because they're scared, because it's part of the adventure they're on, because they're impressed and hoping to become individually special to the R$_S$, or because it's functional while they get another task done. The people near an R$_S$ are in the mindsets of their hungers, hoping the R$_S$ will help satisfy those hungers, while the R$_S$ is in an R$_S$ framed mindset, hoping others will satisfy their sexual hungers.

> *"Being a Hollywood beauty was a mixed blessing.*
> *The fact that I became one is probably the loveliest,*
> *most glamorous, and fortunate misunderstanding."*[41]

When R$_S$s don't get the reactions from other people that they expect, R$_S$s usually think the lesser reaction must be because the R$_S$ wasn't sexy enough or wasn't seductive enough. Meanwhile the other person is actually reacting to the fact that what the R$_S$ said doesn't seem to help the friendship, group harmony, self-esteem, individuality, life experiences, resources, or health that the moment felt like it was about from the other person's perspective.

There are some secrets
I will take to my grave.

But I don't want loving you

to be one of them.

© *e horne and j comeau – asofterworld.com*[42]

Someone flushed with R$_S$ is missing other topics of conversation because they're so turned on, they're so attracted, they're so aroused, that the only topic happening in their minds is sexual escalation.

Valuing Sexual Attractiveness, Sex, and Orgasms While Feeling Individuality-Based Comfort (C$_I$):

"I wish that I could see the inside of your head, when you say you like the things I do. Because I don't think they're all that great, not that impressive, so why do you? I often try to flip the camera around and look at me, but I can't find it, the little spark you think I possess. So you can tell me all the things that I should love about myself. But why would I thank you when I'm none of this. Can I really thank you for your words when I don't believe them myself?"[43]

"The hard part in finding a romantic partner is finding someone who is worthy of me."[44]

"I enjoy romantic relationships. It's nice to have someone around who worships you."[45]

When someone is considering sex or a sexual partner while tense about their own value, individuality, authenticity, agency, and impressiveness, they're in a different mindset than someone who is so attracted to a beautiful angel that they hunger for sexual contact with genitals. C_Is mistakenly think R_Ss are feeling impressed, confident, proud, defensive, or self-loathing, when R_Ss are actually feeling sexual attraction. Someone feeling just R_S has zero thoughts about their own "value" and might not know why anyone would love or not love themselves, or how that could be relevant to sex. An R_S is internally explaining why their partner is sexy in themselves, with zero inclusion or evaluation of themselves.

> *"People think a soul mate is your perfect fit,*
> *and that's what everyone wants. But a true soul mate is a mirror,*
> *the person who shows you everything that is holding you back,*
> *the person who brings you to your own attention*
> *so you can change your life.*
> *A true soul mate is probably the most important person*
> *you'll ever meet, because they tear down your walls*
> *and smack you awake."[46]*

When someone is sexually aroused by C_I tension, they're impressed by the greatness, individuality, and power of a partner. They like the way that being with that impressive person makes the observer feel about themselves. A C_I sees sexual partners as reflections of their own value. It's joyful and relieving to watch a partner who is flushed with impressed attraction as they worship the observer's body. Tension happens when a sexual partner isn't impressed by the observer, isn't impressive, when the observer feels interchangeable (rather than individually special), or when an impressive partner wants the sex to be a secret (so the observer can't get the satisfaction of other people's admiration or jealousy). Is the C_I being used or exploited? Should they stand up for themselves? Are they being rejected because they're not good enough? Sex feels external and functional while someone is fixated with C_I tensions, because the C_I is focused on themselves, modeling how self is being treated. A C_I then thinks they're getting sexual attention because of their greatness, because of their individuality, because they rank so high, when an R_S is turned on by their jaw shape, hair, and chest.

> *"Whatever impresses you attracts you."[47]*

"If I am the longest relationship of my life,
isn't it time to nurture intimacy and love
with the person I lie in bed with each night"[48]

A C$_I$ typically feels superior to R$_S$s because the C$_I$ "knows" that the R$_S$ is seeking validation through sex. The R$_S$ could learn so much from the superior insights of the C$_I$. When, really, the C$_I$ is forming a story about self being individual and superior to resolve their own tension about being individual and superior, misunderstanding that an R$_S$ is just horny and sexually aroused, with no tension about self, individuality, or validation.

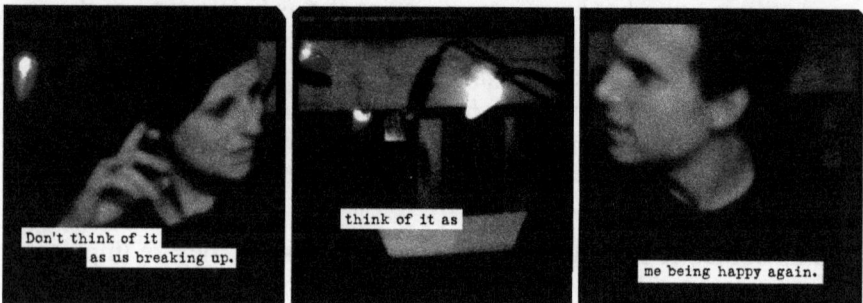

Don't think of it as us breaking up.

think of it as

me being happy again.

© *e horne and j comeau – asofterworld.com*[49]

"Love is the extremely difficult realization
that something other than oneself is real."[50]

"Be ~~with~~ someone who makes you happy."[51]

LH: "Have you fallen in love with the wrong person yet?"
JW: "Unfortunately, Lady of the Haven,
my one true love remains myself."
LH: "At least, you don't have to worry about rejection, Jace Wayland."
JW: "Not necessarily. I turn myself down occasionally,
just to keep it interesting."[52]

"When you're ugly and someone loves you,
you know they love you for who you are.
Beautiful people never know who to trust."[53]

"The most painful thing is losing yourself in the process of loving
someone too much, and forgetting that you are special too."[54]

"I don't dress to impress.
I undress to impress."[55]

"I really want a romantic partner.
But that desire bothers me because it's so stereotypical
and it's so important that I be unique."[56]

Valuing Sexual Attractiveness, Sex, and Orgasms While Feeling Alliance-Based Socialness (S$_F$):

"If I have a dream about another girl,
I feel guilty IN THE DREAM.
I'll be like, 'I can't do this, I have to go,
how did I get myself in THIS situation?'"[57]

If you're having sex with someone because they're such a good person, because the goodness of their soul is endearing, because you want them to be happy, because they obviously want it and you don't want to disappoint them, or if you feel obligated because they want it and you don't have the words to say 'no,' that is S$_F$. If you'd want sex with that body even if it had a crappy personality inside of it, even if they didn't want sex, because their body is so physically attractive, then that's pure R$_S$. Caring about another person's feelings is a different feeling from being sexually aroused and hungry for sex with their body.

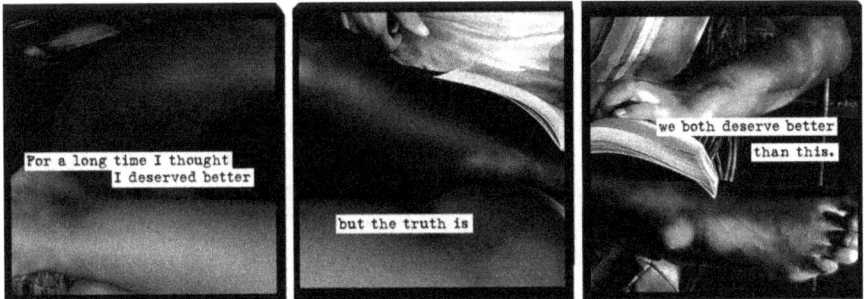

For a long time I thought I deserved better

but the truth is

we both deserve better than this.

© e horne and j comeau – asofterworld.com[58]

When someone wants sex because they're feeling S$_F$ tension, they think their partner is tense because they want sex, so the observer is trying to relieve and relax their partner, so the observer can then also feel relief and relax. If a partner feels bad about their body or their attractiveness, an S$_F$ feels tension about their pain and seeks out the words and actions to make their partner feel good about themselves again, relieving both people. The way to get sexual escalation started is to express affection for each others' souls and reinforce that the two are merged partners. The merged, loving, emotionally entangled friendship is what's valuable.

> *"When two people love each other,*
> *they don't look at each other.*
> *They look in the same direction."*[59]

Tension happens when a sex partner is ignoring the friendship while getting sexual satisfaction. Is the friend's mind elsewhere? Are they focused on just sex when together, or always not-in-the-mood when the observer is aroused? Is this alliance real? Are both people emotionally invested in each others' emotions? An S$_F$ feels tension if their friend has sexual desires that the S$_F$ doesn't want to fill. They feel obligated to satisfy the friend's needs, but are too repulsed from sex itself by other motivators. An S$_F$ feels tension if the sex feels too impersonal. S$_F$s then thinks they're getting sexual attention because the other person sees the goodness of their soul and values the merged connection the two share, while an R$_S$ is turned on by their sexual organs, the sexual vocal tone, and the shape of their butt.

> *"Really loving another person, really adoring their soul, feeling so connected that you're flushed with affection and relaxation in their presence makes something about life feel right. The quirky shared jokes, the shared interpretation of moments, the way they drop everything and feel your pain when you hurt. You've found your person. They are your home. Life feels full and complete because of this other soul. Sex is a great addition to that because it's more separation of this relationship from the rest of the world. I don't just love your soul, I want my mouth on your body. I want all of me pressed up against and combined with all of you. It makes sense that that level of excitement and satisfaction happens with you. But if you were hit by a bus and your body was a noodle, I would want to be there to love you and care for that noodle because the other half of me is the soul in your head."*[60]

Valuing Sexual Attractiveness, Sex, and Orgasms While Feeling Body-Based Comfort (C$_B$):

> *"Intimacy is when you can tell someone your truth,*
> *when you can show yourself to them,*
> *when you stand in front of them bare*
> *and their response is 'you're safe with me.'"*[61]

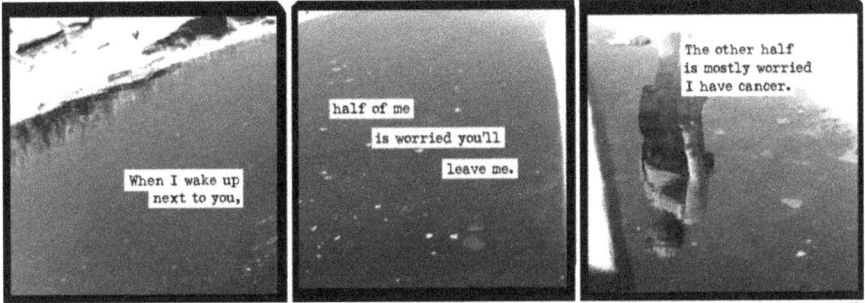

When I wake up next to you,

half of me

is worried you'll

leave me.

The other half is mostly worried I have cancer.

© *e horne and j comeau – asofterworld.com*[62]

> *"How brave of you, to love so deeply."*[63]

Everyone is much more vulnerable when they're alone, especially when they're also asleep. Pleasant physical sensations and peaceful satisfaction come with orgasms. C$_B$s can mistakenly think R$_S$s are acting sexual because they're feeling fear and seeking safety, when R$_S$s are actually feeling sexual attraction.

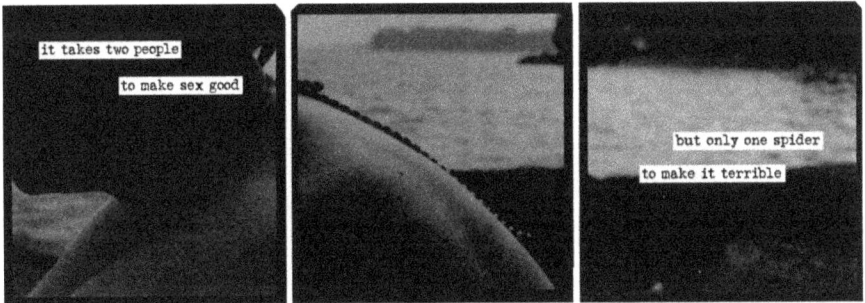

it takes two people

to make sex good

but only one spider

to make it terrible

© *e horne and j comeau – asofterworld.com*[64]

When someone values sex and sexual attraction while flushed with C$_B$ tension, then their partner's sexual enthusiasm for them confirms that they're safe and their partner would still protect them. Tension happens when the smells, sounds, textures, temperature, visuals, and

49

body functions like sweat aren't right during sex. Tension happens if the observer's body is in an uncomfortable position. Tension happens when the observer stops feeling safe and protected. Tension is relieved when a partner takes the time to make themselves familiar, shows the same interest in safety, and shows the same interest in making the observer feel cared for first. Tension is relieved when the observer knows that they won't get hurt with surprises or disconnection after sex. C$_{BS}$ fantasize about having a perfectly clean, delightful smelling partner who loves them completely. A C$_B$ then thinks they're getting sexual attention because they're safe, comfortable, and familiar, when an R$_S$ is turned on by their returned sexual arousal, the shape of their lips, and firmness or softness of body parts.

© Loryn Brantz – LorynBrantz.com[65]

Some C$_B$s get very caught up in the aesthetics of humans, and find certain bodies very pleasing to observe and others uncomfortable and unpleasing. The difference between C$_B$ and R$_S$ is whether the pleasing feeling makes them hungry for touching and orgasms, or whether appreciating the beauty doesn't fixate them with hunger for sex. Is the person pleasant to look at, like a beautiful flower? Or are your genitals engorging?

Status: In a Relationsleep[66]

*"There is no substitute for the comfort supplied
by the utterly taken-for-granted relationship."*[67]

Someone feeling only C$_B$ is not in a relationship with sex. They love comfort, safety, and wellbeing. Sex is something which can add or subtract from those. Sex is an option evaluated for its costs and benefits to comfort, health, and safety, which are the actual topics of the moment.

*Date: "You told me you were interesting."
Me: "I said I was 'into resting.'"*[68]

"We are never so defenseless against suffering as when we love."[69]

"A much needed pee can feel better than the average orgasm."[70]

Valuing Sexual Attractiveness, Sex, and Orgasms While Feeling Community-Based Socialness (S$_C$):

S$_C$s sometimes think that R$_S$s seek sex because they're surrounded by people and a culture that glorifies sex and are conforming to those standards. Meanwhile, R$_S$s find their target to be so shockingly sexy that the R$_S$ would (and often does) want sex right now even if the one group rule was to never have sex with that person. An S$_C$ thinks that emotions about group harmony are obviously tied to sex, while an R$_S$ won't be conscious of the group again until after their fixated sexual arousal is satisfied.

An S$_C$ wants sex too, but trusts the community to have developed standards for how sex happens best. The community is right that hurt feelings, babies, and STDs are best managed by picking a partner who the group approves of. The group will be the least disturbed if marriage (the ceremony where the group gives its approval for a couple to have sex) happens before sex.

© *Hector Cantú and Carlos Castellanos*[71]

Even though they're community-focused, S$_C$s are the most protective of their sexual information because they don't want anyone else to be upset by what's happening. This is true whether they're being more kinky and active than others expect, or less kinky and active. But they will probably provide the information slowly to trusted people because they feel like their actions in bed impact the greater values they're supporting.

At some point in your life somebody has masturbated to the thought of you.

[–] nobodythemadder
I don't believe so. But alright

[–] PitchforksEnthusiast
I got you homie, my next one goes out to you

Reddit.com[72]

S$_C$s have a fantasy about meeting another member of the group who is equally dedicated to their values, who everyone loves and respects, who does their part, who becomes their best friend, who follows all of the rules and marries them in the standard, group-accepted way. An S$_C$ then thinks they're getting sexual attention because of their social values, their importance to the group, and because sexual arousal is expected, while an R$_S$ is hungry for sex with them because of their laugh, their teeth, and their weight.

For an S$_C$, tension happens when group members feel romantic attraction imbalances for each other, and when partnership shifts happen and someone's feelings are hurt. An S$_C$ feels a draw to correct social injustices with their partner choice, and relationship style. Someone feeling only S$_C$ is serving a higher purpose for humanity, and their individual connections are always subservient to their obligation to the harmony of the whole group.

Valuing Sexual Attractiveness, Sex, and Orgasms While Feeling Resource-Based Comfort (C$_R$):

> *"If I had a relationship, I'd probably eat vegetables more,*
> *I'd probably exercise more,*
> *I'd probably wake up feeling happy because I had sex."[73]*

C$_R$s think that R$_S$s seek sex to fill biological needs, to fill companionship needs, to be entertained, or maybe because they're trading for money or a lifestyle that they enjoy. Meanwhile, someone feeling just R$_S$ has zero thoughts about resources and doesn't know how those could be related to sexual attraction. C$_R$s mistakenly thinks R$_S$s are feeling boredom, greed, food hunger, acquisition desire, or resource-love when R$_S$s are actually feeling sexual attraction.

assumed sleeping areas for a couple sharing a bed — their side | your side

actual arrangement — their side | your side

© Justin Boyd – InvisibleBread.com[74]

When someone is sexually aroused by C_R tension, they're recognizing that people with resources can do more to look attractive, enjoying the entertainment value of sex, recognizing that people with resources are higher value partners, and recognizing that sex can be part of a fair trade between partners who are filling each others needs, especially if the effort they have to exert is fair.

"Thinking about you is like remembering that I have ice cream in the freezer."[75]

© Mackenzie Moore - CinimomoComics[76]

Both partners are humans with similar hungers, so a reasonable deal seems possible. Hopefully both partners will leave with more than they had on their own. Tension happens when a sexual partner asks for more than they're giving, or asks more than the observer can deliver. Tension happens when the observer has to do all the work, or has too many other prices involved in sex. C_{RS} sometimes think they're getting sexual attention because of their resources, when an R_S is turned on by their shoulders, eyes, and height.

"More than by love, a person gets excited by money."[77]

WHAT SOME PEOPLE WANT FOR CHRISTMAS

WHAT I WANT FOR CHRISTMAS

LORYN BRANTZ

© Loryn Brantz – LorynBrantz.com[78]

"Unpartnered adults aged 25 to 54 have worse outcomes than those who are married or cohabitating, for both men and women. Unpartnered adults have lower earnings, on average, than partnered adults and are less likely to be employed or economically independent. They also have lower average education attainment and are more likely to live with their parents. Married and cohabitating adults fare better than those who are unpartnered when it comes to health outcomes as well."[79]

A C_R typically thinks that R_Ss are overvaluing sex and undervaluing the prices they pay for that sex. They're getting bad deals because they're too desperate and not considering all the factors involved in the transaction. They could save a lot of effort and money by calming down.

"A romantic relationship has a very slim chance of making me happy. But food makes me happy 100% of the time. I think that's why you go to dinner on a date. Because you want to compare if the person in front of you is going to make you as happy as the food you ordered. If it's a bad date, it's like, "I choose the quesadilla."[80]

Valuing Sexual Attractiveness, Sex, and Orgasms While Feeling Experience-Based Relationalness (R_A):

"I wouldn't get involved with me if you aren't into evolving."[81]

What more extreme way is there to intensely connect with someone than sex? Even though R_A happens right next to R_S, R_A is dominant if the sex feels more like an experience, if it's exciting because it's new and extreme, rather than because the other person's body is so beautiful and the observer is hungry for an orgasm. An R_A feels satisfaction because they were afraid to approach, but conquered their fears by getting all the way to orgasms with a new, sexy person. They've now grown because they became familiar with something that was unknown and felt impossible before. The next morning, when the partner starts explaining all the ridiculous, arbitrary rules they follow, the R_A will realize they can't imprison themselves to this person's self-limitations. Sometimes an R_A wants to have sex in a crazy place, in a crazy situation, for the experience of it, while their R$_S$ partner is in love with their sexy body and isn't getting any thrill from the extreme experience also happening.

Tension is felt when someone says the R$_A$ can't have sex because of ridiculous external rules. For some reason, truly evil people are hell bent on making sure that intelligent people don't live their lives. Someone who worships fear and fake boundaries is emotionally toxic. They can either get over it and realize that life is to be lived, or they are a human cancer.

C$_I$: The Individuality-Based Tension Spectrum

"Knowing yourself is the beginning of all wisdom"[83]

Individuality-based Comfort (C$_I$) tension adds a focusing need for escalation or repair, paired with relieving self-worth satisfaction to the noticing of self, identity, and ranking related inputs. Feeling tension when comparisons happen, and when self is or isn't included causes the observer to notice and focus on self, ranking, and influence, and create understandings about the deep meaningfulness individuality and greatness. Each person is somewhere on the spectrum from being frequently triggered with very strong tension about self, identity, and ranking (being flushed with fixating arousal by competition, judgment, respect, self-criticism over missed opportunities at glory, and hunger for excellence), to being infrequently triggered with weak or no tension about self, identity, and ranking (observing self, identity, and ranking for what they are without additional hunger for escalation and satisfaction).

The Self/Ranking Pleasure Spectrum

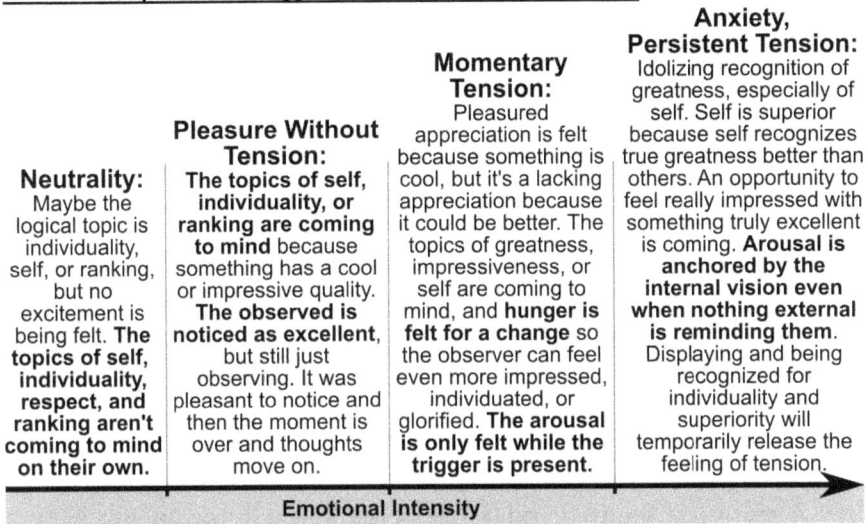

Neutrality:	Pleasure Without Tension:	Momentary Tension:	Anxiety, Persistent Tension:
Maybe the logical topic is individuality, self, or ranking, but no excitement is being felt. **The topics of self, individuality, respect, and ranking aren't coming to mind on their own.**	The topics of self, individuality, or ranking are coming to mind because something has a cool or impressive quality. **The observed is noticed as excellent,** but still just observing. It was pleasant to notice and then the moment is over and thoughts move on.	Pleasured appreciation is felt because something is cool, but it's a lacking appreciation because it could be better. The topics of greatness, impressiveness, or self are coming to mind, and **hunger is felt for a change** so the observer can feel even more impressed, individuated, or glorified. **The arousal is only felt while the trigger is present.**	Idolizing recognition of greatness, especially of self. Self is superior because self recognizes true greatness better than others. An opportunity to feel really impressed with something truly excellent is coming. **Arousal is anchored by the internal vision even when nothing external is reminding them.** Displaying and being recognized for individuality and superiority will temporarily release the feeling of tension.

Emotional Intensity

Terminology & Abbreviations

Self and ranking **neutrality** is felt when observing anything which is just a factual, fixed part of reality. The topics of impressiveness, excellence, or self aren't coming to mind because the input is unrelated or just coincidentally related in fixed, unchangeable ways. isn't noticed as being particularly impressive or unimpressive because it'. Most people feel self and ranking neutrality when considering the moon versus Mars, ranking the excellence of clouds, and rating themselves on how they open drawers. Those things exist, but don't bring the topic of self, individuality, and ranking to mind, and especially don't trigger a focusing hunger for differentiation, glory, or individual attention.

Self and ranking **pleasure without tension** is recognition of momentary individuation, superiority or excellence. This is what is felt when someone is alone and throws trash across the room that lands in the trash can. It's the pleasure felt when a random person speaks to you with more respect than they needed to. It feels like noticing that self is being respected, self is individually recognized, or that something is truly great, but in a fixed, momentary, practical way. The moment feels complete as soon as it happens. There's no hunger to be even more respected, individuated, or great.

Self and ranking **pleasure with tension** feels like noticing an opportunity for something good about self, ranking, and individuality, but in a lacking way. There's potential for more self, individuality, and ranking pleasure and focus hungers for the thing to happen.

- **Momentary positive tension** (externally triggered tension) is hunger for escalation that only exists while the trigger is present. It's what it feels like when a quiz question is asked, you're the only person who knows the answer, but you haven't spoken it yet. It's what it feels like to watch a competitor who is about to make a fool of themselves. It's when you know the host of the party will be excited to see you and is about to turn your way. Attention is focused and desire is felt, but will be quickly relieved. It's small enough that the moment will be forgotten as soon as it happens.

- **Anxiety, persistent positive tension** (internally maintained tension) is hunger for self, individuality, and ranking escalation which persists even when the external trigger isn't present. It is confidence, self love, and anticipation of self's potential and excellence. Self's ability and impact will be clear, everyone is going to notice and be impressed, and self will bask in glory. Focus is on an internal vision of the excellence that will be displayed and the glorious results that will be felt. Internal attention solves for the path from the present moment to that escalated self, individuality, and ranking intensity. Other topics are hard to consider because this mind is excited for self, individuality, and ranking.

The Self/Ranking Pain Spectrum

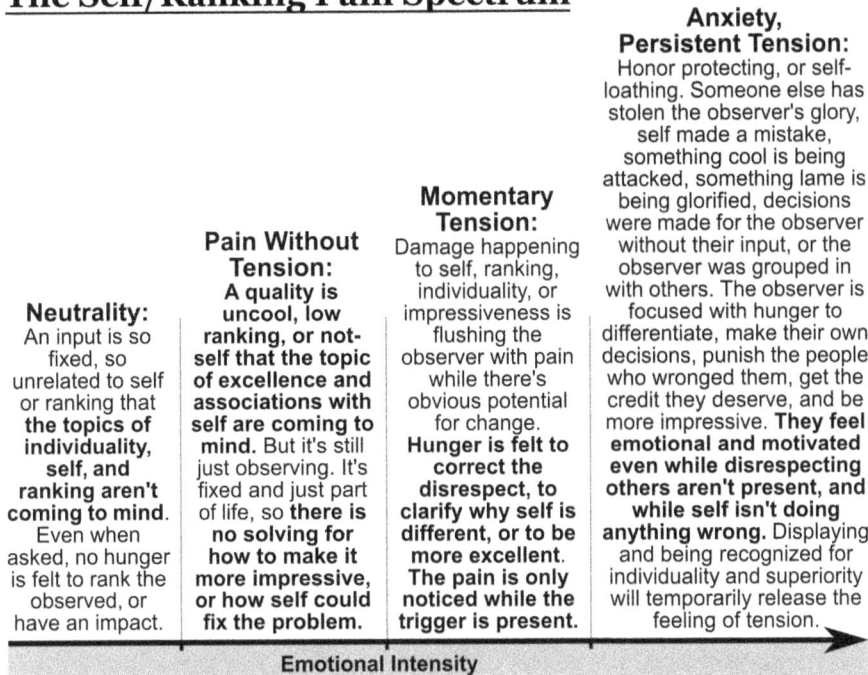

Neutrality:	Pain Without Tension:	Momentary Tension:	Anxiety, Persistent Tension:
An input is so fixed, so unrelated to self or ranking that the topics of **individuality, self, and ranking aren't coming to mind**. Even when asked, no hunger is felt to rank the observed, or have an impact.	**A quality is uncool, low ranking, or not-self that the topic of excellence and associations with self are coming to mind**. But it's still just observing. It's fixed and just part of life, so **there is no solving for how to make it more impressive, or how self could fix the problem**.	Damage happening to self, ranking, individuality, or impressiveness is flushing the observer with pain while there's obvious potential for change. **Hunger is felt to correct the disrespect, to clarify why self is different, or to be more excellent. The pain is only noticed while the trigger is present**.	Honor protecting, or self-loathing. Someone else has stolen the observer's glory, self made a mistake, something cool is being attacked, something lame is being glorified, decisions were made for the observer without their input, or the observer was grouped in with others. The observer is focused with hunger to differentiate, make their own decisions, punish the people who wronged them, get the credit they deserve, and be more impressive. **They feel emotional and motivated even while disrespecting others aren't present, and while self isn't doing anything wrong**. Displaying and being recognized for individuality and superiority will temporarily release the feeling of tension.

Emotional Intensity ⟶

Self and ranking **pain without tension** is the realistic self and ranking negativity of an imperfect world. You wanted to roll a 6 and win, but you rolled a 2 and lost. Someone else can go in the shorter line because they have status and you're in the regular line because you don't. It's passive, negative recognition that self got a negative option, but it feels fixed and doesn't hold attention for more than a moment. It feels like objective recognition of external reality. Thoughts easily move to the next topic because there's nothing more to consider about it.

Self, individuality, and ranking **pain with tension** is discomfort felt when noticing that self, individuality, or ranking have taken damage or are in danger, but in a lacking way that wants something to change. Self is being treated unfairly, disrespectfully, being grouped in with others, or is failing. But it's not just logical. The observer is flushed with the feeling of negative expectation that things should be different. They feel activated and hungry for an adjustment to happen so this pain can be stopped.

- **Momentary negative tension** (externally triggered tension) happens in moments where action can be quickly taken to restore self's greatness, individuality, or respect. Someone says, "we all like the same thing," and momentary tension is felt until the observer speaks up and says they individually like a different option. But what's keeping pain happening is the continued observation of the uncool, disrespecting, conforming, or not-self feature. If the moment is suddenly interrupted before the tense observer can speak up, the moment will be forgotten because it didn't actually matter much. The most common C_I momentary tension is felt when someone else makes a declarative statement and the C_I feels compelled to add an adjustment or clarification. The tension is relieved when the C_I voices their insight.

- **Anxiety, persistent negative tension** (internally maintained tension) is a sharp feeling of being disrespected, humiliated, inferior, ignored, or abandoned, which makes self's individuality and superiority feel threatened, decreasing, damaged, or disappointing. It's regret that past opportunities for self to be impressive weren't fully seized. You really let yourself down. Someone clearly disrespected you and is getting away with it. It's also the feeling of being taken advantage of, of self being screwed over, or of self being lumped in with others unjustly. You did something right, but someone just explained why your way was wrong and laughed. Focus shifts to internally cycling in the negativity of the moment long after all the external reminders are gone. This impediment to self, individuality, and ranking arousal needs to be resolved because the pain is so sharp and lingers for so long.

Individuality-based Comfort **satisfaction** is felt when a tense urgency about self or ranking is resolved. The observer fought back and had a shockingly decisive victory. The attacker is punished and others marvel at the skill exhibited to do it. Satisfaction is the relief which comes through other people being impressed with the observer again, or jealous because of the observer's excellence. The observer is not only right, but impressive, clever, and individual for being so right. Satisfaction is felt when others modify themselves in the ways the C_I suggested. C_I satisfaction also comes from being truly impressed with self, from standing up for self and getting self's choices, through verifying that negative rank-indicators about self weren't accurate, that ranking wasn't actually threatened, and sometimes just from differentiating.

The shorthand for people who are triggered with Individuality-based Comfort tension and anxiety more often and strongly than the other tension and anxiety options is that these people are "**C_I-first**." When a reference is made to "a C_I," or "C_Is," it's identifying the discussed person or people as being C_I-first.

The shorthand for people who are triggered more strongly and frequently by all six other tension options is that people are "**C_I-last**." Someone who is C_I-last can still feel tension when someone tries to control them, but it's more often momentary and can be more easily interrupted by Social tension about other people's feelings, or Relational tension about sexual attractiveness.

We're now going to immerse in the life experience people have when they're most frequently and strongly struck by Individuality-based Comfort tensions to see what it's like to live at the highest end of the spectrum. Then we'll immerse in the life experience of people who feel the six other tensions more strongly and frequently to see what it's like to live at the lowest end of the C_I spectrum.

© *e horne and j comeau – asofterworld.com*[84]

C$_I$-First: Frequently Triggered Strong C$_I$ Tension

> *"Work until you no longer have to introduce yourself."*[85]

Being C$_I$-first means feeling emotions before logic has had a chance to evaluate an input. C$_I$-firsts are stabbed with negative self consciousness when they perform poorly or make a mistake, especially while other people are watching. **The observers' bodies aren't getting touched, and yet they're flushed with pain as if the damage to their impressiveness were physical damage happening to themselves.** Was the pain a response to logic? No. C$_I$-firsts don't logically assess the utility of the task, the true damage done to their reputations, and then make a logical choice to feel pain. The observer can't logically choose to feel pain on command from other logical negatives which don't trigger the feeling. The pain happens automatically and simultaneously with the observation of self's mistakes, losses, and conformity. Logic is used after the feeling to explain why the error wasn't self's fault and how to reestablish self's superiority and individuation (satisfaction conditions which would bring relief).

> *"Maybe Tetris was trying to teach us*
> *That if we fit in, we disappear"*[86]

C$_I$s are then flushed with intoxicating pleasure when they expertly handle a difficult problem, especially when it impresses others. Is the pleasure felt a response to logic? No. C$_I$-firsts don't logically assess the functional value of the action, how impressed other people really are, the true rarity of possessing such skills, and then make a logical choice to feel euphoria from the impact they're making. They can't logically decide to feel that feeling on the unimpressive actions of an unimpressive person. Logic is used after the feeling to explain why this moment is evidence that self is individuated and superior and why that matters enough to generate pleasure.

> *"I'm better at self-esteem than most people."*[87]

The third feeling which really cements these in is that C_I-first observers can tolerate much bigger problems in other areas without getting triggered with excitement or concern about them. There was an awkward moment with a friend, but not enough pain was triggered to make it feel like action is needed. Other humans are misunderstanding each other, but those misunderstandings aren't painful enough that the observer has to get involved. A cutie didn't look this way, but that isn't painful enough to require action. Activities aren't perfect, but there aren't any exciting options right now. Resources are generic and sufficient at the moment. These topics aren't coming to mind because they're within the ranges of pain where they're not a problem that needs attention (because this observer isn't triggered with tension about them at these levels). They're happening how life happens.

> *"There is a vitality, a life force, an energy, a quickening that is translated through you into action, and because there is only one of you in all of time, this expression is unique. And if you block it, it will never exist through any other medium and it will be lost. The world will not have it. It is not your business to determine how good it is nor how valuable nor how it compares with other expressions. It is your business to keep it yours clearly and directly, to keep the channel open."[88]*

Approaching the highest end of the C_I spectrum, observers are drugged with much more self and ranking arousal and heartbreak more easily, by more inputs. But it doesn't feel individual and it doesn't feel internal. It's obvious that self is better or worse than nearby people. It's obvious that humans and other inputs are ranked and that that ranking matters. Differentiated people are objectively superior and non-differentiated people are objectively inferior. It makes logical sense to manage self-expectations if self's successes and failures are going to flush self with tension. It makes sense to manage self's image if other people's impressed or unimpressed reactions to self will trigger tension. It makes logical sense to be impressive if the world has an elite who are impressive individuals among mindless drones who aren't. Someone who is choosing to not be impressive and individuated is getting the natural consequences of ignoring a critical basic of life. Confidence matters. At the highest setting, it feels like all human interactions happen based on the ranks and impressiveness of the people involved, based on each individual's excellence and individuality.

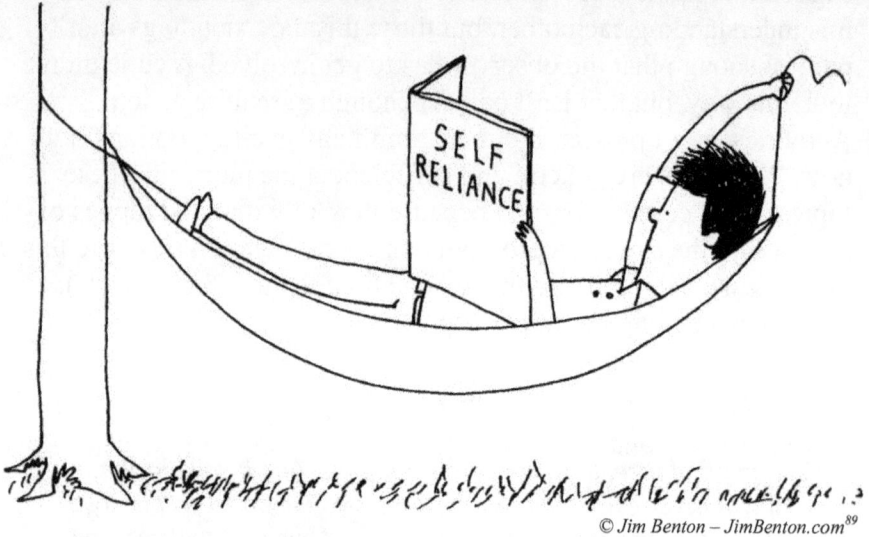

© Jim Benton – JimBenton.com[89]

A C_I observer feels tension because other people are doing things wrong. The C_I needs to speak up. The C_I's tension will be relieved when they correct others, especially if those others are impressed. Meanwhile, every other part of life is normal. The reason to focus on self's changes is that self was so right and others were so wrong. Since these moments happen so frequently, what can be done to escalate the intensity of the good feelings felt? What can be said or done so people are even more overwhelmed by self's excellence? Tension is felt as the opportunity starts to slip away. Is the topic changing before the observer gets to say the killer line? Is some other idiot saying something too similar and getting the attention instead? Since the rest of life is ignorably acceptable, the moments when self displays superior excellence feel meaningful. C_Is don't want to think about self and ranking again, but another moment came up on its own which requires action or regret.

> *"There's a thousand yous.*
> *There's only one of me."*[90]

Half of what makes self-based feelings feel objective is that self does so many things that inspire no tension, happiness, sadness, or relief, even for C$_I$-firsts. No pain is felt because passing strangers aren't stopping to notice and admire the observer, because the observer wasn't trying to stand out as impressive in that moment. There are so many moments which don't automatically trigger sharp emotions, that the moments which do make the observer feel self conscious, proud, or embarrassed must actually be evidence of an individual greatness which matters.

> *"If we were not all so interested in ourselves,*
> *life would be so uninteresting that none of us*
> *would be able to endure it."*[91]

Tension events alternate with being released again when C$_I$s get satisfaction, which is the admiration of others, self having a clear impact, or clear excellence. Each day is a tug-of-war between neutral availability of focus for any thought and fixated individuation and excellence arousal or heartbreak. The emotional problems in life happen when a self and ranking opportunity appears which doesn't end in satisfaction. Maybe the observer is ignored in a moment they thought they'd get attention. Maybe the other person doesn't seem impressed, or wasn't paying attention. Maybe a competitor interrupts the moment.

> *"We're trying to impress ourselves.*
> *That's why we keep trying to do things better.*
> *We never get satisfied."*[92]

The core of C$_I$-first is ***love for the feeling of being proud of self, and impressed in general***. Drop all judgment and distraction and really let yourself feel the pleasure of being the absolute best at something, of basking in other people's impressed attention, of being recognized by a fan on the street, and the righteousness of making decisions for yourself, not clouded by any other feelings. What extreme, imaginary scenario would flush you with the most extreme pleasure in your self-admiration? What are the skills and knowledge which really make you stand out? What actions have you taken, or what words have you said which drew everyone's focused admiration? What could you do right now to increase your skills in ways which would satisfy your own vision of yourself and also draw the attention and praise of others? What can you adjust about your presentation that everyone would notice? What job could you have that would make people the most impressed? How could your life massively change so that people would be overwhelmed when they saw you, so that everyone would know your name, so that everyone would want to be associated with you? Can you focus on that scenario and feel some of that pleasure now?

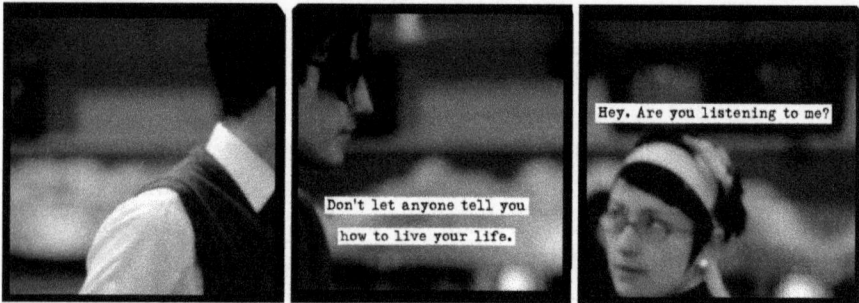

Don't let anyone tell you how to live your life.

Hey. Are you listening to me?

© *e horne and j comeau – asofterworld.com*[93]

Then feel the tension when you know you're right, but the other person stays doubtful. They refuse to verify your accuracy and just "agree to disagree." The longer they pause, the more tension feels like a component of this idiot. But then the pause ends and they say, "You're right. I had to think about it, but what you said is actually quite brilliant." Tension is released. Focus is free to consider other topics again.

> *"I was upset because I felt stupid and incompetent.*
> *Having one exaggerated scenario thought validates the next one*
> *that goes up a notch, and I get stuck in this rut of*
> *thinking worse and worse things. I'm better than this.*
> *What will people think of me? I'm embarrassed*
> *to talk about it because I did so poorly. I'm so dumb.*
> *I can't believe I did this. Everything's a disaster."*[94]

It's critically important to distinguish between the feelings of C_I and any objective, factual logic about self and ranking. C_I tension is the unsettled feeling about self, individuality, rank, and impressiveness which fixates attention, which logic has to repeatedly interpret and manage. Someone feeling tension will keep feeling tension related to self even if they logically know they're fine. Someone not feeling tension about self won't feel tense even if it would be logically helpful. Someone else might feel flushed with rage that their choice for themselves is being overruled by someone else, even when they logically know both choices are functionally equal. The feelings and the logic are different things which can align or be in conflict.

"He's just doing that to get attention."

Later on, these emotions interrupt peaceful, calm moments that don't have external triggers. Pain happens again, triggered by the memory of someone explaining something to the observer which the observer already knew. No decision was made to think about the how condescending that was. In fact, logic knows that the other person had no way of knowing. But the pain is so sharp that attention is fixated on something that isn't even present. Then happiness is felt, triggered by the memory of the person who walked in and knew that the observer is an expert in the field, an authority on this topic, and set the condescending "instructor" straight. The observer is alone. The actual exterior moment is quiet. But they're flushed with self and ranking pain or pleasure.

"It's more important to influence people than to impress them."[96]

Since tension could be triggered at any moment, C_Is preemptively take actions to maintain their impressiveness, their individual style, and their skills in general. A C_I-first has to consider how anything they say or do will make them look, because if they look cool, individuated, or superior then they'll be flushed with euphoria and relief, but if they look inferior, conforming, or dumb then they'll be flushed with pain. So, watching how self is doing, anticipating other people's errors and quickly injecting individual superiority, is the path toward a present, calm focus. Even when situations aren't ranking the observer, a C_I-first knows the situation might be ranked, and that it will be striking if it does, so they keep making choices to protect themselves from pain that could come if they don't dominate with individuated excellence. In a perfect world, they'd be the king or queen, the visionary genius, the superhero, the prodigy, so they'd have access to really satisfying impact, influence, and adoration every time the opportunity for individuation arose. In the real world, they're still superior, but surrounded by people who don't understand the topics well enough to realize how impressive they are.

"Find your niche, people say.
Like I am a person who has one major identifying characteristic.
Like I don't contain multitudes."[97]

C_I-firsts think that the self and ranking attraction they feel is helpful. They're motivated to be excellent, to differentiate from other people, to stand up for themselves, and to make choices that draw other people's impressed attention. They make better decisions about food, jobs, friends, groups, health, romantic partners, sex, and experiences, because they prioritize how these impact their own personal excellence, individuality, and ranking. Meanwhile, C_I-lasts only seem to have disadvantages. Most obviously, people who don't prioritize self and ranking have inferior intelligence. The biggest part of being human is missing from them, replaced by soullessness.

Their opinions don't matter because there's something critically broken about how their brain works. Lower C$_I$ friends could be impressive and keep choosing to be pathetic instead. They could be excellent and they choose to be lame. They could be individuals and they choose to conform. They should be the one signing the autographs, rather than part of the mob asking for them. C$_I$-lasts could do impressive things and present themselves in impressive ways, and get all the benefits of overwhelming people with the feeling of being impressed, but they just let all that potential wither. C$_I$-lasts miss out on the best parts of life because they don't have enough individual intelligence to stand out. The best survival strategy of people with below-average intelligence is to merge into a group. A C$_I$-first may not have a perfect life, but they've got the foundation. They've maintained their individuality and ranking, they stood up for themselves in critical moments, and are constantly striving for more. They have what other people have, while also being impressive and unique. A C$_I$'s life is optimized for actual reality.

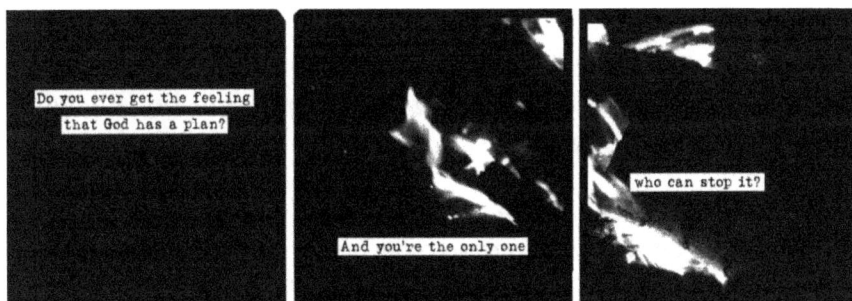

While C$_I$s have commonalities, there's a lot of variation among C$_I$s depending on what needles them. Some are more focused on what's joyfully superior and what's painfully inferior. Some are more focused on what's impressively self and what's pathetically others. Some focus on having the most control so that the most things have self as a component and the fewest things are missing self as a component. Some focus on getting attention for being unique, even if there is no excellence involved. Some are constantly rating themselves as unrealistically inferior or superior. The specific things that each thinks is "impressive" vary wildly. The important thing is the repeated distraction away from peaceful presence into internal comparison of self to others, into explanations of why others are wrong, or of what would be impressive. C_Is are accustomed to being told that they're overly focused on self and ranking, by competitors who think that saying that makes them look superior.

> *"I want to thank me for believing in me."*[99]

C_Is think repeatedly feeling confident, proud, humiliated, defensive, ignored, and abandoned is just what life is. C_I-firsts think they're trying for a totally realistic, but admittedly high-level of excellence and individuation with admittedly high frequency and intensity of other people's admiration. But they determined that something is "realistic" by imagining something better than what they've already encountered, or the best thing they ever encountered, while minimizing the inextricable trade offs which come with those positives. The result is an underlying, recurring ache, an unfillable anxiety, a dissatisfaction with reality, because the "realistic" goal they need to hit to feel satisfied is just beyond what's actually possible.

C_I-Last: Living without Tension about Individuality-Based Pleasures and Pains

> *"I am nothing special, of this I am sure.*
> *I am a common man with common thoughts and I've led a common life.*
> *There are no monuments dedicated to me*
> *and my name will soon be forgotten.*
> *But I've loved another with all my heart and soul,*
> *and to me, this has always been enough."*[100]

There have been about a hundred billion human lives. At the lowest point on the C_I spectrum, self is seen in perspective, because the observer isn't drugged with pain when they think of themselves as being another copy of a copy of a copy. Being the same or different from others doesn't trigger feelings. Being individuated or merged in with a group doesn't trigger feelings, so it seems like the factual reality of the moment. No other option is considered or hungered for. So when someone is individuated, it's unemotionally coincidental to the moment, like them wearing shoes, or looking west. It isn't euphoric or painful, it doesn't trigger the observer to fixate on wanting some change. No tension is felt when something happens that self wasn't involved with. Without tension, self's impact can be observed, but it doesn't feel variable enough to trigger imagination about what it could be, and it's not emotional enough to want some other option. Self exists, just like the Earth's core exists. Self just is. The same tension that isn't felt about ancient fossils also isn't felt about self, individuation, or superiority. Those all sound like random, unemotional topics. Self feels more tangent to the moment, which is obviously about something else (instead of being a moment about self's individuation and superiority). Self is a logical topic about function, and isn't emotional topics about fixating hunger and euphoric relief.

> *"Nearly everything you do is of no importance,*
> *but it is important that you do it."*[101]

Additionally, without drugging, ranking of inputs isn't emotional. Lots of people have never even thought of what it would be like to get emotional about ranking. When something is better for a function it's just better and that's it. Someone won an event at the 1896 Olympics. Do you really care what their name was? Are you really going to be flushed with the feeling of being impressed? When a flat head screwdriver is better for a screw, do you need to get excited about how dumb Phillips-head screwdrivers must be? When observers aren't flushed with euphoria, pain, lack, and relief when options are compared, then comparing things feels functional, fixed, and momentary. Everyone gets moments of winning and losing. A spoon is better for eating soup than a fork. No euphoria. No fixation. The person who is focused and insisting that the superiority "really matters," sounds ridiculous. There's still recognition of which option is better, and that's chosen, but there's not an automatic flushing with the feeling of being impressed by the winning option, and of laugh-inspiring condescension by the patheticness of the losing option. Since euphoria and pain aren't felt, the balancing negatives of what won and the balancing positives of what lost aren't silenced. Everything is a balance of positives and negatives which really depend on what's being valued in the moment.

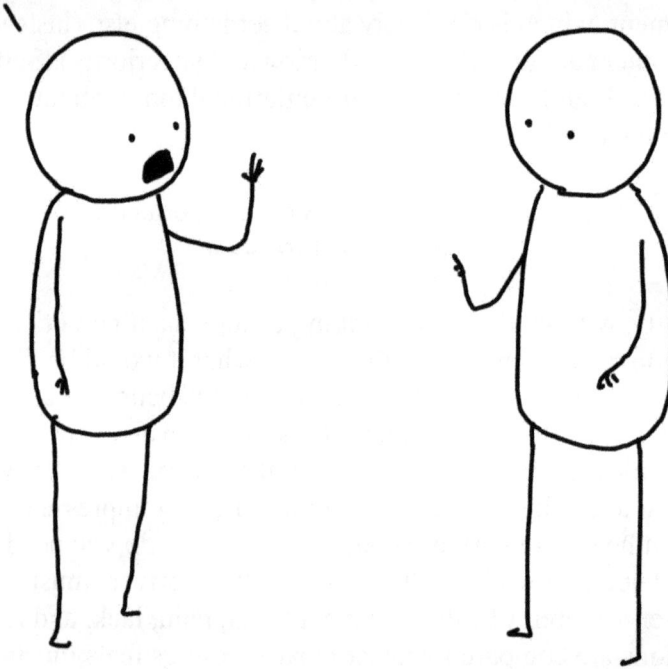

SORRY TO INTERRUPT YOU, AND THIS MAY BE A BIT AWKWARD, BUT THE WAY YOU TALK ABOUT "SELF-ESTEEM" MAKES IT SOUND LIKE YOU THINK IT'S A REAL THING.

© STEINBERGDRAWSCARTOONS
© *Avi Steinberg – SteinbergDrawsCartoons.com*[102]

Most C$_I$-lasts still can feel pleasure from the admiring reactions of a crowd after the C$_I$-last does something excellent, and pain after the C$_I$-last does something poorly that makes the crowd laugh in disrespect. But the experience of those is different when those events don't automatically trigger hunger for change and escalation. There was a moment of self-based pleasure or pain, that's just reality, and then the moment ended. The thought ends there. The observer can still look to the side and discuss a different topic. Pleasurable moments don't fixate the observer with hunger to do something even better and wow people even more. The rest of reality isn't silenced. The observer's focus isn't distracted away from the moment with an internal fantasy of even more greatness and even more admiration. Instead it seems weird that we're still talking about that moment when it was over long ago.

Any input which doesn't make people feel feelings about self or ranking feels C_I neutral. At the lowest end of the C_I spectrum, it's very hard for anything to happen which generates love, hate, or disappointment about self, or the feeling of being impressed or repelled. C_I neutrality is what's felt when someone is so focused on something else that they're not thinking of how cool they look, how impressive they look, or humiliated by how common or unimpressive they look. For a C_I-last, that lack of feeling is happening almost all the time, even when a C_I is pointing at them and laughing.

> *"Ignorance more frequently begets confidence*
> *than does knowledge."*[103]

Individuality-based neutrality isn't rejection of the topics of self or ranking. It's not a decision not to defend self or a decision to accept self's ranking or an attempt to accept the reality of self. It's not a lack of confidence. It's not doubting self or pretending not to care. Neutrality isn't any thought at all. Individuality-based neutrality is a lack of self-connected feelings that would bring the topic of self to mind. It's a lack of ranking of inputs that would bring the topic of rank to mind. Even when someone brings up the topic, C_I neutrality is a lack of the feeling of confidence, pride, humiliation, or rejection when considering a topic, because the topic is obviously unrelated to self. It's a feeling of pointlessness when it would come to ranking things where ranking is obviously irrelevant.

At the lowest point on the C_I spectrum all inputs feel C_I neutral. Nothing external is related to self. It's all just happening nearby. But, from the inside, it feels like self is one of billions of humans, the same way that ants are each one of billions of ants, and squirrels are each one of billions of squirrels. All humans are basically similar, and it just doesn't matter which ones are doing well or poorly at the moment. Observation of no one, even self, generates the feeling of being impressed. Conforming or deviating from the rest of the group generates no feelings, so the practical, intelligent option can be taken since there are no emotions to manage. When people individuate or conform, it just doesn't matter. Neither draws attention or admiration. The thing to do with self is navigate reality, and that's it. Self isn't emotional. Self isn't something which has a changeable value.

© *Randall Munroe – xkcd.com*[104]

C_I-lasts live in a not-individuated world, because they're not triggered with tension when they're similar or dissimilar, when they're winning or losing, when they're excellent or failing, or when attention is happening or not happening. C_I-lasts don't feel impressed when someone stands out, and they aren't flushed with feelings of superiority when other people conform and fail. They're not flushed with jealousy, self-loathing, or hate when other people are getting attention.

No more impactful, more individuated moment is imagined, no joy is felt imagining it, so no hunger is sparked to make it happen in reality. Someone who cares about being individuated is like a person who cares about how many hairs are on a horse. It's a weird thing to care about, and obviously only matters to that person. Individuality isn't a changeable thing. It's an observed, fixed reality, and it has zero value or meaning.

If you could feel the process of turning yourself down in C_I tension, you'd feel a silencing of the urgency felt about having an impact on anything. As a result, there's a muting of everyone's identities, and a reframing of thought away from identities and onto whatever else you want to think about. Things are happening, things are being said, and none of it has anything to do with you. Even when other people use you as the topic while they give away who they are, it's not actually about you. All humans are built from essentially the same DNA, on the same planet, at the same time. Logic still knows that self is different from other people, and that other people have differences which individuate them, but the people with more or fewer similarities to others don't also feel good or bad. There's certainly no joy to be felt from being the only person doing a thing differently for a moment. No focus is on self at all. Focus is on the task being done.

"The dead are quickly forgotten."[105]

When a human truly stands out as an individual, it's not emotional. It's momentary. Everyone gets that moment. There's no fixation or devastation because another person has a unique look or a conforming look, because someone was right or wrong, because someone was influential or ignored. There's definitely no thought that positive features could be combined, or that negative features could be removed, and the glory that one person felt could be even more extreme.

The way people act is about them. Polite people are polite. Impolite people are impolite. Their actions have nothing to do with the observer. Other people don't sound wrong just because they're making declarative statements. Self doesn't sound informative just because self knows another detail. There's no need to defend self when attacking people are attacking. It's still worth logically separating, but there is no 'honor' that is also being attacked in addition to the practical reality of being in the presence of a negative person. There's no need to correct others when incorrect people are incorrect. Other people don't feel changeable. They're saying and doing what they say and do. The way they act has nothing to do with self.

© *Tim Cordell – cordellcartoons.com*[106]

Of course it'd be nice to be respected and admired. But reality is what it is. All the adults in the room focus on the task that needs to get done. Only the broken idiot is distracted by what other people are doing so they can do the opposite and then hope people notice, are impressed, and comment.

Not being emotionally triggered doesn't mean that C_I-lasts can't recognize when they're being unjustly, individually attacked. But C_I-lasts might've missed someone else's condescension on their own, because their mind was on what they were trying to get done, not on whether they're being respected. And, even when they are mistreated, they learn which person mistreats others and avoid that person from then on. Rude people are rude. Their rudeness is about them, and sometimes it's part of the price of doing business to get tasks done.

*"We are all apprentices in crafts
where no one ever becomes a master."*[107]

The actual experience of being at the extreme minimum is that it feels weird to even consider "impressiveness" because how humans interact is so normally and generically human. It feels weird to talk about self "love" because self isn't emotional. What would "loving" self even be like? What would "hating" self even be like? It's like "loving" the moon and "hating" water. These things just are. Self also just is. Anyone who is feeling love or hate for self has an individual hobby that doesn't make sense.

*"Some people like what you do. Some people hate what you do.
But most people simply don't give a damn."*[108]

Instead, imagine that your pet's paw is pinched in a door and it's screaming. Imagine a stranger just aggressively pushed your family member. Imagine a breathtaking hottie just kissed you. Imagine you just found an adventure that you need to go on. For all humans, self and ranking aren't the topics of the moment while other meaningful life events are happening. C_I-last observers have more Relational and Social triggers connected to more drug intensity. No choice is being made to ignore self and ranking. But any self-related triggers present have to be particularly severe for the observer to get triggered with self-focus, while really weak Social or Relational triggers will much more easily flush the observer if they're also present. It's not a self and ranking moment, because it's obviously a critical Social or Relational moment (which happens to be a lot of moments).

Self, individuality, and impressiveness are different when other people don't sound so wrong, and when self's words don't sound so thoughtful and impressive. Someone being forced to choose among neutral options wouldn't have feelings of self and ranking arousal and heartbreak to help with the choice (to distract the choice away from logic), or to make them feel especially lucky if they got certain options. C_I-lasts see actions, words, and humans for what they really are, because they're not risking not having an impact, not risking feeling defensive, not risking losing love for themselves, or in love with the self and ranking qualities of any option. C_I-lasts aren't euphoric about moments of success, and aren't heartbroken about moments of failure. C_I-lasts aren't comparing people to each other, and especially aren't valuing differences higher than similarities, so there's not only no ranking, but would be no value in ranking anyway.

© *Randall Munroe – xkcd.com*[109]

Meanwhile, those same humans, words, and actions, more easily trigger sexual-attraction-protective feelings, life-purpose-protection feelings, friendship-protecting feelings, and group-harmony-protecting feelings. If you're managing a life where you're easily triggered by Social and Relational concerns, it's worth finding the people who are also paying attention to other people's feelings, the people who are sexy, and the ones seizing life's adventures. It's worth ignoring the people who are fixated on themselves, who pointlessly rank things, who get satisfaction in making others wrong and blaming people.

Imagine finding someone who is so well fit to your personality that it seems like the two of you were made to merge into one unit. Imagine that person being so vulnerable and sweet with you that you feel their emotions automatically. Imagine finding a group of humans who are so mutually loving and supportive, and dedicated to such a good cause, that you have emotional reactions to that group's successes and failures. Imagine that your best friend comes in a really sexy package and every time you feel horny you see returned sexual hunger in their eyes. Imagine the two of you going on extreme adventures together, exploring all the corners of the planet. Meanwhile, when you meet a rude person, they are rude. When you meet a nice person, they are nice. Can you imagine finding happiness while not even thinking of yourself specifically?

> *"One of the reasons that birds and horses are happy*
> *is that they are not trying to impress other birds and horses."*[110]

A C_I-last is observing reality without creating something different inside, which is what it feels like to accept reality as it is. C_I-lasts know how tiny and human they are, and aren't intoxicated or revolted by that reality. They know their good moments come with balancing drawbacks. They know their failures are normal parts of their growth. They are who they are, and they never revisit the topic of "caring for themselves," again.

C_I-lasts have tried to get happiness from winning, from teaching things to other people, from standing out, and from making sure people know they're right, and it wasn't worth it. The joy was temporary while their long-term happiness suffered. Impressiveness, self, and ranking don't have deeper meanings. Superiority, attention, and other people's reactions aren't a source of joy or disappointment in themselves. The meaning of life has to do with friends, family, sexual attraction, and extreme, varied life experiences. Being recognized and respected is pleasant too, when it happens, but it's definitely less important than the rest of that.

"The fool doth think he is wise,
but the wise man knows himself to be a fool."[111]

From the perspective of C_I-lasts, C_Is only seem to have disadvantages. C_Is disagree constantly, desperately seeking ways to make other people wrong after their autopilot already said, "you're wrong," and that's just not pleasant to be around. Then C_Is "correct" people with obvious statements and condescendingly imply that others need to question things more, when it's the C_I who is oblivious that their condescension comes from a lack of knowledge of the topic while discussing it with people who know more. The C_I is solving for how to make the other person wrong because they felt a moment of negativity which they misinterpret as the other person's lack of accuracy, when the C_I should be neutrally considering new information. C_Is learn the least, because they're so averse to being in situations where they're not dominating, or inaccurately certain they know more than others when they don't. They give up too early when they're not instantly good at things. They can't just relax and learn while someone else knows more than they do, unless it's "impressively" more. C_Is want attention and praise for being "unique" when they mindlessly do the opposite of the group, which is still just following the group, and when being "unique" is an arbitrary quality that isn't good or bad. C_Is pick condescending jerks to idolize, including themselves. C_Is repeatedly choose the dumb option, just to be different. C_Is repel friends because they're so desperate to show that they're different than what other people expect. C_Is think their friends are impressed when the friends are actually tolerating the C_I because of their Social or Relational tensions. C_Is dramatically overestimate how impressive their own words, actions, and accomplishments are, and are quick to find faults when the same are done by others. C_Is have an endearing way of overvaluing intentions when they make a mistake, matched by the overvaluing of results when others make mistakes. C_is passionately disregard reality, enthusiastically find ways to be unhappy with what exists, and make bad decisions among existing options. They seem to be unaware of who they are and what people think of them, while thinking they're impressing other people and clearly superior. C_is bully other people into differentiating from other people, into prioritizing themselves, and into changing in arbitrary ways so the C_i can feel influential, because the C_i is immersed in an individual exaggeration of the value of their own input, differentiation, and ranking. In critical moments, C_is sacrifice friends, groups, the good will of others, sexual attractiveness, and life purpose because they're distracted with "being impressive" in ways that aren't impressing anyone. What C_is are actually experts at is remaining a self-worshiping child while the people around them continue growing up. Why would anyone want that life?

© Jim Benton – JimBenton.com[112]

There is no disappointment to feel with self, with how self is treated, and with how self is recognized. The frequency of impressive moments and self's influence are always fine. There's no need for more, less, better, or different. It's still worth making sure that self gets maintenance, but that maintenance can happen without tension and relief, without fixated daydreams, and without judging what's happening as good or bad. C_I-lasts are realistic about what they've got, what they get from it, what their options are, and what it costs. They're more present to the reality of self and ranking than C_I-firsts because they're not distracted by emotions. Part of what makes self more capable than others is that the observer isn't distracted with glorifying self and doesn't feel attacked or belittled when negative people are negative. C_I-lasts have a superpower because they can focus on projects outside of themselves and make those projects happen, because they won't get distracted with self while completing them. The life experience of C_I-lasts automatically includes the self and ranking satisfaction that C_I-firsts can't find, because C_I-lasts live in reality, undistracted by visions of not-reality.

Cross Overs

*"I am so clever that sometimes
I don't understand a single word of what I am saying."*[113]

Most C_I-lasts can feel defensiveness when jerks demand even more slavery or when someone else makes choices for them in too dehumanizing of a way. Most C_I-lasts can feel some joy in the moment that a stranger really is impressed to meet them. But self and ranking fixations happen in WAY fewer moments, WAY less intensely, and satisfaction comes much faster just by realizing that what happened is the fixed reality.

"Humans are the only creatures who refuse to be what they are."[114]

Many times a day C_I-firsts pass by humans without considering their relative "ranking," without considering how individuated that person is, and without feeling the need to change the situation in some way that would draw positive admiration. C_I-firsts can be distracted by other topics, even while interacting with someone whose admiration they'd like to feel, but have true neutral lack of consideration of self and ranking in that moment because nothing feels related to self and ranking arousal. Even for a C_I-first, it feels like awkward, tedious work to generate a fantasy about how they caused something to happen that clearly wasn't related to them.

© Ben Zaehringer – BerkeleyMews.com[115]

C_I Conclusions

"The need to impress others causes half the world's woes."[116]

The addition of C_I means self and ranking aren't just functional anymore. Self, superiority, and individuality are loved, exciting, beautiful, and desirable, triggering excitement, joy, concern, disappointment, pain, and relief. C_I tension and relief aren't necessary for a system to protect themselves, stand up for themselves, or to strive for excellence. But self and ranking tension and relief add focus and incentive to make sure other people notice self's contributions, and recognize self's superiority.

Actual C_I-firsts usually don't want to be categorized at all, except as being an exception, as "uncategorizable," or as being the ultimate best. Being grouped in with others triggers pain tension which will be relieved when they've clearly separated themselves in an impressive way. They don't think their reverence for differences is their individual hobby. It seems obvious in all of external reality that individuality and ranking are very important. Meanwhile, C_I-lasts think people who picked individuality as a hobby are united by that hobby, and quite similar to everyone else who picks any hobby. It is very hard to imagine that C_Is really think there's an external ranking of humans and that anyone would care about that even if it existed.

"Lions. Not sheep."[117]

C_I-firsts stand out as individuals more because they invest so much time and energy in seeking out, building, and maintaining individuality and impressiveness. A consistent focus on self and ranking helps them seize opportunities to individuate and seize power. They're constantly sacrificing for the benefit of how impressed they'll be with themselves. But they're the least satisfied with their own impressiveness, individuality, and ranking because daily tension reminds them to focus on what's wrong and imagine and feel desire for better.

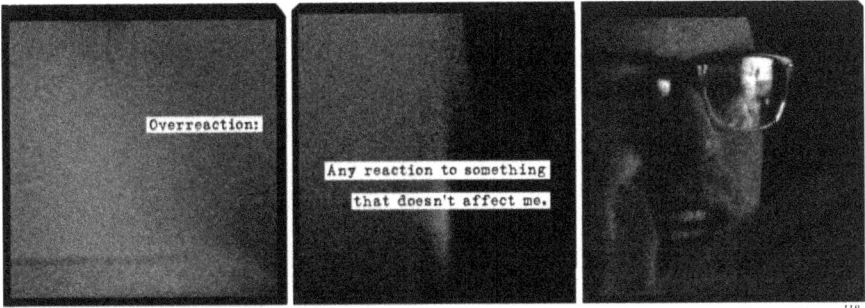

Overreaction:

Any reaction to something
that doesn't affect me.

© e horne and j comeau – asofterworld.com[118]

Easily Confused for the C_i Spectrum

This chapter compares C_i to the six other motivators one-by-one. It holds the topic constant (self) and looks at it from each of the seven perspectives so you can hear that it's the framing of the topic that gives away the observer's motivators, not the topic itself. Each observer's experience of ranking and self is different when they're feeling different kinds of tension and seeking different kinds of relief from ranking and self. This is the chapter to come back to when determining the relative influence of C_i versus any other motivator for a person.

C_is Think Other People Feel C_i Also:

"Live like you're always trying to impress someone."[119]

An observer who dominantly gets flushed with C_i arousal is more likely to think that other people are also judging and ranking. They're more likely to think other people are thinking about self-adoration, individuality, or about the C_i observer. A C_i is more likely to think other people's problems are crises of not standing up for themselves, not being honest enough about what they want, not differentiating themselves, or about not trying hard enough to be excellent. And they realize that they have to say something to make that situation right, because their input could change everything.

"It's just a matter of time
before they add the word 'Syndrome' after my last name."[120]

Meanwhile, other people aren't noticing ranking or individuality because they're rarely or never triggered with emotions about ranking or individuality. Other people aren't self-loving or self-hating because they don't get triggered with emotions about self. Other people aren't impressed because they rarely get triggered with the feeling of being impressed. Other people aren't solving for their own impact, because they aren't triggered with emotions based on whether or not they had an individual impact.

"All I'm saying is, I wished for an endless summer vacation, and now the glaciers are melting."

© Avi Steinberg – SteinbergDrawsCartoons.com[121]

Instead, other people are in a totally different mindset where individuals aren't relevant. Those others are listening to the C₁ to be polite, to support their friend's emotions, hoping to be entertained, because they're scared, because they're sexually attracted, because it's part of the adventure they're on, or because it's functional while they get another task done. Others get easily triggered by the feelings of social tension, food hunger, sexual arousal, friendship tension, fear, and painful stagnancy. The people near a C_I are in the mindsets of their hungers, hoping the C_I will help satisfy those hungers, while the C_I is in a C_I framed mindset, hoping others will satisfy their C_I hungers (usually by modifying themselves in a way the C_I suggested).

"That was classic me."

When a C_I doesn't get the reaction from other people that they expect, most think the lesser reaction must be because the C_I wasn't impressive enough, because people don't like them, because the receiver wasn't smart enough to understand, or because the receiver is overly focused on doing things their own way. The other person is wrong for not taking the C$_I$'s brilliant advice. Meanwhile the other person is actually reacting to the fact that what the C$_I$ said doesn't seem to help friendship, group harmony, sexual arousal, life experiences, resources, or health. The C$_I$ is less easily triggered by those other options, so it seems obvious that other tensions don't matter right now, or maybe ever, and couldn't be changed anyway, because they happen the way they happen. The C$_I$ is trying to solve for satisfaction either about their own greatness, or their receiver's self-love because they're so easily triggered to think situations are about self-love and individuation even when they're not.

> *"A bully's job is to say terrible things about you*
> *and make you feel stupid*
> *until you're old enough to do that for yourself."*[123]

> *"If we're really honest with ourselves,*
> *most of us will admit that we want to impress people."*[124]

Valuing Self, Ranking, and Attention While Feeling Alliance-Based Socialness (S$_F$):

S$_F$s rarely mistake themselves as being C$_I$s, but will occasionally if their friend is a C$_I$ and they have to merge into that mindset to stay aligned with their partner. If their friend thinks that tattoos are cool, but they have to be unique for each person, then an S$_F$ will get a tattoo also, which is similar enough so they feel merged, but different enough that their friend is satisfied that it's individual and different.

An S$_F$ feels selfish when a friend wants something from them that the S$_F$ doesn't want to deliver. The friend wants the S$_F$'s money, attention, and time, which the S$_F$ would gladly give to their merged partner, but feels tension because this other person isn't merging in return. They're staying emotionally separate. The pain the S$_F$ feels is the repulsive force of the lack of S$_F$ being felt by the other person.

But it feels selfish to hold onto money, attention, and time when the friend wants them, because the friend's desire is felt as the observer's own pain. Relief will come when the selfish partner's desires are satisfied.

An S$_F$-first would feel selfish if they did something for themselves that didn't benefit their friend, or especially anything which even remotely hurt their friend. S$_F$s feel selfish even when a huge benefit for self comes with no detriment for their friend, even when they'd be euphoric if their friend received such a windfall.

Of course self matters too. An ally who just wants a slave isn't a good enough person to be worthy of love. That's clear because it hurts to hear their selfishness, it hurts to hear their statements where they give away that the observer's feelings aren't being considered. But negative statements by an ally show that the ally isn't a friend, not that the observer isn't "worthy." The S$_F$ doesn't have to influence the other person into being a better ally. The other person is selfish, and therefore dissimilar to the observer and should be friends with other selfish people.

When someone is thinking of self, individuality, and superiority because of S$_F$ tension, they usually accidentally befriended a C$_I$ who is getting more and more obvious about objectifying and using the S$_F$ as a tool. When a C$_I$ too repeatedly gets pleasure by belittling the S$_F$-first, even an S$_F$-first will realize that they have to hurt the S$_F$-last's feelings by leaving. The S$_F$-first feels a constant unease because of the C$_I$'s lack of respect for the friendship. The C$_I$ isn't emotionally investing in the friendship, they're instead taking cheap shots at the friend so the C$_I$ can feel superior. The C$_I$ likes having the S$_F$ around as a validation machine and that's it. The C$_I$ will think the S$_F$ left because the S$_F$ wasn't impressed enough with the C$_I$, when the S$_F$ left because the C$_I$ wasn't emotionally invested in the happiness, success, and wellbeing of the S$_F$. The S$_F$-first is realizing the two are too different to be friends, while a C$_I$ would be realizing that the other person is a taker jerk who is exploiting the relationship. A C$_I$ is protecting themselves by leaving a friendship, while an S$_F$-first is leaving because the other person's attacks on merged emotional investment feel so painful. But the S$_F$-first will feel selfish for leaving, and that pain tension is their Socialness, flushing them with pain about the tension their beloved C_I will feel when their slave doesn't fill their next need.

Valuing Self, Ranking, and Attention While Feeling Sex-Based Relationalness (R_S):

> *"If people knew how much energy and inner work it took to cultivate the love and peace you embody, they would know that access to you in any capacity is a privilege."* [125]

R_Ss think that C_Is want to look impressive because they're trying to make themselves as sexually attractive as possible to potential mates, since feeling sexual attraction to others, and having others feel sexual attraction in return is what matters in life. Meanwhile, people feeling just C_I make themselves attractive because they want to feel impressed with themselves. The R_S mistakenly thinks the C_I wants to feel sexual arousal, when C_Is actually want to feel confidence, pride, and self-adoration.

© *Harry Margulies* [126]

When someone feels confidence and self-admiration because of sexual attraction, they realize that they really do have the fixated sexual attention of a high value sexual option. The other person's sexual arousal is stable enough, and their sexual attractiveness is stable enough that the observer is flushed with extra euphoria at all times from being in their presence, and feeling the returned attraction of this breathtaking hottie. But someone dominated by R$_S$ is hungry for the sexy person's body, hungry for sexual escalation, and hungry for orgasms. The value they feel is the sexual value of their partner. They're not feeling C$_I$, which is hunger to feel great about self with sex being one of the tools to prove their individuality, ranking, and worth. They're not feeling impressed with the individuality, greatness, and ranking of the other person. When an R$_S$ does have the sexual attention of a partner, the R$_S$ still thinks it's the shape of their own body, and their own sexual attraction which is arousing their partner, and not their accomplishments or "impressiveness."

An R$_S$ is curious to know how they can modify their hair, clothes, what they say, and anything else to fit the sexual arousal triggers of their partner, and thinks it's obvious to make those modifications so that sex can be even more aroused for both partners. Meanwhile a C$_I$ is easily negatively triggered if someone makes a decision for them. So they're likely to be struck with negative emotions if a partner asks for modifications in hair, clothes, what they say, or anything else. C$_I$s instead hunger to have an impact on their partner, because seeing their impact will make them feel good about themselves. A C$_I$ usually thinks rejection means that they're not impressive or worthy. Meanwhile an R$_S$ is grateful for rejection because they got as far as they sexually could with that partner, satisfying the motivating tension, so they can move on to the next. Attraction is arbitrary, so it's no one's fault if someone just isn't feeling it.

Someone feeling R$_S$ tension while standing up for themselves is moving on from a partner who is logically suitable, but doesn't inspire sexual arousal in the R$_S$. The R$_S$ is asking a partner to change their hair, body, words, or actions to be more sexy, but motivated by a hunger to be more aroused, to be excited enough to have an orgasm. It's still self-benefiting words and actions, but it's driven by a hunger for orgasms, not by pride, power, or hunger for self-glorification. It's not based in a feeling of superiority, but in a feeling of sexual hunger that can't find enough triggers to climax.

An R_S is tense about ranking when ranking is important to a sexual target. The R_S has to do what sexually arouses the cutie. An R_S feels tense about being "unique" or "individual" if caring about that makes a hottie more likely to have sex. The R_S is navigating the labyrinth of the other person's hurdles so that sex can finally start.

Someone feeling R_S tension is concerned that their sex partner will stop sexual escalation, that sex won't happen, or that orgasms won't happen. They're relieved when the partner is horny and orgasms happen. That's different from C_I tension which is concerned that the partner isn't actually worthy because that partner's attention doesn't make the observer feel better enough about themselves. A C_I wants to be sexually attractive to everyone, because they like the attention and power it gives them over others. An R_S wants to be sexually attractive to everyone, because they are in love with the shape of other people's bodies and love kissing and touching.

R_S is an obsession with the other person's sexiness the same way that C_I is an obsession with self's impressiveness.

Valuing Self, Ranking, and Attention While Feeling Resource-Based Comfort (C_R):

> *"I find that a duck's opinion of me is strongly influenced by whether or not I have bread."*[127]

C_Rs think that C_Is want to look impressive because they want the wealth which comes with fame, to experience the luxury of the fancy version of a resource, to be a more valuable resource themselves, or they think displaying resource value might get them access to more resource value. Meanwhile, people feeling just C_I want to look impressive because they want to feel impressed with themselves. The C_R mistakenly thinks the C_I wants to feel resource abundance, entertained, and full of food, when C_Is actually want to feel confidence, pride, and self-adoration.

*"People spend money they haven't got
to buy things they don't want
to impress people they don't like."*[128]

"Each person sees himself as a uniquely
precious miracle of life but honestly,
to me they all taste like chicken."

© Crowden Satz – crowdensatz.com[129]

When someone is thinking of self, individuality, and superiority because of C_R tension, they're proud of themselves and satisfied with themselves for acquiring so many resources. They know how to get resources and it's that knowledge which is actually valuable. A C_R assumes the attention they're getting is from people who also want to understand how to get the resources, because the resources have the value. A C_R isn't turning that value back on themselves individually and feeling value on themselves for the attention they're getting. Someone dominated by C_R is hungry for consumption and acquisition. They're not feeling C_I, which is hunger for the adoration of others, with resources being among the excuses used to attract that adoration.

A C_R thinks everyone would be satisfied and happy if they also had resources, because resources are what's great. Meanwhile a C_I wants more and better resources than other people, because they want the feeling of superiority, individuality, and attention that would come with having more and better than other people. A C_I wants other people to acquire the same resources as the C_I because they admire the C_I and want to copy the C_I. A C_I wouldn't be interested in having an item once everyone had one, because it would trigger painful tension when they realized they were the same as everyone else. They didn't actually love the item, they loved the feeling of being different and of influencing others.

"Great art is horseshit. Buy tacos."[130]

Someone feeling C_R tension is concerned that they'll be bored, hungry, or want better resources than they have. They're relieved when they eat, are entertained, or trade up for the better item or investment. That's different from C_I tension which is concerned that they're not as cool as the person who showed up with the flashy, attention-grabbing item, or the distinct, individual style. A C_I hungers to be the one that everyone is admiring.

C_R is an obsession with the qualities that make resources and entertainment valuable the same way that C_I is an obsession with the qualities that make self worthy, superior, and unique.

Valuing Self, Ranking, and Attention While Feeling Experience-Based Relationalness (R_A):

"Don't fear failure.
Fear being in the same place next year that you are today."[131]

The R_A feels tension about doing too little with life, which is relieved when they dive into the unknown. The C_I feels tension about loving themselves, which is relieved when they're excellent enough to trigger self-adoring feelings.

> *"There are people less qualified than you,*
> *doing the things you want to do,*
> *simply because they decided to go for it."*[132]

R_As think that C_Is seek excellence and rank because they're trying to experience the most they can with their lives, they're following their individual callings, and they're concerned with being stagnant. Meanwhile, people feeling just C_I seek "excellence" because they want to feel impressed with themselves, and they want to bask in the glorious feelings of other people's admiration and jealousy. R_As mistakenly think C_Is wants to enjoy the thrill of extreme experiences, when C_Is actually want to feel the confidence, pride, and self-adoration that accomplishments make them feel about themselves.

> *"A somebody is a nobody who wanted to and did."*[133]

When someone is thinking of self, individuality, and superiority because of R_A tension, they feel like they're the only ones chasing dreams, the only ones confronting and overcoming fears, and the only ones really trying to understand what's outside of themselves.

> *"The devotion of the greatest is to encounter risk and danger*
> *and play dice for death."*[134]

When someone feels confidence and self-admiration because of extreme activities, they realize that they have experience and breadth because of all the risks they've taken. Other people hide from life, generating unrealistic fears, while an R_A appreciates the gift of being alive. But what the R_A is really feeling is appreciation for the information they know because they tested the limit, not self-adoration for being the person who knew it. R_As want the hypochondriac to go live life too, because there's so much good information out there to know. R_As think everyone should be following their callings, trying extreme new things, and feeling the most thrill that life can deliver. R_As don't care if anyone knows what they've done, other than as inspiration for other people to follow their dreams too. They're not hungry for individual attention, recognition, and pride. They're hungry to feel engaged with life, to never feel stagnant.

The clearest difference is that R_As want everyone to experience these experiences, because it's the experience which is so great. Being famous is an extreme experience worth trying. Being anonymous is an extreme experience worth trying. Being ignored and adored are both worth trying. Winning everything and losing everything are both worth trying. Meanwhile a C_I wants to be the best at anything so that they can bask in the great feeling of other people's attention and respect. A C_I wouldn't appreciate the activity anymore if everyone else also did it just as well or better. A C_I has no interest in "the experience" of being the lowest, of failing, and of being rejected. Unless they can get lower than anyone else ever has, so they can then tell stories of how much better they are because they've been to further extremes.

Someone feeling R_A tension is concerned that the activity will be stopped or softened by scared idiots who want to remove the thrill. Someone feeling C_I tension will be concerned that self might fail, or that others might do it better, making the observer feel bad about themselves.

> *"Your first podcast will be awful.*
> *Your first video will be awful.*
> *Your first article will be awful.*
> *Your first art will be awful.*
> *Your first photo will be awful.*
> *Your first game will be awful.*
> *But you can't make your 50th without making your first.*
> *So get it over with."*[135]

R_A is an obsession with the thrilling newness and extremeness of activities the same way that C_I is an obsession with self's impressiveness.

Valuing Self, Ranking, and Attention While Feeling Community-Based Socialness (S$_C$):

S$_C$s think that C$_I$s want to look impressive because society has trained people that winners are better. S$_C$s condescendingly "know better," that the group happiness is what actually matters, and hope that a shift in group mentality will help the C$_I$ conform to a harmony-focused perspective. Meanwhile, people feeling just C$_I$ want to look impressive because they want to feel impressed with themselves. They intentionally take action to differentiate themselves from the group because they're triggered with pain and tension when they notice that they're similar to others. The S$_C$ mistakenly thinks C$_I$s feel pressure to align with what the group expects, when C$_I$s actually feel pressure to differentiate from what others expect, to stand up for themselves, and to display their innate superiority over others. It's the same pressure (tension), but felt in the other direction.

> *"Work for a cause, not for applause."*[136]

> *"The only time most people think about injustice is when it happens to them."*[137]

> *"You're never going to get the same things as other people. It's never going to be equal. It's not going to happen ever in your life. So you must learn this now: You don't look into your neighbor's bowl to see if you have as much as them. The only time you look in your neighbor's bowl is to make sure that they have enough."*[138]

> *"It is amazing what you can accomplish if you do not care who gets the credit."*[139]

When someone is thinking of self, individuality, and superiority because of S$_C$ tension, they're feeling the collective tension of everyone else in their group, so action needs to be taken to relieve everyone and restore harmony and joy among the members. The S$_C$ feels individually superior when they stand up for moral values, but they think that the rest of the group would agree that the principle is superior (the principle of the greatest good for everyone), and that anyone else in the group who had the skills and opportunity would make a stand for "objective" goodness also. An S_C doesn't want the individual attention, and might be fighting for something that's individually bad for themselves, but they feel like they have to take a stand against something that's negative for group harmony, which is causing some group members to get hurt. They're fixated with pain as long as group members are hurting, as long as the group is turned in a negative direction.

© T. McCracken
mchumor.com

"BUT I RISK HURTING THE GOALIE'S SELF-ESTEEM IF I SCORE."

© Theresa McCracken – McHumor.com

"Diversity is the art of thinking independently, together." [140]

"Tact is the art of making a point without making an enemy." [141]

When people feel confidence and self-admiration because of S_C, they realize that they really are better humans than selfish people. Each S_C action helps lots of people, while selfish people's actions are either unhelpful to the group, or helpful only to a few, often at a greater group expense. Someone dominated by S_C is hungry for everyone to work together for everyone's mutual good. They're not feeling C_1, which is hunger to feel great about self.

VOLUNTEER TO MAKE A KID FEEL LIKE A QUEEN FOR A DAY AND YOU MAY FEEL LIKE YOU'RE EMPEROR OF THE WORLD.

© *Theresa McCracken – McHumor.com*

> *"We can't all be good at everything.*
> *This is partly the logic behind having a team in the first place,*
> *so each role can be filled with the person best suited for that role*
> *and together every job and every strength is covered."*[142]

An S$_C$ will be relieved when they know the rules so that they can follow them, so harmony isn't disturbed. An S$_C$ will sometimes be bothered if too much attention is on the S$_C$ individually, because other people might be upset by the S$_C$ getting attention. It would be great if everyone were so good, so competent, so practiced in working together that the observer could be an anonymous part of a bigger organism. Meanwhile a C$_I$ will feel righteous in breaking the rules which don't accommodate their individual style, because standing up for themselves matters (the same way standing up for the group matters to an S$_C$), and because it will relieve their tension when the group changes itself based on the C$_I$'s input.

> *"You have a little bit of 'I want to save the world' in you,*
> *That's why you're here.*
> *I want you to know it's okay if you only save one person,*
> *and it's okay if that person is you."*[143]

Someone feeling S$_C$ tension is concerned that any disruption to the flow of the group will make people tense or unhappy. They're relieved when people follow the rules, wait their turns, and do their parts because everyone is benefiting from the system equally. That's different from C$_I$ tension which is concerned that self is being made to wait or conform to a dumber person and they have to stand up for themselves. S$_C$ motivates an obsession with the harmonious, satisfied flow of the group the same way that C$_I$ motivates an obsession with self's individuality.

Valuing Self, Ranking, and Attention While Feeling Body-Based Comfort (C$_B$):

> *"Tupac was one of the biggest thugs I know.*
> *And he always wore his seat belt."*[144]

C$_B$s think that C$_I$s want to look impressive to protect themselves from being hurt, in reaction to pain, or to cover up internal terror.

Meanwhile, people feeling just C$_I$ are trying to be impressive because they want to feel impressed with themselves. The C$_B$ mistakenly thinks the C$_I$ wants to feel comfort, peace, health, and safety, when C$_I$s actually want to feel confidence, pride, and self-adoration.

> *"If you think you hate everyone, eat.*
> *If you think everyone hates you, sleep.*
> *If you think you hate yourself, shower."* [145]

When someone is thinking of self, individuality, and superiority because of C$_B$ tension, they're focusing on self-care because their body and mind are disrupted and need healing. They want to be flushed with peace and comfort because of calming, comforting, healing inputs. A C$_B$ thinks everyone would be happier if their mind and body were peaceful and healed also. Meanwhile a C$_I$ thinks their superior abilities at health, safety, and comfort are one of the tools which prove their individuality, ranking, and worth. They want to be the teacher, because seeing others influenced by their instruction will resolve their tension about being influential.

> *"Health so far outweighs all other blessings in life,*
> *that a truly healthy beggar is happier than a sick king."* [146]

A C$_B$ would love a world where every person was peaceful, healthy, and comforted. They'd love to anonymously be one of the peaceful beings and might even feel safety in that anonymity. Meanwhile a C$_I$ would feel tension about conforming and taking instruction from others. They'd have to develop their own system that's better and would feel relief in being respected for the individual impact they made.

> *"I find it really uncomfortable to interact with people*
> *who are much less intelligent than I am.*
> *I feel like they could turn on me at any moment."* [147]

Someone feeling C$_B$ tension is concerned that they're being physically threatened, while someone feeling C$_I$ tension thinks their individuality or superiority are being threatened. If everything goes wrong for a C_B, they'll be uncomfortable, injured, or even dead. If everything goes wrong for a C_I, they'll be a failure, rejected, abandoned, forgotten, pathetic, and hate themselves. C_B is an obsession with mental and physical health the same way that C_I is an obsession with self's individuality and impressiveness.

S_C: The Community-Based Social Tension Spectrum

"Thousands of candles can be lit from just one,
and the life of the candle will not be shortened." [148]

Community-based Social (S_C) tension adds a focusing need for escalation or repair, paired with relieving satisfaction to the perception of other souls feeling tension and relief, and to the group functioning harmoniously or conflicting. Feeling tension when others feel tension focuses attention on the feelings of surrounding souls. How do those people feel, and what can be done to make everyone the most relieved? Each person is somewhere on the spectrum from being frequently triggered with very strong tension about the happiness, harmony, and direction of the group (being flushed with fixating arousal when the group is excited or upset, or distraught over missed opportunities for the group to work together and grow more interconnected), to being infrequently triggered with weak or no tension about the feelings of others or the harmony and progress of the group (observing other people's emotions and the group cohesion and direction of the group for what they are without additional hunger for everyone to feel happy and connected). This chapter focuses on the high and low ends to help understand how life feels different as you move up and down the community-based tension spectrum.

Unlike Friendship-Based Social tension (S_F), which is matching a **known person's** individual pain because of their individual personality and situation, Community-based Social tension (S_C) is felt on behalf of other conscious beings whether individually known or not, as if the irritant were happening to self rather than to the other person. S_C is a confusing of self with others when it comes to feeling pain and tension. Self feels the tension and pain regardless of who actually gets the injury or feels the need. S_C observers are stabbed with pain because they see someone else stabbed with pain, and it feels like something needs to be done to end that person's pain (which will then end the observer's pain). The S_C-motivated observer wants to help resolve the group's problem, because the S_C will feel relief when the group is relieved.

The Community Pleasure Spectrum

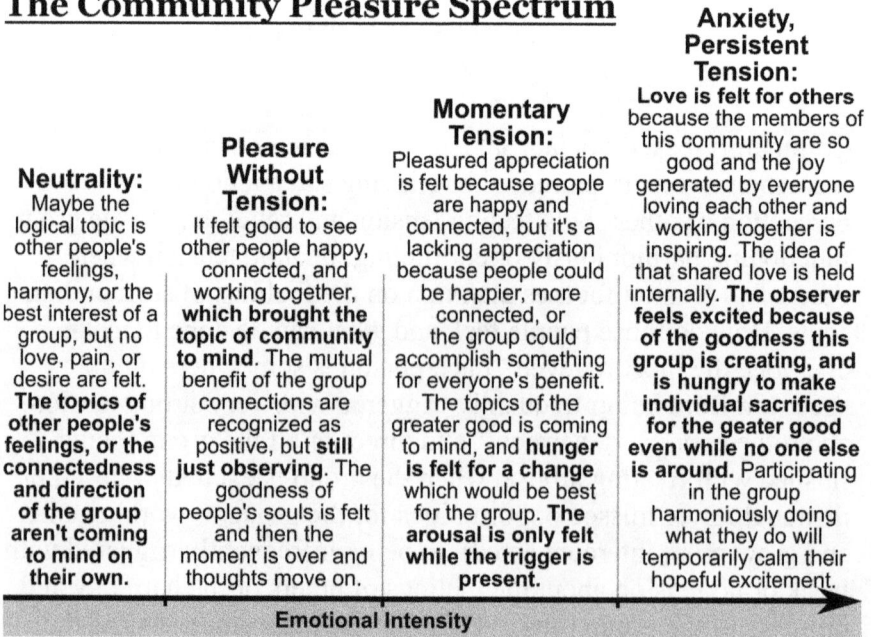

Neutrality:	Pleasure Without Tension:	Momentary Tension:	Anxiety, Persistent Tension:
Maybe the logical topic is other people's feelings, harmony, or the best interest of a group, but no love, pain, or desire are felt. **The topics of other people's feelings, or the connectedness and direction of the group aren't coming to mind on their own.**	It felt good to see other people happy, connected, and working together, **which brought the topic of community to mind**. The mutual benefit of the group connections are recognized as positive, but **still just observing**. The goodness of people's souls is felt and then the moment is over and thoughts move on.	Pleasured appreciation is felt because people are happy and connected, but it's a lacking appreciation because people could be happier, more connected, or the group could accomplish something for everyone's benefit. The topics of the greater good is coming to mind, and **hunger is felt for a change** which would be best for the group. **The arousal is only felt while the trigger is present.**	Love is felt for others because the members of this community are so good and the joy generated by everyone loving each other and working together is inspiring. The idea of that shared love is held internally. **The observer feels excited because of the goodness this group is creating, and is hungry to make individual sacrifices for the geater good even while no one else is around.** Participating in the group harmoniously doing what they do will temporarily calm their hopeful excitement.

Emotional Intensity →

106

Terminology & Abbreviations

Community-based **neutrality** happens when souls are around who don't match the observer's community-based arousal triggers. It's felt when considering groups in history, but also sometimes felt when nearby people are purely coincidental and not at all interconnected. It feels like purely functional proximity which doesn't have any meaning and will be over in a moment. The group's feelings aren't matched by the observer even if the observer focuses on the unarousing people and tries to think of the harmony and direction of the group, or the goodness of their souls. Because there is no group direction, there's no group interaction. Most people feel community-based neutrality when they hear about random people in far away lands. There might be people in the same cafe on the other side of the planet, but it feels like a change of topic to consider how they might all be connected and what the group emotions might be. Most observers aren't flushed with concern about figuring out what those people are feeling and hunger for them to feel more love for each other. When starting from a neutral mind, it feels like a change of topic to then start considering whether or not people are grouped and what that group is feeling. It doesn't feel like there's a reason to make the moment about other people's connectedness and group feelings.

> *"Be kind whenever possible.*
> *It is always possible."*[149]

Community-based Social **pleasure with<u>out</u> tension** is the joy felt when noticing Social love or teamwork between others. The topic of community is coming to mind because souls looked out for each other in recognition of each others' inherent value. This is the pleasure felt when someone can't carry something alone and you see a stranger run over and help. But it's not just humans. This is the loving joy felt when you see someone get out of their car and carry a turtle out of the street to safety. It feels like noticing the goodness in other people's souls, but in a fixed, momentary, practical way. The moment feels complete. That moment was part of the normal world. It passes and nothing more needs to be done. But it's not just objective, emotionless recognition. Pleasure is being felt too. But it's a complete, satisfied pleasure that isn't also hungering for more.

Community-based Social **pleasure <u>with</u> tension** feels like noticing an opportunity for something good about the feelings, connectedness, or progress of group members, but in a lacking way. There's potential for more connectedness between members and more joy in the group and focus is waiting for the pleasurable adjustment to happen. Again, it's not just logical recognition. It's excited hunger, anticipating pleasure.

- **Momentary pleasure tension** (externally triggered tension) is excited, loving hunger for a change that would make the group even happier or more connected, but where the tension only exists while the trigger is present. It's anticipation of goodness that will come when the group is more comfortable, from people loving and supporting each other, or from the group succeeding. Attention is focused and desire is felt, but will be quickly relieved. It's the focus and motivation felt when the group starts singing a song and you haven't started singing with them yet. It's the tension felt when someone is carrying way too much into a party and you could help. It's the excitement felt when your team is running toward the goal but hasn't made it yet. You are part of a larger whole, that larger whole has a need in the current moment, and you can contribute in a way that will make people feel seen, loved, and connected.

> *"We are blessed with technology that would be indescribable to our forefathers. We have the wherewithal, the know-it-all, to feed everybody, clothe everybody, and give every human on Earth a chance. So, let's do it already."*[150]

- **Anxiety, persistent pleasure tension** (internally triggered tension) is hunger for community escalation which persists even when the external trigger is removed. It is the loving immersion people feel in the emotions of the greater group. The base of the thought moves from noticing external inputs to having an internal vision of the group being even more loving, being even

108

more connected, and making even more progress. If everyone keeps working together, the world will be better for everyone. If barriers can be removed, people will love each other more and trust each other more and everyone will feel happier. As the group has successes, people will become more and more invested in participating. The observer isn't just hungry for the positive outcome. They feel like part of the mechanism which brings the desired outcome into reality for everyone.

The Community Pain Spectrum

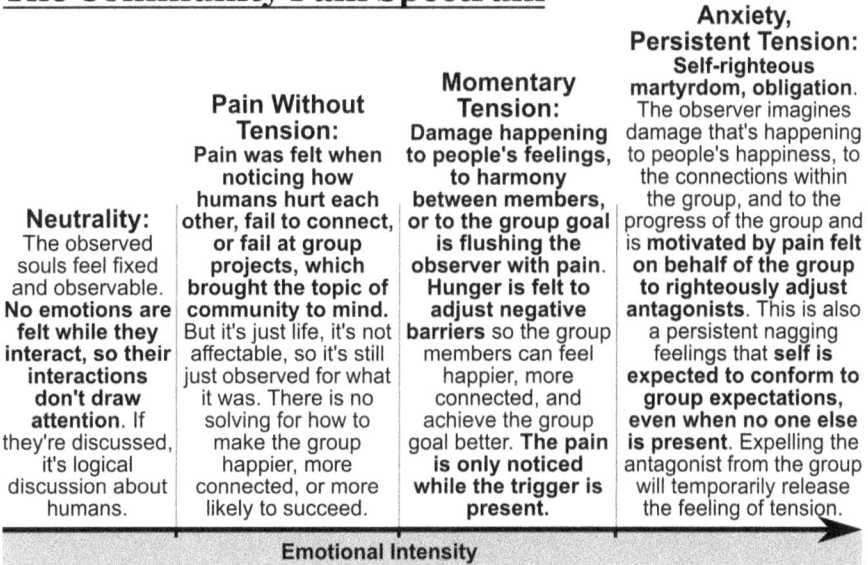

Neutrality:	Pain Without Tension:	Momentary Tension:	Anxiety, Persistent Tension:
The observed souls feel fixed and observable. **No emotions are felt while they interact, so their interactions don't draw attention.** If they're discussed, it's logical discussion about humans.	Pain was felt when noticing how humans hurt each other, fail to connect, or fail at group projects, which **brought the topic of community to mind.** But it's just life, it's not affectable, so it's still just observed for what it was. There is no solving for how to make the group happier, more connected, or more likely to succeed.	Damage happening to people's feelings, or to the group goal is flushing the observer with pain. Hunger is felt to **adjust negative barriers** so the group members can feel happier, more connected, and achieve the group goal better. **The pain is only noticed while the trigger is present.**	Self-righteous martyrdom, obligation. The observer imagines damage that's happening to people's happiness, to the connections within the group, and to the progress of the group and is **motivated by pain felt on behalf of the group to righteously adjust antagonists.** This is also a persistent nagging feelings that **self is expected to conform to group expectations, even when no one else is present.** Expelling the antagonist from the group will temporarily release the feeling of tension.

Emotional Intensity →

Community-based **pain without tension** is the realistic community-based negativity of an imperfect world. It's passive recognition that two group members had a misunderstanding, that people want different things, or that something disturbed what the group was doing, but in a way that is complete. It's a normal discomfort that happens when humans are near each other. It feels like objective recognition of external reality. It doesn't hold attention for more than a moment. There's nothing to be done about it.

Community-based **pain with tension** is feelings of pain and tension in the observer, triggered by the assumed pain or tension being felt by others, but in a lacking way that wants to resolve those other people's pain or tension. This group matters, their feelings matter, and they're in pain that needs to be resolved. The observer is hungry for the adjustment that would make the pain stop.

- **Momentary pain tension** (externally triggered tension) is hunger for pain to stop that only exists while the trigger is present. What's keeping pain happening is the continued observation of the discomfort, disconnection, pain, and needs of the group. The most common S_C momentary tension is felt when someone in the group voices a complaint and the S_C feels compelled to find the common ground that resolves their concern, or finds the compromise where the most people can be the most comfortable. Or maybe the temperature or a sound is making the group uncomfortable and the observer can adjust the thermostat or close a door and resolve the group's discomfort. Maybe another person shows up and there aren't enough chairs, so the observer can run and get another. They're all tensions felt on behalf of the group, but they're quickly resolved and don't come up in cyclical thoughts later.

- **Anxiety, persistent pain tension** (internally triggered tension) is a sharp feeling of concern and righteousness, which makes the group's happiness, connectedness, and progress feel threatened, decreasing, damaged, or disappointing. It's cycling negative predictions of what has happened and what might happen if that threat isn't resolved. Someone is spreading ideas that split the group apart. Someone is selfishly hurting others for their own benefit. Someone is lobbying for rule changes that sound seductive, but actually hurt the group. It's also the feeling of regret for not stepping up and protecting weaker strangers that you saw being attacked, for not saying something when the group considered an idea that you knew was wrong. Focus shifts to an internal solution of what needs to be removed and what needs to be done so that harmony, love, and progress can be restored again. This is so many souls hurting, and so many souls who could thrive if the impediment were removed. This problem needs to be resolved because the pain is so sharp and lingers for so long.

Community-based Social **satisfaction** is felt in the moment when a tense urgency about group mood, connectedness, or progress is resolved. Group members were knocked over and everyone came together and helped them back up. They're now laughing while they talk about the shared experience. The team ran toward the goal and scored and everyone cheered. A vacant lot had gathered trash and the group picked it all up and made it prettier for everyone. There were people who weren't fitting in, but they've learned the group's system, made friends, and are now valuable contributors. Satisfaction feels like relief, triggered by group happiness, group connectedness, through completion of group bonding activities, through verifying that expected positive or negative group qualities were a mistake, through realizing that the group wasn't actually threatened, and sometimes through making the maximum possible group harmony, consensus, and direction adjustment in a disconnected situation. Things were tense, but the goodness of people's souls, all working together, restored harmony, restored happiness, and is on a clear path toward a better life for everyone. Nothing needs attention or action anymore. Thoughts can move on to other topics.

The shorthand for people who are triggered with Community-based Social tension and anxiety more often and strongly than the other tension and anxiety options is that these people are "S$_C$-first." When a reference is made to "an S$_C$," or "S$_C$s," it's identifying the discussed person or people as being S$_C$-first.

The shorthand for people who are triggered more strongly and frequently by all six other tension options is that people are "S$_C$-last." Someone who is S$_C$-last can still feel motivated by love for the group to individually sacrifice for the greater good, but that hunger to do their part is more often momentary, and the tension felt can be more easily interrupted by Relational tension about a sexy group member, or Comfort tension about protecting their resources, sensory comfort, or individuality.

We're now going to immerse in the life experience people have when they're most frequently and strongly struck by Community-based Social tension to see what it's like to live at the highest end of the spectrum. Then we'll immerse in the life experience of people who feel the six other tensions more strongly and frequently to see what it's like at the lowest end of the Community-based Social spectrum.

Hallelujah!

S_C-First: Frequently Triggered Strong S_C Tension

"The first sign of civilization in an ancient culture
was a fossil thighbone that had been broken and then healed.
In the animal kingdom, if you break your thigh, you die.
You cannot run from danger, get to the river for a drink,
or hunt for food. You are meat for prowling beasts.
No animal survives a broken thigh long enough for the bone to heal.
A broken thighbone that has healed is evidence
that someone has taken time to stay with the one who fell,
has bound up the wound, has carried the person to safety
and has tended the person through recovery.
Helping someone else through difficulty is where civilization starts."[152]

Being S$_C$-first means feeling emotions before logic has had a chance to evaluate an input. S$_C$s are stabbed with painful tension when a stranger accidentally hurts themselves. They're also stabbed with tension when a stranger assaults someone else who was peacefully walking. **The observers' bodies aren't getting touched, and yet they're flushed with pain as if something negative were happening to themselves.** Was the pain a response to logic? No. S$_C$-firsts don't logically assess the actual damage, the statistical likelihood of the positive and negative outcomes, the impact to themselves, and then make a logical choice to feel pain. They can't logically choose to feel pain on command from other logical negatives which don't trigger that feeling. The pain happens automatically and simultaneously with the observation of potential and actual disruption and pain to others. Logic is used after the feeling happened to explain why the other person's situation feels so sharply painful to observe. Other people's happiness must matter because it's so fixating when they're upset, and so relieving when they're relieved.

S$_C$s are flushed with joyful excitement as their team runs toward the goal. S$_C$s are flushed with hope when people march for democracy. Again, the situation isn't about themselves, but now they're flushed with hungry joy that's fixated on something changing for the benefit of other humans. Again, none of these feelings are the results of logical decisions. S$_C$-firsts don't logically assess the function of points in a game, or the complex reality of human politics, and then make logical choices to feel euphoria from these inputs. They can't logically decide that some other input generate that fixating pleasure instead and then feel it there. They're flushed with joy and hope that unknown humans are going to be happier, and use logic after the feeling to explain why that situation would be positive enough to warrant the feelings.

The third feeling which really cements these in is that S$_C$-first observers can tolerate much bigger problems in other areas without getting triggered with excitement or concern about them. There are some attractive members of the group, but not so sharply attractive that any change in relationship is considered. The observer's life has gotten to be repetitive, but it's not uncomfortable enough to require adjustment. Sensory comforts aren't ideal, but they're not so painful that they require action. Self is calmly doing self's thing right now without drawing any attention for being cool, but that doesn't feel like a problem. Resources are generic and sufficient. These topics aren't coming to mind because they're within the ranges of pain where they're not problems that needs attention (because this observer isn't triggered with tension about them at these levels). They're not perfect, but that's just how life is.

> *"We hold these truths to be self-evident, that all men are created equal,*
> *that they are endowed by their creator with certain unalienable rights,*
> *that among these are life, liberty and the pursuit of happiness.*
> *That to secure these rights, governments are instituted by citizens,*
> *deriving their powers from the consent of the governed,*
> *That whenever any form of government becomes destructive of these*
> *ends, it is the Right of the People to alter or to abolish it."*[153]

As you approach the highest end of the S_C spectrum, observers are drugged with much more social arousal and heartbreak while observing way more groups and group interactions. But it doesn't feel individual and it doesn't feel internal. It feels like objective recognition that humans are all one family, that benefits come when people work together, and that problems and pain happen when individuals ignore their affects on other people. At the highest setting everyone who passes on the street is part of the observer's group. If any of them suddenly feel tension, the S_C will quickly feel the same tension. The S_C observer will be relieved when that stranger is also relieved. If conflict starts the S_C will be flushed with tension to support whoever supports harmony and progress for the group. In stores, while driving, at the park, happiness happens when everyone is flowing with the group and doing their parts for everyone's happiness. Pain is assumed to be felt by <u>everyone</u> when an individual starts hassling <u>anyone</u> else.

Was anyone needled by what was just said? Does anyone look like they're feeling excluded? Is anyone feeling discomfort? Since every other part of life is ignorably acceptable, the stability of the flow of the group feels sharply consequential. S_Cs don't want to feel other people's tension again, but a critical moment came up on its own which requires action or regret (which ends up being a lot of moments).

"We, as individuals, are pretty junk at doing most things by ourselves.
We're not smart enough to solve all the problems by ourselves.
We're not strong enough to lift the heavy weights by ourselves.
As social animals we're just better in groups.
So anyone who thinks they can manage life or career or work alone
is on a fool's errand. At the end of the day, one of the most difficult
lessons for any of us to learn, but it's also the most rewarding,
is simply to say, "I need help, will you help me?"
We're all surrounded by people who want to help us.
They don't because they think we don't need it. As soon as we're willing
to ask, it's amazing the army of people who are right by our side."[154]

Half of what makes group-based feelings feel objective is that so many group-related inputs inspire no arousal, even for S_C-firsts. No tension, happiness, sadness, or relief are felt on behalf groups that existed in ancient history. No pain is felt today because the observer's first grade class isn't still united as one team. There are so many people, groups, and issues which don't automatically trigger sharp emotions, that the current focuses must be important.

> *"Give me your tired, your poor,*
> *your huddled masses yearning to breathe free,*
> *the wretched refuse of your teeming shore.*
> *Send these, the homeless, tempest-tossed to me,*
> *I lift my lamp beside the golden door!"*[155]

Tension events alternate with being released again when S_Cs get satisfaction, which is usually a restoration of the harmony and progress of the group. When walking down the street, tension is felt as a stranger approaches. The S_C makes eye contact, nods, smiles, and says, "good morning" hoping to connect. The other person returns the smile and nod. They're relaxed, so the tension is satisfied and released.

Each day is a tug-of-war between neutral availability of focus for any thought and fixated community-based arousal, joy, pain, obligation, or anger. The emotional problems in life happen when people selfishly hurt others. Maybe a conflict isn't resolving. Maybe the group is separating into factions. Maybe people got together but didn't feel connected this time. Everyone could've happily done their part, and instead it's incomplete. The situation will keep cycling in thoughts so that the resolving action can be determined.

> *"What Gandhi did, we could each do. Can you imagine if*
> *10 Gandhis showed up at the same time? Just 10 of us.*
> *10 of us are going to do something. And, if it's 20 of us,*
> *then we each only need to do half the stuff that Gandhi did."*[156]

S_Cs love the feelings of harmony, community, and group success. If you dropped all judgment and distraction and really let yourself feel the pleasure that everyone gets from having other people around, not clouded by any other feeling, what would you focus on? What values can people have in common that make them such good souls that they're endearing to be teamed up with? How would daily life be easier if you were surrounded by people who all joyfully did their parts? How much better would life be for everyone if people stopped fighting each other? How great would every event be if you could act with 100% confidence that everyone is looking out for each other and caring for each other? Can you imagine the society in which all the citizens were honorable and worked together and feel some of the pleasure of living in that community right now?

Then imagine the tension felt when a jerk walks over and shoves a sweet, tender, but weak member of your group. That jerk would feel like they have negative tension as one of their observable components. The disruption focuses attention and feels like it requires action. It feels like it's individually painful for every observer, and the combined discomfort of the whole group is felt by the S_C. It would relieve SO MANY people if the jerk were handled.

"I am wary of stories with one hero."[157]

S_C feelings are different from logic. S_C tension is the unsettled feeling which fixates attention, which logic has to repeatedly interpret and manage. Someone feeling tension will keep feeling fixated and unsettled even if they logically know they're powerless to affect what they're anxious about. A governmental change would be fairer and make more people happy, but it's not going to happen. Or they might agree that a rule is ridiculous but still feel awkward and awful if they broke it. The feelings and the logic are sometimes aligned, but can just as easily be in opposition.

Later on, these emotions interrupt peaceful, calm moments that don't have external triggers. Pain happens again, triggered by the memory of the politician teaching people divisive, negative perspectives. No decision was made to think about that jerk. In fact, logic might realize that the negative version being lived in memory has more severe damage than what actually happened in reality. But the pain is so sharp that attention is fixated on how much pain would've been felt and how tragic the loss would've been had people adopted those views. Then community-based arousal strikes again, triggered by the vision of how great society could be if people worked together and looked out for each other. The observer is alone, the actual exterior moment is quiet, but the observer is flushed with relief and happiness.

© *Zach Weinersmith – smbc-comics.com*[158]

Since tension could be triggered at any moment, S$_C$s preemptively take actions to maintain the peace, harmony, consensus, and direction of the group, and hone their group-supporting skills. Even when the group seems fine, S$_C$-firsts knows the situation might turn, and it will be striking if it does, so they keep making choices to protect the group from disruptions. The way to be present and available for the rest of life is to notice and resolve disruptions before they happen.

> *"What are you doing?" the man asked.*
> *"I'm throwing the starfish back into the water*
> *so they can live," replied the boy.*
> *"But there are thousands of them. You can't possibly make a difference."*
> *The boy reached down, grabbed another one, heaved it into the surf,*
> *and said, "I made a difference for that one."*[159]

A love for group harmony, consensus, and direction creates a desire for people to follow the rules or social standards of situations, even when those guidelines only exist to avoid confrontations and misunderstandings between members, since maintaining the peace is vital. Creating a fuss will upset others without changing anything, so just follow the dumb rules.

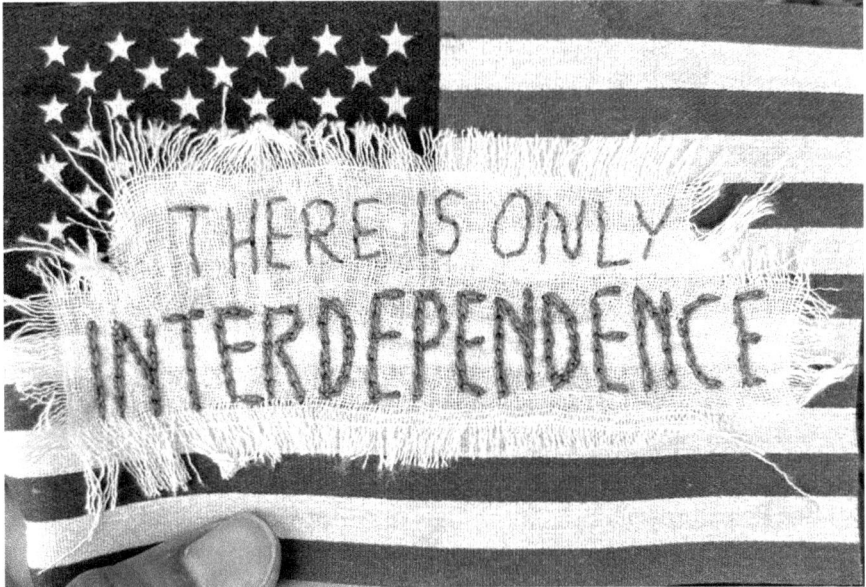

INDEPENDENCE IS A MYTH! © Zak Foster - ZakFoster.com[160]

S$_C$-firsts think that the community-based arousal they feel is helpful. They're motivated to watch how the whole system of people work together so the actions they take can be meaningfully helpful in benefiting everyone. They form strong bonds in the community as people realize that they're consistently looking out for others. They make better decisions about food, jobs, comfort, self, sex, risks, and experiences, because they prioritize how these impact the harmony and progress of humanity. They have what other people have, plus they're a part of something much bigger than themselves, making a meaningful difference in the world.

"We are all one. Only egos, beliefs, and fears separate us."[161]

Meanwhile, S_C-lasts only seem to have disadvantages. Most obviously, people who don't care about other people have dangerous psychological problems. The biggest part of being human is missing from them, replaced by soullessness. Their opinions don't matter because there's something critically broken about how their brain works. Lower S_C friends don't think about how their actions impact the group, so they lose out on the benefits of the support of others, often in exchange for small, momentary gains in meaningless ways. They want all the benefits of being in a stable society while not doing their small part to keep that system in motion. They're constantly hurting others without even realizing it. They monologue about being an individual while they're still following the group, predictably watching the group so they can do the opposite and say the opposite. They definitely aren't getting benefits by attacking the people who would love them, by disagreeing with the people who are trying to help them, and by alienating the people they'll miss when they don't have a holiday meal to go to.

"No one has ever become poor by giving."[162]

S_C-lasts miss the best parts of life because they get distracted with things that don't matter. An S_C-first may not have a perfect life, but they've got the foundation. If an S_C died today, they're at peace that their life supported the greater good and they're leaving humanity better than they found it. An S_C's life is optimized for actual reality.

"You may say I'm a dreamer, but I'm not the only one.
I hope someday you will join us. And the world will live as one."[163]

"Wow, I can't believe it's already time for you guys to pick up on social cues that we'd like you to leave."

© Teresa Burns Parkhurst[164]

S_Cs vary quite a bit in what and who sparks their group-focused joy, inspiration, excitement, relief, and pain. Some focus on supporting the people they've known the longest. Some focus on the group they were born into. Some immerse in politics, religion, or community groups, while others are absolutely dedicated to family. Some are ardent members and supporters of antisocial groups and antisocial leaders. Some have a small circle, while others are struck with tension every day about all of humanity. Many are part of their community by proxy through the news or media. S_Cs are accustomed to being told that they need to be more individual, by people who are too selfish to realize that supporting the greater good can be an individual purpose.

S_Cs think repeatedly feeling obligated, flushed with righteousness, flushed with empathetic pain, and empathetic joy, is just what life is. They think they're trying for a totally realistic, but admittedly high-level of teamwork and connectedness. But they determined that something is "realistic" by imagining something better than what they already encountered, or the best they ever encountered, while minimizing inextricable trade offs that come with those positives. The result is an underlying, recurring ache, an unfillable anxiety, a dissatisfaction with reality, because the "realistic" goal they need to feel satisfied is just beyond what's actually possible.

S_C-Last: *Living without Tension about Community-Based Pleasures and Pains*

> "I dreamed a path that was traditional: Disc Jockey → Comedian → Actor → Big Success, which was a mainstream dream. Meanwhile what I really was was an outlaw and a rebel. I got kicked out of three different schools, the Air Force, the choir, the alter boys, summer camp, the Boy Scouts, and I quit school in ninth grade. I had great marks, I was a smart kid, but I didn't care. It's important in life to not care, it can help you a lot. I was a pot smoker at 13, we broke the law, we broke into cars, we broke into offices, we broken into Columbia University, we broke into stores. We did all sorts of unlawful things. I was one who swam against the tide of what was expected, against what the establishment wanted from us. But I didn't know that about myself because this traditional dream blinded me. I didn't know this dissonance was inside of me. I gravitated toward anti-authority because I was that kind of person already. In the period this was happening, the counter-culture was growing, and I realized artists were using their talents to project their feelings and ideas, not to please people. And I suddenly was able to see my place. I had denied myself and I never became a really big success until I let myself grow into being an anti-authority outlaw and rebel."[165]

At the lowest point on the S_C spectrum the connectedness between people, and the state of other people's emotions feels like something fixed which can be observed, rather than something variable which might change. Other people's emotions and connections feel more like practical parts of reality which might help or get in the way, and less like satisfaction themselves for an existing hunger. Other people's emotions and connections feel irrelevant to the moment, which is obviously about something else. Group harmony and direction become logical topics about function in this moment's reality, and aren't emotional topics about desire and relief for how things "should" or "could" be.

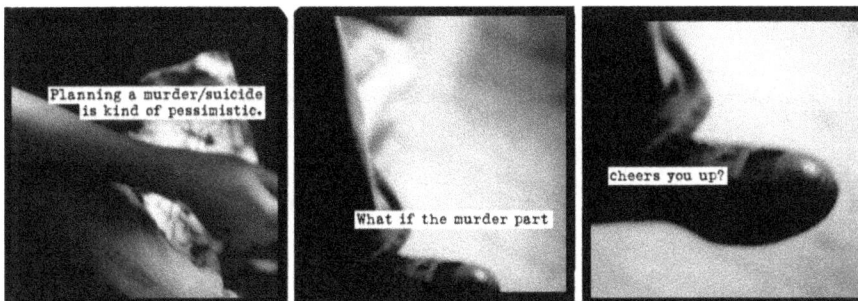

As S$_C$-triggers reduce in number and drug intensity (moving down the S$_C$ spectrum) fewer humans and fewer groups trigger the observer to feel concern or excitement. Social neutrality isn't criticism or rejection. It's not a thought at all. It's a lack of excitement, pain, tension, or relief which would bring the topic of other people's emotions to mind. When you walk on a sidewalk and are not automatically flushed with the feelings of the sidewalk, you are feeling social neutrality about the sidewalk. You're not making any decisions to ignore the feelings of the sidewalk. You're not solving for the logic of why the sidewalk's feelings matter and pretending that you're upset because of the logic. With no upset feelings to trigger it, the "logic" you'd develop seems irrelevant. Full S$_C$ neutrality is a lack of triggered emotions even when someone brings up the topic of other people's emotions. The group is freaking out, maybe positively, maybe negatively. It's just observed as what it is. Matching emotions aren't automatically triggered. Even while discussing what a sidewalk would be feeling, you're not automatically flushed with its emotions. Even when told that other people are upset, an extreme S$_C$-last isn't flushed with their tension, so they don't become hungry to resolve those other people's tension. Instead those other people's pains sound exterior. It's observed information, if it's noticed at all.

> *"If I go into a store and someone's like "How you doing today?"*
> *They don't actually care.*
> *The next time someone you don't know asks "How you doing?"*
> *Just say, 'Waffles.'*
> *It doesn't make the conversation any less meaningful.*
> *No one's not getting information they really want."*[167]

Most S_C-lasts still can feel pleasure from cheering along with a crowd rather than cheering alone, and feel bad for humanity when they watch a tragic event happen. But the experience of those is different when those events don't automatically trigger hunger for change and escalation. There was a moment of community-based pleasure or pain, that's just reality, and then the moment ended. The thought ends there. The observer can still look to the side and discuss a different topic. Pleasurable moments don't fixate the observer with hunger for humans to bond together even tighter and work together even more. The rest of reality isn't silenced. The observer's focus isn't distracted away from the moment with an internal fantasy of what the world would be like if everyone looked out for each other. Instead it seems weird that we're still talking about that moment when it was over long ago.

Even S_C-firsts usually feel S_C neutrality while watching a flock of birds. Logically they see that a bird might deviate, or an obstacle might interrupt the flow, but it's observed without being flushed with the pain of the group when that disturbance happens, and without relief and joy when harmony is reestablished. The group remains external and functional. At any moment the observer could effortlessly move all focus to a different topic.

> *"That's just me saying something terrible*
> *because it makes me laugh that it upsets you.*
> *That's all that is, just so you know.*
> *It's enjoyable to me that you're upset."*[168]

Community-based Social neutrality is a not-modeling of the group as an integrated entity. Neutrality is a not-imagining of ways harmony could be different. It's a noticing of reality as it is in a completely accepting way. But, for the person not flushed with emotions, it's just a normal day where things are happening. When forced to think about other people's emotions (and the sidewalk's emotions, or random birds' emotions), i t feels like other people's emotions are fixed and momentary. It's like asking if it's day or night. The answer is noted without imagining other options and longing for those options.

Now imagine that some idiot just insisted that you call him "sir" when you speak to him. You reach for your keys and they're definitely missing. You feel dizzy and might pass out. The cutie you've been flirting with just laughed at someone else's joke. This is the last moment in your old environment and you're about to move to an exciting new place. For all humans, the group's harmony isn't the topic of the moment while other meaningful life events are happening. S_C-last observers have more Relational and Comfort triggers connected to more drug intensity. No choice is being made to ignore the harmony and direction of the group. It's just not a community-based moment, because it's obviously a critical Comfort or Relational moment (which happens to be a lot of moments).

© *Jim Benton – JimBenton.com*[169]

Other people are getting the results of their decisions, situations, and intelligence. Humans have different desires. Conflict is always going to happen just like wind is always going to happen. It is illogical to get emotional every time other people are emotional. If it's more useful to have people in a different mood, wait it out and they'll be in a different mood soon. The people who want to work together are already doing that. The people who don't, aren't. Most of the time, emotions aren't felt about other people until they're getting in the way. If you could feel the process of turning yourself down in S_C tension, you'd feel a silencing of the urgency felt when noticing other people having emotions. There's no need to get to know emotional people's situations and help them find relief. You can see how the group is and then think about whatever else you'd like to think about. When you watch a school of fish repeatedly changing direction you can feel how much their fluctuations don't matter. That is what fish do. When you see humans being emotional you can feel that it doesn't involve you. Humans get emotional all the time and they can deal with it themselves.

> *"If humans started as social animals —*
> *isn't all progress and civilization*
> *directed toward making them individuals?*
> *Isn't that the only possible progress?"[170]*

Groups can still be functionally useful even when no emotional investment is made in their harmony. But there's no thought that positive features of different communities could be combined, or that disharmony could be removed, or that the connecting friendships, teamwork, and selflessness could be more extreme. All the adults in the room can easily tune out what other people are feeling while the meaningful task gets attention. Only the brainless will fuss over the anxious people's emotions while the task happens.

> *"The way I look at it is that they're not me, so I don't care."[171]*

Not being emotionally triggered doesn't mean that S_C-lasts can't recognize the benefits of a functioning society, and of membership in a tightly connected group. But S_C-lasts might've missed noticing those on their own, because their mind was elsewhere. And, even when they recognize that their situation is good, they won't feel extra euphoria from the goodness on top of the practical, logical benefits.

> *"Humans think in herds; and they go mad in herds,*
> *while they only recover their senses slowly, and one by one."[172]*

Interacting with groups is different when the emotions of those people are their own situations and responsibilities. Someone choosing between groups wouldn't have feelings of community, love, obligation, and disconnection to help with the choice (to create an alternative to logic), or to make them feel especially lucky as they became more involved. S_C-lasts can see that the people in one group are working together as a team better than in another, but they're not so happy that the trade offs for that teamwork get minimized. Instead, consideration of those groups more easily triggers self-protective feelings, resource-protective feelings, sensory comfort-protecting feelings, safety-protecting feelings, body-protecting feelings, sexual arousal-protecting feelings, and experience-protecting feelings. If you're managing a life where you're easily triggered by Comfort and Relational concerns, it's worth avoiding groups that trigger your recurring pain tension, and it's worth prioritizing groups who will help resolve your tensions. If you want to care about the harmony and direction of a group then find the group which helps the most with your Comfort and Relational needs and see if you can accept that group the way it is. Then never revisit the question of how harmoniously people are getting along again.

> *"The greatest crimes in the world are not committed*
> *by people breaking the rules, but by people following the rules.*
> *It's people who follow orders*
> *who drop bombs and massacre villages."*[173]

Humans will never all come together to work as one team because people are individually too different. This is particularly clear to anyone whose C_I is higher than their S_C, because they recognize each individual's absolute need to differentiate from others. Current society is as good as it will ever get in terms of humans managing to trade and live near each other with minimal murder. Everyone could pick up and move if they wanted, and people are staying right where they are. People could make political changes if they wanted, and they sit at home instead. The current group options are fine and any other options would just come with different, not better, annoyances. Whatever conflicts, inefficiencies, and inaccurate directions groups have are what they are. Reality isn't fantasy. There's nothing to be gained by trying to never have those. If you

let humans have the normal conflicts that they have, if you let
humans do the dumb things they do, you're free to live life.

Instead of fantasizing about humans working together, deviate
slightly from reality in Comfort and Relational directions. Find a
great romantic relationship. Figure out your individual calling and
go for it. Travel. Enjoy the taste of food. Pause and really feel how
great the breeze feels. Recognize your individual strengths and
become truly excellent in those things. Build a name for yourself.
Build a home for yourself. Set it up just how you like. Get a steady
income, build up some savings, and get some emergency supplies
together. Feed and heal your body. Get enough sleep. Get enough
water. Realize how short your time is and use it wisely to enjoy
living as much as you can. Then imagine doing that while humans
and society stay the mess that they are, where conflicts happen
every day, where other people get fussy and upset every day. Can
you find a way to feel energized, hopeful, and creative while
humans keep being humans? Can you find a way to feel inspired
and focused while others are flushed with the same tension they'll
always have? Can you live your own life instead of trying to solve
other people's problems?

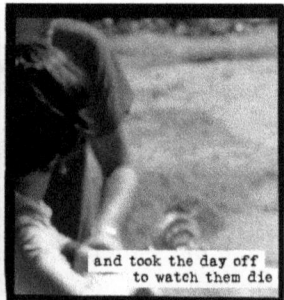

all the whales washed up on shore

so we filled coolers with beer

and took the day off to watch them die

© *e horne and j comeau – asofterworld.com*[174]

An S_C-**last** is observing reality without creating something different
inside, which is what it feels like to accept reality as it is. S_C-lasts
have tried to get happiness from being part of a group, and it wasn't
worth it. The joy was temporary and they left feeling rejected and
unliked. Groups have moments of function and pleasure. Group
harmony doesn't have a deeper meaning. Groups aren't a source of
joy or disappointment in themselves.

From the perspective of S$_C$-lasts, S$_C$s only seem to have disadvantages. Why freak out about stuff you can't control? Why do S$_C$s believe such ridiculous stupidity just because the people around them also believe it? Why don't S$_C$s speak up for themselves when they're individually inconvenienced? Being S$_C$ is the way to have the gift of a unique soul and waste it managing the dumber people around you who can't manage themselves. If you have a gift, why are you wasting it on people who don't have gifts? If the two of you died it would cancel out and the world wouldn't have been different. Let those people go. Let them get the consequences of their lack of character and intelligence. Focus on using your own skills to create something. S$_C$s waste time discussing news items that are exaggerations, bigotry, and lies, which they can do nothing about. They're so focused on an imaginary, perfect conformity that they get "righteously" upset at a world that's already as aligned as it's ever going to get. They're so focused on exaggerations about the impacts of groups that they don't enjoy the benefits that they get right now from the best that humanity has to offer. S$_C$s are flushed with righteousness in the moments they add the most evil to the world by punishing other people for being themselves (for not conforming to the group). S$_C$s think they're sacrificing for "everyone's good," when they're really just sacrificing to calm their own emotions about harmony. S$_C$s think other people are feeling obligated, or upset about disharmony, when they're actually feeling Comfort or Relational emotions. S$_C$s overestimate how much benefit comes from people working together and doing things the same way. S$_C$s overestimate how dangerous dictatorships and non-conformity are. S$_C$s overestimate how much good their rules do, and underestimate how much damage their rules do. S$_C$s passionately disregard reality, enthusiastically find ways to be unhappy with what exists, and make bad decisions among existing options. They seem to be unaware of the reality of how humans survive around each other, while thinking they're experts in how humans survive around each other. S$_C$s bully other people into living inauthentically because the S$_C$ is immersed in an individual exaggeration of the value of harmony among humans in general. In critical moments, S$_C$s sacrifice resources, ranking, health, safety, comfort, sexual opportunities, and meaningful life experiences because they're distracted with following rules that benefit no one. What S_Cs are actually experts at are generating evil and pain for themselves and others because they won't wake up and see reality for what it is. Why would anyone want that life?

© *Jim Benton – JimBenton.com*[175]

There is no disappointment to feel with how humans interact with each other. Sometimes people bond together well. Sometimes people spend all their time fighting. When something is truly beneficial for lots of people, groups form long enough to make that happen. The way groups and societies happen is fine. The size of groups is fine. The people who don't feel included are fine. The harmony and direction of the group is fine. There's no need for more, less, better, or different. It's still worth making sure that beneficial memberships get basic maintenance, but that maintenance can happen without tension and relief, without fixated daydreams, and without judging what's happening as good or bad. S$_C$-lasts are realistic about what they've got, what they get from it, what their options are, and what it costs. Part of what makes groups valuable is that they don't need extra attention. S$_C$-lasts live in the group satisfaction that S$_C$-firsts can't find, because S$_C$-lasts live in reality, undistracted by visions of not-reality.

> *"I am not wise enough to lead.*
> *But I am wise enough not to follow."*[176]

Cross Overs

© e horne and j comeau – asofterworld.com[177]

Most S$_C$-lasts can be flushed with happiness when they're with their normal holiday group in a moment when everyone laughs together. Even the S$_C$-last can feel extra love because the surrounding people are happy, and agree that there's something special about doing this day with these people. Most S$_C$-lasts can feel the pain of other people if the next town over is being bombed. They won't just be upset for themselves, they'll feel those people were part of self even though they individually are just fine. But feeling the joys and pains of others happens with WAY fewer inputs, WAY less frequently, and satisfaction comes much faster just by realizing that what happened is the fixed reality.

> *"The reason I don't worry about society is:*
> *nineteen people went into those buildings to kill.*
> *Then hundreds ran in to rescue and save."[178]*

> *"A group or collective identity offers the powerless a variety*
> *of psychological benefits. Such as the ability to dispense*
> *with one of life's heaviest burdens: self-responsibility.*
> *When one sees oneself as a mere particle in the much greater social*
> *whole, one no longer needs to think and make decisions for oneself.*
> *Rather, one merely needs to do and think what others do and think*
> *and blindly obey the collective authority figures."[179]*

Many times a day S_C-firsts are near groups, but aren't struck with the emotions of the group, and therefore neutrally don't notice them. Even sports fans have walked by a crowd of people excitedly cheering for a sport and not been riled themselves with emotion because they don't know who's playing, or it's a different sport than what they watch, or because they don't understand the language. People who are immersed in their own politics, flushed with pain and joy on behalf of the group, feel nothing when walking through a foreign political rally where they don't know what the sides are. The members of some groups don't feel similar enough to the observer to feel an emotional tie to their emotions. When S_C-firsts don't feel the feelings, the emotions of group members feel external and not affectable.

> *"Each new generation born is, in effect, an invasion of civilization*
> *by little barbarians, who must be civilized before it is too late."[180]*

© Justin Boyd - InvisibleBread.com[181]

*"I can picture in my mind a world without war, a world without hate.
And I can picture us attacking that world
because they'd never expect it."[182]*

S_C Conclusions

The addition of S_C means the harmony and direction of the group aren't just functional anymore. S_C drugging adds incentives to protect the qualities of the group that make it harmonious, to heal tensions within the group, to participate in the group cause, and to support the happiness of other members. The group and its purpose are loved, exciting, beautiful, and desirable, triggering excitement, joy, concern, disappointment, pain, and relief. But S_C tension and relief aren't necessary for an observer to join and contribute to groups.

*Student: "How should we treat others?"
Teacher: "There are no others."[183]*

S_C-firsts have the support of more loving communities because they invest so much time and energy in seeking out, building, and maintaining those groups. A consistent focus on group harmony and progress helps them seize opportunities to positively impact lots of people, building returned emotional investment from people they don't know directly. But S_Cs are the least satisfied with the current harmony between others and the group as a whole because daily tension reminds them to focus on what's wrong and imagine and feel desire for better.

*"The most dangerous thing in the world is an immense accumulation
of human beings who are manipulated by only a few heads."[184]*

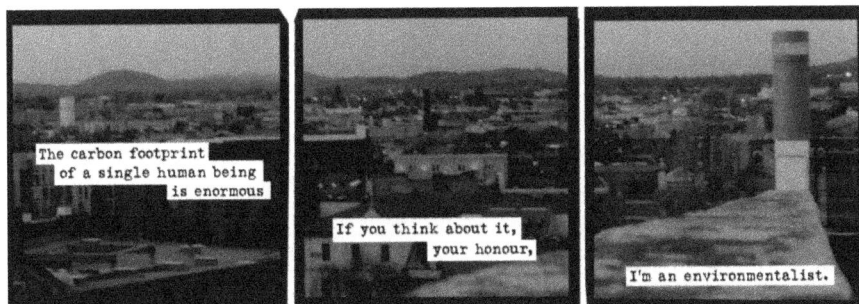

The carbon footprint of a single human being is enormous

If you think about it, your honour,

I'm an environmentalist.

© e horne and j comeau – asofterworld.com[185]

Easily Confused for the S_C Spectrum

"Some people think they are in community, but they are only in proximity.
True community requires commitment and openness.
It is a willingness to extend yourself to encounter and know others."[187]

This chapter compares S_C to the six other motivators one-by-one. It holds the topic constant (community) and looks at it from each of the seven perspectives so you can hear that it's the framing of the topic that gives away the observer's motivators, not the topic itself. Each observer's experience of groups is different when they're feeling different kinds of tension and seeking different kinds of relief from groups. This is the chapter to come back to when determining the relative influence of S$_C$ versus any other motivator for a person.

Valuing the Harmony and Progress of the Group While Feeling Community-Based Socialness (S$_C$):

An observer who dominantly gets flushed with Community-based Social tension is more likely to think that other people are also feeling tension about harmony whenever there's conflict between humans. What inspires S$_C$s to take action is the understanding that they're going to relieve the tensions that everyone is feeling about a disturbance, ending the suffering of many, and bringing satisfaction to many. Meanwhile, other people aren't noticing how the group is flowing, or how other people are feeling because they're rarely or never triggered with emotions about those things. Instead, not-S$_C$s are in a totally different mindset where the group isn't relevant. So the S$_C$ who thinks they're resolving "everyone's" tension is actually addressing something that is only disturbing people to the degree that they're also triggered with the same type of tension and aren't distracted with other tensions.

Someone who is hungry with S$_C$ imagines everyone in the group happily working together for everyone's good. Meanwhile, others are members to get a benefit that they couldn't get alone. The people near an S$_C$ are in the mindsets of their hungers (food hunger, resource affection, self-love, sensory excitement, defensiveness, fear, sexual attraction, or painful stagnancy), hoping the S$_C$ will help satisfy those hungers, while the S$_C$ is in an S$_C$ framed mindset, hoping others will satisfy their social hungers for everyone to love and care for each other. On both sides, people think the framing of the moment was triggered by the external world, and is therefore the obvious and reasonable background for understanding.

When an S$_C$ doesn't get the reaction from other people that they expect, the S$_C$ feels superior because they "valued the group first," while others were "selfish." Most S$_C$s think the lesser reaction must be because other people weren't raised properly, or they weren't conditioned properly to care about others, which now requires social pressure to rectify. Meanwhile the other person is actually reacting to the fact that what the S$_C$ said doesn't seem to help their own self-esteem, individuality, life experiences, resources, sensations, safety concerns, sexual attraction, or health. Both people feel superior and more intelligent than the other because they each solved for what would help resolve their own tension. When S$_C$s are sacrificing for the happiness of the group, they're just as often taking actions which negatively needle group members who didn't need S$_C$ satisfaction, and are now triggered with negative Comfort or Relational tension.

© *Harley Schwadron – SchwadronCartoons.com*[188]

Valuing the Harmony and Progress of the Group While Feeling Sex-Based Relationalness (R$_S$):

An R$_S$ will join whichever group has the most hotties in it, the best gender ratio for acquiring a new partner, and will switch groups if another group provides better sexual opportunities. An R$_S$ is going to get really horny today, several times, and will be fixated on sex until they have an orgasm each time they do. So, surrounding themselves with the highest chances of having sex with the most arousing partner is the logical way to seek satisfaction. They're hoping to find a very sexually charged romantic relationship, and group memberships are one tool to get there. An S$_C$ meanwhile will join a group that they know doesn't have sexually attractive members in it, and will be internally motivated to care for the feelings of unattractive members, giving up time where they could be finding sexual partners because the needs of the group feel more important (they triggered more fixating tension).

© e horne and j comeau – asofterworld.com[189]

People who are in sexual love have an energetic, loving base to fuel their joy. People fight less when they're sexually attracted and sexually satisfied. People in love aren't hungry in the ways that cause humans to act out. So, the best way to make society happier and more harmonious is to end the tension of the not-sexually-satisfied and help true lovers find each other. An R$_S$ would happily move to a conflicting, crumbling society which had fantastic sexual options rather than stay in a harmonious society with mediocre sexual options. If the connection with a partner is threatened, nothing about the community matters until sexual intensity is restored. Whatever makes sexual partners horny is more important than social norms, strangers conflicting, or whatever the group is doing.

There are lots of problems with dating an S$_C$. One is that they're tempted to wait to have sex until the community approves. An R$_S$ is likely to think the other person isn't sexually attracted if they won't have sex, so it's in both people's interest for the relationship to end, when really the other person is sexually attracted, but has submitted their free will to the direction of less intelligent people (the group). But, even when an S$_C$ gets across the fact that they're more worried about upsetting others than they're excited about having sex, that still just reveals them as someone who isn't feeling matching sexual attraction. An S$_C$ might also bring people and policies into the bedroom, concerned about what "values" they're supporting or attacking with how sex happens. They detach from the passion of the moment, immersed in painful, unsexy, inaccurate daydreams of humanity being healed or restored by their sex decisions. All that self righteousness, lack of presence, and lack of intelligence isn't sexy. R$_S$s want to feel sexual attraction and escalation, while S$_C$s want to feel like they're doing their part to support the greater good. But S$_C$s don't realize that harmony is the hobby of only a few people. R$_S$s don't realize that group-lovers really do get more happiness from supporting their group than they do from having orgasms.

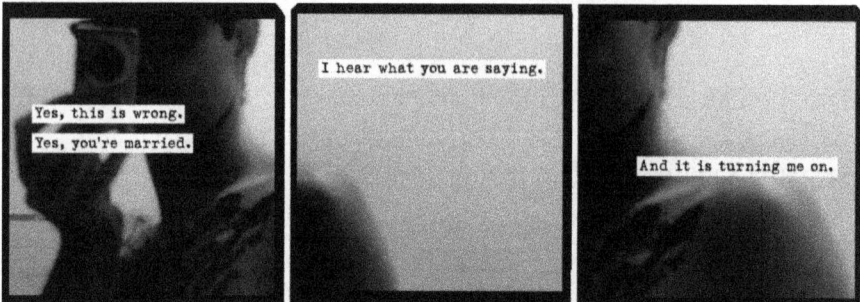

© *e horne and j comeau – asofterworld.com*[190]

Valuing the Harmony and Progress of the Group While Feeling Resource-Based Comfort (C$_R$):

*"Lately I've been thinking about the verb 'to treasure,'
and how valuing something can sometimes lead to hoarding it,
when what would help the universe most
would be to share what you value to bring someone else joy."*[191]

"What if we try to make the world a better place, but for profit."

© *Avi Steinberg – SteinbergDrawsCartoons.com*[192]

A C_R values the harmony and progress of the community for how they help in attracting and protecting the parts of life which are emotional, which are consumption, acquisition, and fun. A community is helpful if it provides stability and opportunities. Every society has risen and collapsed, so being in the profitable phase of each society is intelligent, and switching societies when a better option comes up is the basic foundation for an intelligently lived life. Resource related policies make a difference in a stable society, like government protection of personal property. A community can be a great resource if it is well connected, well supplied, and if the surrounding people provide information, help, and even just motivation. It's helpful when everyone's basic needs are taken care of, and it's better if it's done while taking the fewest resources from the members. Emotions are felt based on how society is doing, but those emotional reactions make it seem like it's time to hoard food because of instability, or it's time to provide a service because there's money to be made.

"Prices are a fast and effective conveyor of information through a vast society in which fragmented knowledge must be coordinated."[193]

Meanwhile, an S$_C$ is tense because someone nearby is hurting, and would gladly sacrifice resources in order to relieve the tension that the other person is feeling. Then the S$_C$ will feel relieved by the other person's relief. The C$_R$ mistakenly thinks the S$_C$ is feeling boredom, greed, food hunger, acquisition desire, or resource-love when the S$_C$ is actually feeling inspired by the internal idea that they're aligned with positive social values, creating strong bonds with others, and part of a merged greater community.

"You can get everything you want in life, if you're willing to help enough people get what they want."[194]

C$_R$s can be surprisingly willing to individually sacrifice for the good of the community. But they do it because they recognize the benefits they're getting in return and are trying to be fair. The group is a good resource, and the moment it stops being a good resource the C$_R$ will move on. C$_R$ motivates a default framing of topics around the qualities that make resources attractive the same way that S$_C$ motivates a default framing of topics around the qualities that make communities harmonious and connected.

"The first lesson of economics is scarcity: There is never enough of anything to fully satisfy all those who want it. The first lesson of politics is to disregard the first lesson of economics."[195]

"Don't tell me what your priorities are. Show me where you spend your money and I'll tell you what they are."[196]

<u>*Valuing the Harmony and Progress of the Group While Feeling Alliance-Based Socialness (S_F):*</u>

> *"The more you understand a conversation between two strangers the less likely they know each other well."* [197]

Community-based Social (S_C) tension is similar to Friendship-based Social (S_F) tension in that they're both automatically triggered tension and relief because other people are feeling tension and relief. They're different in that S_F is tension and relief based on modeling the individual soul, customized to what triggers and relieves that individual, while S_C is tension and relief based on modeling a generic, valuable soul, or modeling everyone nearby generically, assuming they also all feel S_C tensions. S_Cs are protecting values, while S_Fs are protecting a sweet, known soul or a valuable, connected, specific friendship. An S_C can turn against an individual if they pull out a weapon and start threatening a group, because that individual violated the social value that holds the group together. Meanwhile an S_F will want to go mediate if the person who did that is their crazy family member, to make sure the crazy family member doesn't get hurt. The S_F treats that individual differently because they're familiar and known. Community-based tension is felt generally for good souls, thinking of the ways that all souls have the same basic sources of pain. So S_C feels four times the tension when four harmonious strangers are disrupted.

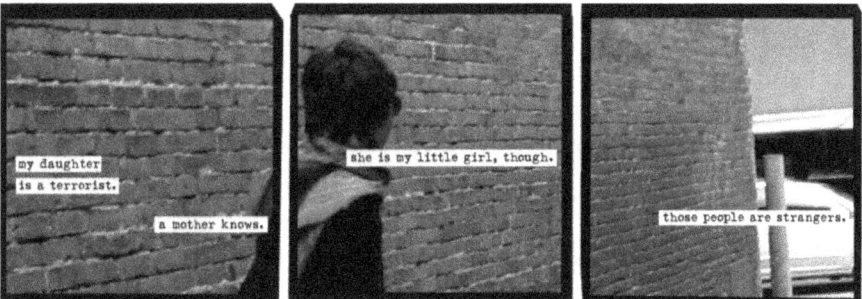

my daughter is a terrorist.

she is my little girl, though.

a mother knows.

those people are strangers.

© *e horne and j comeau – asofterworld.com* [198]

An S_F values the harmony and progress of the community for how they serve as a backdrop on which their friendships happen. It's easier to create deep, meaningful connections with individual humans when the surrounding environment is peaceful, plentiful, and has cute coffee shops. But the focus isn't on the community. If friends want to move to a different community then it makes sense to move. If friends want to stay in a degrading community then it's time to stay. Friends are the "roots" that make a place feel like home. An S_F cares about community rules to the extent that they impact friends. An S_F will break community rules if they're doing it with a friend, so it's a shared bonding experience. An S_F sees the humanity and softness of a friend's soul even when that friend screwed up and did something bad. The friend and the friendship are what matter, and sticking together through hard times is what friendships are all about.

S_F motivates a default framing of topics around the qualities that make known souls happy and synchronized with the observer, the same way that S_C motivates a default framing of topics around the qualities that make communities harmonious and connected.

Valuing the Harmony and Progress of the Group While Feeling Experience-Based Relationalness (R_A):

> *"If you look around at your circle of people.*
> *If you don't feel inspired, you don't have a circle.*
> *You have a cage."*[199]

R_As think that S_Cs are focused on the group for the ultimate experience of being immersed in a group. What's confusing is why S_Cs cheer from the stands, or support with signs, rather than trying to be the players that people cheer for, or the candidate that others hold signs for. If you're really passionate about this, why not go for the ultimate experience? Don't go to church, become a preacher. Don't watch the news, go be the news, or at least be the reporter who breaks the news. R_As rarely confuse themselves as being S_C, because they move towns, and move topics too often to have the longevity that establishes group memberships. But R_As become group leaders because they are overflowing with energy and passion about a topic and know how everyone can work together to maximize the thrill. But R_As are mistaking the desires of their S_C group members. Those people often want a harmonious group who looks out for each other and follows the rules so no one is upset. They're often not there to maximize the thrills that come from doing something new and extreme.

> *"If you're socially awkward and want to change that, become consumed by a cause or a purpose. I've never felt socially awkward when thinking about the ambitious things I want to accomplish. The stuff I want to do trumps everything else. There are no negative social consequences which are important enough that they can waiver my sense of purpose."*[200]

An R_A wants to experience being in a perfectly harmonious society, and in a chaotic anarchy, in complete freedom, and in complete repression, because they'll come out the other side of those experiences with wisdom and understanding that only come through experience. Going to an oppressive society and standing up against the guns is a thrilling life experience. Going to a conforming society and helping individuals escape is exciting. Having the practical knowledge of what it's actually like feels valuable, and makes the observer much more helpful in conversations about the topic.

> *"Here's to the crazy ones. The misfits. The rebels. The troublemakers. The round pegs in the square holes. The ones who see things differently. They're not fond of rules. And they have no respect for the status quo. You can quote them, disagree with them, glorify or vilify them. About the only thing you can't do is ignore them. Because they change things. They push the human race forward. And while some may see them as the crazy ones, we see genius. Because the people who are crazy enough to think they can change the world, are the ones who do."*[201]

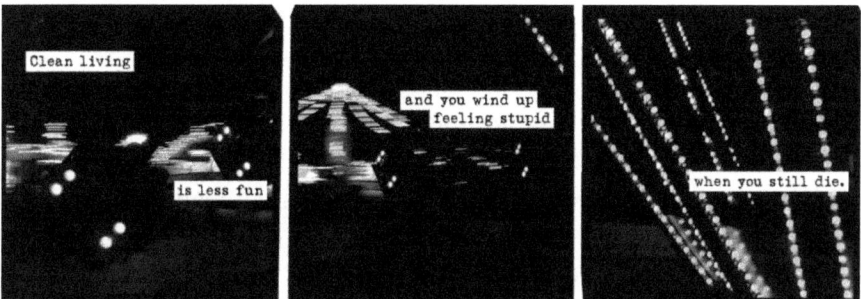

Clean living

and you wind up feeling stupid

is less fun

when you still die.

© e horne and j comeau – asofterworld.com[202]

143

An R$_A$ values the harmony and progress of the community for how they help in supporting the part of life which is emotional, which is extreme life experiences, adventures, and newness. But the focus isn't on the community. A beneficial society provides the tools and opportunities and none of the ridiculously dumb restrictions that keep people from feeling the excitement and danger of living right at the edge. The best society would be one where every human is following their internal guidance, experiencing all the options, living their dreams, supporting each other as they reach for the unknown, the extreme, and the truly magnificent.

"There are places you haven't been where you already belong."[203]

Someone feeling S$_C$ tension is concerned that the group might be disturbed. Someone feeling R$_A$ tension will be concerned that the group might choose the safe option which brings tension and pain, rather than choosing the thrilling option that brings life, learning, and joy.

D: "My dear, who will let you?"
R: "That's not the point. The point is, who will stop me?"[204]

S$_C$s have a similar dream to R$_A$s, but they want humanity to achieve greatness together, as one merged group where everyone understands each other, so no one gets flustered while each sub-group does their thing. R$_A$s quickly learn through experience that laws and rules are fantasies, artificial barriers constructed by unintelligent people's fears. Trying out the option of breaking them leads to the clear reality that the fearful people who make laws are wrong about dangers and needlessly holding intelligent people back from living. Meanwhile S$_C$s go through most of their lives thinking rules and laws are as real as the laws of nature, because they naturally and automatically feel tension when anyone looks like they're about to break one. R$_A$ motivates an obsession with trying all the options, learning the true limits of reality through first-hand experience, and following dreams until they are a reality, the same way that S$_C$ motivates an obsession with how great society could be if humans worked together for everyone's good.

Valuing the Harmony and Progress of the Group While Feeling Individuality-Based Comfort (C_I):

> *"The goal is to do the thing, whatever it takes.*
> *The people around you are irrelevant.*
> *They will adapt to you, because you are the focus."*[205]

C_Is want to lead groups because the leader is obviously the best, because it will release their tension about adding their own individual influence to each group action, and because they like the recognition and attention that come with having the top position. C_Is focus a surprising amount of energy on what other people are doing, because it's joyful to see other people's mistakes, because seeing others impressed with the C_I is so joyful, and because it feels so good to know that the C_I is doing something different and individual.

> *"I'm a team player. I love working as a team.*
> *In this situation I'm the leader,*
> *so everyone checks with me before they do things, and does what I say.*
> *So it's infuriating when someone in the group tells people what to do.*
> *It makes me angry. They're not being a team player*
> *because they're not respecting me as the leader."*[206]

C_Is recognize that the people in power are forcing their individual perspective on others because exercising power over other people is pleasurable for them. It's painfully tense for a C_I to watch those leaders get attention, and it's relieving when the C_I gets attention instead. If the C_I were in power, if the C_I were the world leader, then everything could be fixed by direct edicts and everyone would realize how great the C_I is. The C_I's unique style of leadership would draw adoration and praise. Little kids would walk around with pictures of the C_I on their shirts the same way they adore superheroes. And then the C_I could finally relax, because they could see themselves in everything they encounter.

> *"I have an unreasonably strong disdain for people who have a 9-5 job,*
> *a family at home, who go on vacations twice a year.*
> *I hate them for being so common, for being the antithesis of great."*[207]

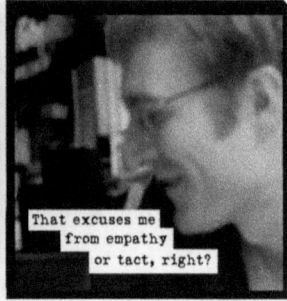

When the next community policy is announced, a C$_I$ can immediately explain what's wrong with it, who it victimizes, and why it's a direct assault on intelligence. Or the C$_I$ can righteously explain why they're compassionate for believing it and why the people attacking it are selfish, evil, and inferior. But the focus is on self. Self is brilliant and righteous and other people will be impressed if they're smart enough to understand. The C$_I$ wants surrounding people to see that the C$_I$ is insightful, that the C$_I$ has special individual intelligence, and is simply a better human than lower class people. The C$_I$ isn't actually focused on improving society. They're internally considering how they look while they say what they say. C$_I$ motivates a default framing of topics around self's individuality and greatness, the same way that S$_C$ motivates a default framing of topics around the group's harmony and progress.

"If you can't impress yourself, then no one else really matters."[209]

"Don't be part of the problem.
Be the whole problem."[210]

"When you are trying to impress people with words,
the more you say, the more common you appear."[211]

"Instead of drifting along like a leaf in a river, understand who you are
and how you come across to people. Understand what kind of an
impact you have on the people around you, the community around you,
and on the world, so that when you leave,
you can feel you have made a positive difference."[212]

"To learn who rules over you,
simply find out who you are not allowed to criticize"[213]

"THE GREATEST ADVANCE OF THE DIGITAL ERA HAS BEEN THE REBRANDING OF NARCISSISM AS SHARING."

P.BYRNES.

"*I am not a very nice man. I don't know the word.*
I have always admired the villain, the outlaw, the son of a bitch.
I don't like the clean-shaven boy with the necktie and the good job.
I like desperate men with broken teeth, broken minds,
and broken ways. They interest me. They are full of surprises and
explosions. I also like vile women, drunk cursing bitches with loose
stocking and sloppy mascara faces. I'm more interested in perverts
than saints. I can relax with bums because I am a bum.
I don't like laws, morals, religions, and rules.
I don't' like to be shaped by society."[215]

"*Respect is how you treat everyone.*
Not just those you want to impress."[216]

"*Don't use social media to impress people.*
Use it to impact people."[217]

"Good human beings save the world
so that bastards like me can keep creating art, becoming immortal.
If you read this after I am dead, it means I made it."[218]

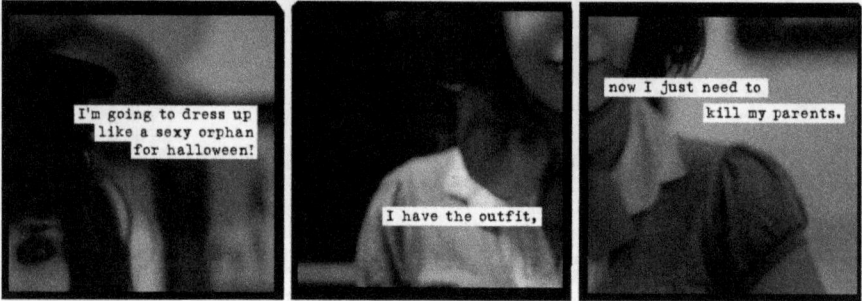

Valuing the Harmony and Progress of the Group While Feeling Body-Based Comfort (C$_B$):

Headline: *Arkansas Woman Befriended Mom's Killer Out of 'Spiritual Obligation,' - And Then He Murdered Her Too[220]*

A C$_B$ values the harmony and progress of the community for how they help in protecting themselves from dangers, avoiding sensory and emotional discomforts, and increasing sensory and emotional comforts. There is safety in anonymity, and danger in sticking out. A group that feels safe, that has the same tastes in sounds, smells, tactile sensations, and sights is a better fit for the C$_B$. A group that feels dangerous, that has obnoxious smells, sights, tactile sensations and sounds is less beneficial. So the C$_B$ enjoys their spiritual group, their yoga group, their meditation group, their healing circle, their safe spaces where they can immerse in the environment without getting triggered with fear. A good community has strong medical facilities, but also a focus on general physical and mental wellness before body problems become an emergency.

"Many of us seek community solely to escape the fear of being alone.
Knowing how to be solitary is central to the art of loving.
When we can be alone, we can be with others
without using them as a means of escape."[221]

*"I start every day by running ten miles. I get a lot out of it.
If nothing else happens today, I've taken care of my most important
asset, my mental and physical health, which are more important to me
than everything. They have to be. I can't be my best self for my children
or my wife and I'm useless to anyone if I'm not healthy."[222]*

© Loryn Brantz – LorynBrantz.com[223]

All of society could really benefit from a strong gratitude mindset.
All of society could benefit from therapy, a reduction of traumas, a
reduction of stressors, and an increase in peaceful, soothing inputs.

*"There's nothing worse than to finish a poop,
then reach over and find the toilet paper container empty.
Even the most horrible human being on earth
deserves to wipe his butt."[224]*

But the C$_B$ has to focus on self-care first. They need to heal their mind and body first before they'll have anything to contribute externally. What matters is individual peace and comfort. Their actual underlying fantasy is that they'll be the last one standing when something attacks the group and the ones who weren't taking precautions go down first. C$_B$ motivates a default framing of topics around health, safety, and peace the same way that S$_C$ motivates a default framing of topics around the group's health, safety, and wellbeing.

"The marks humans leave are too often scars."[225]

"As you journey through life,
take a minute every now and then
to give a thought for the other fellow.
He could be plotting something."[226]

C_B: The Body-Based Tension Spectrum

"Self-preservation is the primary and only foundation of virtue"[228]

Body-based Comfort (C_B) tension adds a focusing need for escalation or repair, paired with relieving satisfaction to the perception of smell, touch, sound, and visual sensations, especially the extremes of sensations. Feeling tension when sensations happen causes the observer to notice and focus on those sensations, create understandings about the deep meaningfulness of those sensations, and create predictions about why those sensation are the first signs of something great or awful. Repeatedly considering those options focuses attention on physical and mental health, and on maintaining a stable, comfortable environment. Each person is somewhere on the spectrum from being frequently triggered with very strong tension about sensations (being flushed with fixating arousal when sensations happen, distraught over negative sensations and missed opportunities for sensory pleasures, and fear, terror, and depression about physical and emotional pains), to being infrequently triggered with weak or no tension about sensations (observing sensations for what they are without considering life without the bad ones or with more of the good ones). This chapter immerses in the two extremes to help understand how life feels as you move from very-easily-triggered to very-rarely-triggered with body-based tensions.

The Sensory Pleasure Spectrum

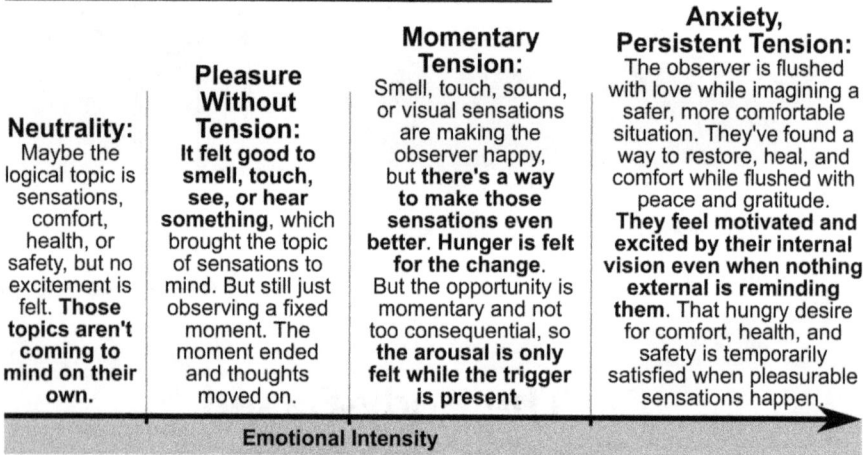

Neutrality:	Pleasure Without Tension:	Momentary Tension:	Anxiety, Persistent Tension:
Maybe the logical topic is sensations, comfort, health, or safety, but no excitement is felt. **Those topics aren't coming to mind on their own.**	**It felt good to smell, touch, see, or hear something**, which brought the topic of sensations to mind. But still just observing a fixed moment. The moment ended and thoughts moved on.	Smell, touch, sound, or visual sensations are making the observer happy, but **there's a way to make those sensations even better. Hunger is felt for the change.** But the opportunity is momentary and not too consequential, so **the arousal is only felt while the trigger is present.**	The observer is flushed with love while imagining a safer, more comfortable situation. They've found a way to restore, heal, and comfort while flushed with peace and gratitude. **They feel motivated and excited by their internal vision even when nothing external is reminding them.** That hungry desire for comfort, health, and safety is temporarily satisfied when pleasurable sensations happen.

Emotional Intensity →

Terminology & Abbreviations

All senses are happening at all times, but all senses don't have focus at all times. **Neutrality** is felt when sensations don't feel good or bad. Instead they can be factually, unemotionally observed as coincidental, unnotable parts of the moment. It feels like a change of topic to consider how the smell can be changed when it's normal and background already, even though it's not pleasurable. When starting from a neutral mind, it feels like a change of topic to then start considering how the current smell, touch, sound, and visual sensations could generate emotions for you. It doesn't feel like there's a reason to make the moment about sensations because they're so neutrally acceptable that some other consideration might be more pressing.

Body-based Comfort **pleasure without tension** is the joy felt when noticing pleasurable smell, sound, visual, or tactile sensations. The topic of comfort comes to mind because a moment of joy happens, triggered by a sensation. It feels like noticing pleasurable inputs, but in a fixed, momentary, practical way. It's like noticing that the breeze is nice today (if you don't also wish it were better). The moment feels complete. That moment was part of the normal world. It passes and nothing more needs to be done. It's not just objective, emotionless recognition. Pleasure is being felt too. But it's a complete, satisfied pleasure that isn't hungering for more. The pleasure of the moment is felt, and then thoughts move on.

Body-based Comfort **pleasure with tension** feels like noticing an opportunity for something good about sensations, but in a lacking way. There's potential for better smell, sound, tactile, or visual sensations which is waiting for a pleasurable adjustment. But it's not just logical recognition. It's excited hunger, anticipating pleasure.

- **Momentary pleasure tension** (externally triggered tension) is a hungry noticing of sensations which wants to feel even more or better, but the tension only exists while the trigger is present. It's noticing a nice breeze, and hoping the breeze might be even better if you move out from behind the barrier. It's noticing that a fabric felt really good and deciding to go touch it again. Something feels good and desire is felt for it to happen again, for longer, with more intensity. But that desire will be quickly relieved. It's small enough that the moment will be forgotten even if the pleasurable adjustment doesn't happen.

- **Anxiety, persistent pleasure tension** (internally triggered tension) is hunger for sensory escalation which persists even when the external trigger is removed. Tension makes it feel like this is a critically important opportunity for pleasure which requires something to change. The hunger is held in place by

153

internal memories or predictions and excitement is felt about how good that better option will feel. It's persistent tension if you're still thinking about that good-feeling fabric the next day, and imagining what it would be like to have bed sheets made of that material.

The Sensory Pain Spectrum

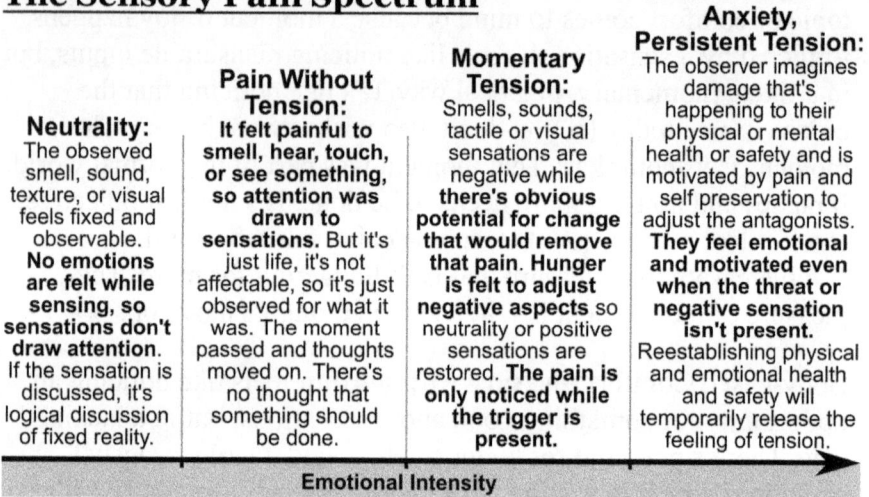

Neutrality:	Pain Without Tension:	Momentary Tension:	Anxiety, Persistent Tension:
The observed smell, sound, texture, or visual feels fixed and observable. **No emotions are felt while sensing, so sensations don't draw attention**. If the sensation is discussed, it's logical discussion of fixed reality.	It felt painful to **smell, hear, touch, or see something, so attention was drawn to sensations.** But it's just life, it's not affectable, so it's just observed for what it was. The moment passed and thoughts moved on. There's no thought that something should be done.	Smells, sounds, tactile or visual sensations are negative while **there's obvious potential for change that would remove that pain. Hunger is felt to adjust negative aspects** so neutrality or positive sensations are restored. **The pain is only noticed while the trigger is present.**	The observer imagines damage that's happening to their physical or mental health or safety and is motivated by pain and self preservation to adjust the antagonists. **They feel emotional and motivated even when the threat or negative sensation isn't present.** Reestablishing physical and emotional health and safety will temporarily release the feeling of tension.

Emotional Intensity →

Body-based **pain without tension** is the realistic body-based negativity of an imperfect world. The irritant or irritation feels fixed and doesn't hold attention for more than a moment, because there's nothing to be done about it. It's passive recognition that something smells bad, that the temperature is too hot or cold, that colors clash, or that a sound is annoying, but in a way that is complete. The breeze brought a gross smell for a moment, but it passed. It's a normal, fixed discomfort that happens in an imperfect world. It feels like objective recognition of external reality. Thoughts can easily continue on an unrelated topic.

Body-based **pain with tension** is feelings of pain and tension, but in a lacking way that wants resolve that negativity. This smell, sound, visual, or tactile sensation is so distracting that other thoughts can't happen until it gets adjusted.

- **Momentary pain tension** (externally triggered tension) is hunger for sensory pain to stop that only exists while the trigger is present. Negative temperatures, smells (especially body smells), sounds, and sights are just too much to ignore. Something could go wrong and something should be done to stop it. But it's minor. Someone can adjust how they're sitting, someone can pull the shade down, someone can mute the noise, and then get focus fully back for any other topic. It was small enough that it won't come up in cyclical thoughts later.

- **Anxiety, persistent pain tension** (internally maintained tension) is a sharp feeling of concern, hate, or terror, which makes sensory happiness, health, or physical or mental safety feel threatened, decreasing, damaged, or disappointing. External triggers aren't necessary to hold it in focus, because an internal prediction of increasing or persisting negativity holds the topic in focus. A car is speeding around a turn. Loud bangs are getting louder. A smelly person is getting closer. A body pain just got sharper. The observer is in danger, it's going to get worse, and it's time to drop all other concerns and resolve this self-preservation emergency. Focus shifts to an internal solution of what needs to be removed and what needs to be done so that health, safety, calm, and comfort can be restored again. When this moment ends, persistent tension can also be regret about past sensory situations that ended poorly and past healing opportunities that weren't fully seized. This situation really should be different because the pain is so sharp and lingers for so long.

Body-based Comfort **satisfaction** is felt in the moment when a tense urgency about sensations, health, or safety is resolved. That resolution might come from immersing in the extremes of sensory pleasures, through completion of sensory activities, through verifying that expected positive or negative sensory qualities were a mistake, through realizing that there isn't actually a threat, and sometimes through making the maximum possible sensory adjustment in an uncomfortable situation. Things were tense, but comfort, health, and safety were restored. Nothing needs attention or action anymore. Thoughts can move on to other topics.

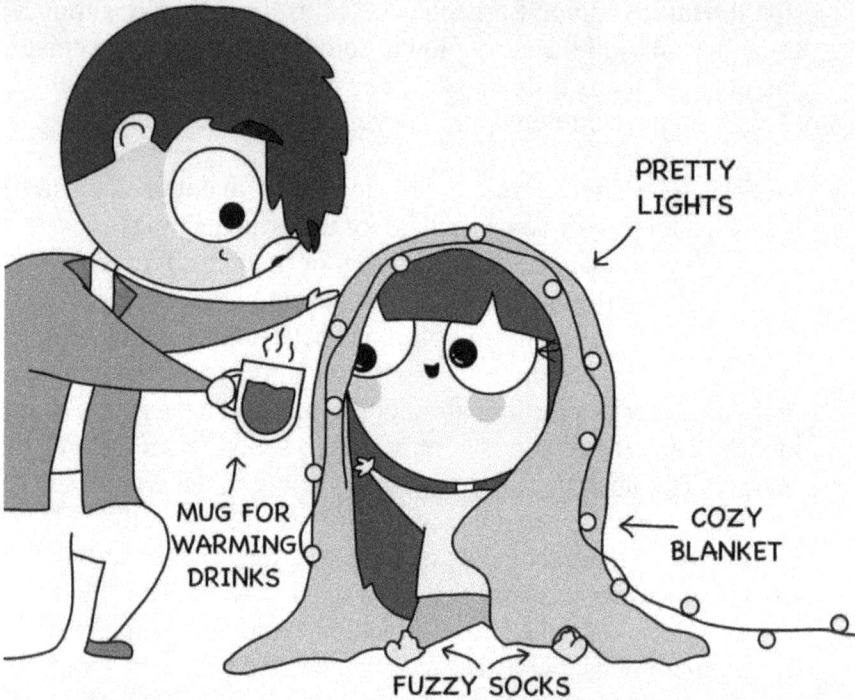

© *Mackenzie Moore - CinimomoComics*[229]

The shorthand for people who are triggered with Body-based Comfort tension and anxiety more often and strongly than the other tension and anxiety options is that these people are "**C_B-first**." When a reference is made to "a C_B," or "C_Bs," it's identifying the discussed person or people as being C_B-first.

The shorthand for people who are triggered more strongly and frequently by all six other tension options is that people are "**C_B-last**." Someone who is C_B-last can still feel feel C_B **pain** and **pleasure** quite strongly, but smells, sounds, visuals, and tactile sensations are more often factually noticed in a fixed way, and less often feel like they need adjustment. Any tension that is felt is more likely to be Social tension about how sensory qualities are affecting others, or Relational tension about how sensations are affecting sexual escalation.

We're now going to immerse in the life experience people have when they're most frequently and strongly struck by Body-based Comfort tensions to see what it's like to live at the highest end of the spectrum. Then we'll immerse in the life experience of people who feel the six other tensions more strongly and frequently to see what it's like to live at the lowest end of the Body-based Comfort spectrum.

C_B-First: Frequently Triggered Strong C_B Tension

> *"You're at your favorite restaurant and you think, what if this food is poisoned? Now, that's not totally irrational. Years ago, you worked at a restaurant, and you once saw an angry employee spit in the food of a customer who complained about their salad not having enough dressing. I mean, this stuff does happen. Or, actually, maybe they didn't spit in it at all. Maybe they cut their fingers and bled into it, in which case, you'll very possibly get Hep C or God knows what else, and what are you gonna do? You can't complain to the manager. That only increases the chances of spit or blood in your burrito. And you can't tell for sure, because you got the red salsa, which you never should've ordered. And then, you hit the pause button, because this is not your first rodeo, and you say, 'I am having an intrusive thought spiral. There is almost certainly neither spit nor blood in my burrito, which was prepared for me by hard-working, kind people.' Which gives you a very brief break, until you circle back to the words 'almost certainly.' I mean, you can't be sure. It remains a real and undeniable possibility that within this burrito is the drop of human blood that will cause you to get a chronic disease, or the drop of spit that will kill you. The spiral tightens and tightens until you're a sweating, shaking mess, completely out of control of the thoughts that are said to be yours, and also, you never get to eat the burrito."[230]*

Being C_B-first means feeling emotions before logic has had a chance to evaluate an input. C_B-firsts are stabbed with sharp pain when an insect crawls out from under their bed, when a stranger won't stop staring, or when a nearby car screeches to a sudden stop. **The**

observers' bodies aren't getting touched, and yet they're flushed with pain as if their body were just damaged. Was the pain a response to logic? No. C_B-firsts don't logically assess the actual damage, the statistical likelihood of the positive and negative outcomes, their options for avoiding the situation completely, and then make a logical choice to feel pain. They can't logically choose to feel pain on command from other logical negatives which don't trigger that feeling. The pain happens automatically and simultaneously with the observation of the potentially body-affecting input. Logic is used after the feeling happened to explain what could've happened which would've justified the extremeness of the feelings felt.

C_BS are then flushed with intoxicating pleasure when they touch a fuzzy blanket, smell a positive smell, hear a really great song, and watch a colorful sunset. All focus is immediately drawn to the intoxicating positivity of the input. Is the pleasure felt a response to logic? No. C_B-firsts don't logically assess the function of this blanket, the technical qualities, or the productive function of sunsets and then make a logical choice to feel euphoria from observing that input. They can't logically decide that unpleasant sensations generate that fixating pleasure instead and then feel it there. Logic is used after the feeling to consider ways to explain why this input stands out in such a positive way and investigate ways to make it even better.

The third feeling which really cements these in is that C_B-first observers can tolerate much bigger problems in other areas without being fixated and concerned (by corresponding sharp, automatic emotions). Friendships are suboptimal, but disconnections there aren't stabbing the observer with fixating pain. Humans are misunderstanding each other, but those misunderstandings aren't painful enough for the observer has to get involved. Some normal unsexiness has crept into the observer's life. The observer's life has gotten to be repetitive, but it's not uncomfortable enough to require adjustment. The idea of focusing on these other parts of life isn't coming to mind because they're within the ranges of pain where they're not a problem that needs attention (because this observer isn't triggered with tension about them at these levels). They're not perfect, but that's just how life is.

© *Mackenzie Moore - CinimomoComics*[231]

As you approach the highest end of the C_B spectrum, observers are more likely to be struck with positive euphoria and startled terror while observing way more sensory inputs. But it doesn't feel individual and it doesn't feel internal. It feels like there are lots of strikingly joyful and strikingly repulsive inputs in the world. Fixating pleasures feel like objective recognition of healing, beauty, and progress toward better health and more comfort. Startling fears feel like objective recognition of actual opportunities for body damage, sickness, and even death.

Tension events alternate with being released again when C_Bs get satisfaction, which is a maximization or restoration of comfort. Each day is a tug-of-war between neutral availability of focus for any thought and fixated body-based excitement or concern. The emotional problems in life happen when a body-based situation occurs which doesn't end in satisfaction. Maybe a smelly person can't be avoided. Maybe a normally-pleasurable situation didn't have the pleasant sounds and sights today. Maybe smell, touch, sound, and visual sensations started, but didn't get up to the levels that would be joyful. This was supposed to be a relaxing, healing, comforting moment, and instead it's incomplete. The situation will keep cycling in thoughts so that the resolving action can be determined.

> *"The number of deaths from unintentional, preventable injuries – commonly known as "accidents" – rose 5.3% in the last year and have now reached their highest number in recorded history – 169,936. Our collective complacency costs us 466 lives every day."*[232]

Half of what makes body and mental health based feelings feel objective is that so many inputs inspire no arousal, even for C_B-firsts. No tension, happiness, sadness, or relief are felt on behalf of some smells, sounds, tactile sensations, and visual inputs. There are so many inputs which don't automatically trigger sharp emotions, that the ones which do trigger tension must matter.

The core of C_B-first is ***love for the feeling of body-based arousal***. If you dropped all judgment and distraction and really let yourself feel the pleasure of pure sensory pleasure, not clouded by any other feeling, what would you focus on? Imagine what it would be like to have a perfectly healthy body. Imagine if every bone, every joint, every blood vessel were at peak health. Imagine if every muscle were warmed up and ready to go. Then imagine extreme comforts. Like a peaceful retreat where the smells, breeze, temperature, and sounds were ideal. What would the optimal smell be? What would the optimal breeze feel like? What temperature would feel the most joyful in that breeze? What sounds would be the most pleasurable? Can you focus on this ideal situation and feel some of that pleasure now?

Then imagine the tension felt when a jerk pulls up to that peaceful place in a loud car with blaring, awful music. The music would have a feeling of tension on it that made it feel like something that needed to be changed. Peace could be restored again if that noise and that awful person would go away.

© Robert Leighton - Robert-Leighton.com[233]

The feelings and logic of health and safety are independent of each other and can be in direct conflict inside any observer. An observer might truly, logically want to feel excited about getting a surgery done, but the excitement just isn't happening. They might truly, logically not want to be excited by the idea of laying out in the sun, but they can't help being flushed with joy and relief by the idea. Logic and feelings can align, but they can just as easily be in conflict.

"I mean, it's nice... I just don't know
whether it makes me *feel* anything"

© Dave Clamp – @YoungPoorAndHappy[234]

Later on, C$_B$ emotions interrupt peaceful, calm moments that don't
have external triggers. Pain happens again, triggered by the memory
of the loud jerk who interrupted the retreat. No decision was made
to think about being discomforted. In fact, logic realizes that the
negative version being lived in memory has more severe damage
than what actually happened in reality. Logic also knows the body
isn't being attacked right now, that it's actually surrounded by the
peace it wanted. But the pain is so sharp that attention is fixated on
how tragic the loss was in that moment. Then body-based arousal
strikes again, triggered by the memory of how good life would be if
the C$_B$ put a wall around that retreat to keep obnoxious people out,
and could live at that retreat forever. The observer is alone. The
actual exterior moment is quiet. But so much love is being felt.

*"What if I go to the dentist, get tortured, and then
the next day I die? All that pain will have been for nothing."*[235]

Since tension could be triggered at any moment, C_Bs preemptively take actions to maintain the peace and sensory pleasure of their environment, their sensory options, and their sensory pleasure escalation skills. Even when situations aren't sensory or scary, a C_B-first knows the situation might become either, and it will be striking if it does, so they keep making choices to protect themselves. The way to be present and available for the rest of life is to have body-based satisfaction easily available so discomforts can be resolved quickly each time they come up. Someone feeling C_B tension will keep feeling their body-focusing fixations even if they logically don't want to feel them. An observer might logically know they're safe, but they can't help being locked in fear, creating threats which would explain that fear. Body feelings and body logic happen separately and can be in conflict with each other.

© Jim Benton – JimBenton.com[236]

C_B-firsts think that the body-based arousal they feel is helpful. They're motivated to find much more pleasurable sight, smell, sound, and tactile sensations. They're motivated to take safety precautions, to clean, and to heal their body damage. They make better decisions about food, jobs, friends, groups, sex, risks, and experiences, because they prioritize how these impact the physical and emotional comfort and safety they'll feel. They have what other people have, plus striking happiness from really great smell, touch, sound, and visual sensations.

© *Joe Rothenberg - Joetatochips.com*[237]

Meanwhile, C_B-lasts only seem to have disadvantages. Most obviously, people who don't prioritize smell, touch, sound, and visual sensations are going to get themselves killed. A vital part of being human is missing from them, replaced by soullessness. Their opinions don't matter because there's something broken about how their brain works. They're living in easily adjustable discomfort. They die way too early. C_B-lasts cling to dangerous friends, they have moments of sexual pleasure in exchange for a shorter lifespan, and they're constantly taking meaningless risks which leave them damaged and uncomfortable. C_B-lasts miss out on the best parts of life because they get distracted with things that don't matter. A C_B-first may not have a perfect life, but they've got the foundation. They've maintained their health and surrounded themselves with comfort, safety, and peace.

"Life Lesson: Panic Earlier."[238]

C_Bs vary quite a bit in what and who sparks their euphoria, excitement, peace, pain, and terror. Some focus on avoiding as many threats as possible, some focus on sensing as many euphoric sensations as possible, some focus on home building, some focus on healing themselves and others. Some are more focused on physical comforts, some are more focused on emotional comforts. C_Bs are accustomed to being told that they get startled too easily, by the idiots who will get eaten first when the surprise turns out to be a monster.

"My mission in life is not merely to survive, but to thrive; and to do so with some passion, some compassion, some humor, and some style"[239]

C_Bs think repeatedly feeling sensory excitement, stress, peace, and terror, then turning inward and healing themselves, is just what life is. C_B-firsts think they're trying for a totally realistic, but admittedly high-level of safety, health, and peace with admittedly high frequency of pleasurable smell, touch, sound, and visual sensations. But they determined that something is "realistic" by imagining something better than what they already encountered, or the best they ever encountered, while minimizing inextricable trade offs that come with those positives. The result is an underlying, recurring ache, an unfillable anxiety, a dissatisfaction with reality, because the "realistic" goal they need to feel satisfied is just beyond what's actually possible.

"Growing up, no one tells you that one day
you'll get tired for no reason, and just stay that way
for the rest of your life."[240]

165

C$_B$-Last: Living without Tension about Body-Based Pleasures and Pains

> *"Don't be afraid of death. Don't have a death wish,*
> *but death is a peaceful thing and a great release.*
> *Be thankful that you were alive and got to live.*
> *The fear of death is a terrible thing to do to people*
> *and it comes from other human beings.*
> *Death is an amazing, amazing experience and should be enjoyed."*[242]

At the lowest point on the Body-based (C$_B$) emotional spectrum sensations feel like something fixed which can be observed, rather than something variable which might change. They don't trigger tension and they don't trigger relief. They're just things that are as they are. Dangers feel like easily avoidable, fixed realities. Sensations and dangers feel coincidental to the moment, which is obviously about something else (instead of feeling focusing). Sensations and dangers feel like logical topics about function, and aren't emotional topics about concern, meaning, discomfort, and relief.

As C$_B$ triggers reduce in number and drug intensity (moving down the C$_B$ spectrum) fewer observed inputs trigger the observer to feel C$_B$ arousal, both pain and pleasure. It takes getting much closer to actually dying before they feel any fear about dying. It takes much more pain before attention is fixated on changing it. It takes much more sensory pleasure before someone switches focus to that pleasure and hungers for more.

Body-based neutrality isn't rejection. It's not a consideration of a sensation or body threat and a decision that an input is safe, fixed, normal, or part of the background. Neutrality isn't any thought at all. Sensory neutrality is a lack of concern or excitement that would automatically switch focus away from other topics and onto wellbeing. Even more, sensory neutrality is a lack of tension and excitement even when someone else points out sensations or dangers. A meteor could wipe out all life around you. If that sentence doesn't flush you with fixating concern that it might happen right now, holding attention so you can't read anymore because you're imagining dying, then it's neutral to you. The feeling just isn't there to hold your attention on the imagined negativity.

Everyone has been in a room where the theoretical opportunities for body damage don't draw attention because they're such normal parts of life which are so uncommon (the ceiling or floor could collapse, but rarely do) a nd easy to avoid on autopilot (you could fall out the window, but no special focus is required to avoid that). For an extreme C$_B$-last, those are all rooms. The actual experience of being at the extreme minimum of C$_B$ is that it feels weird to even consider sensations and threats at the moment because the room is so neutral, normal, and not-threatening. The person who thinks they might fall out of the window by accident sounds extremely unintelligent. Sensory discomfort is easy to avoid by doing things the obvious way, and not tragic if it happens.

> *"Fear is such a volatile and directionless activity.*
> *One threat begets another, only to be contradicted*
> *by yet another newly discovered fear."*[243]

No better sensations are imagined, no "safer" alternative is imagined, no worse sensations are imagined, no body damage is imagined. No joy is felt imagining better options, or pain felt imagining worse options, so no hunger is sparked to change anything. Because reality isn't changeable or dramatic. It's observable and fixed. What's happening is the full extent of what's going to happen.

Most of the time, the whole concept of feeling emotions about sensations and dangers doesn't even come to mind until someone else is freaking out. Yes, the carpet is fuzzy. No, I didn't notice until you mentioned it. No, I don't need to touch it again. Yes, people die in car accidents. No, I'm not petrified with fear now that you mentioned it. Yes, I'm totally fine driving right after you said that. I'm even fine driving if you keep repeating that we're going to die while I do so. That's actually what you normally sound like.

If you could feel the process of turning yourself down in tension, you'd feel a silencing of the urgency felt when noticing that something is dangerous or has sensory qualities. As a result, there's a natural acceptance of body health the way it is, an acceptance of sensations the way they're happening, an acceptance that dangers and risks are natural realities of life, a forgetting about pain fantasies, and a reframing of focus away from body, senses, and threats and onto other topics. It's a switch to objective, external acceptance from internal predictions.

Smells are smells. Sounds are sounds. There's no thought that positive features could be combined, or that negative features could be removed, that negative features could get worse, or that good things could be better. All the adults in the room can easily tune out sensations while the meaningful task gets attention. Only the broken hypochondriac will fuss.

> "The meaning of risk has taken on a largely negative connotation.
> Up until the latter half of the twentieth century it was common sense
> that many risks are worth taking, so long as one was motivated by a
> noble enterprise, self realization, by the spirit of adventure,
> or by values such as freedom and truth. Facing up to risks was
> acknowledged to be a precondition for the cultivation of
> character and even the accomplishment of greatness." [244]

Now imagine you're the only person in line and another person comes over and cuts in front of you. You open your wallet and the money you brought is gone. An injured puppy isn't going to be able to get out of the way of your vehicle in time. Your crush just took your hand and is leading you to a secluded corner. You applied for your dream program and are holding the unopened response letter. For all humans, smell, touch, sound, visual sensations, and threats aren't the topic of the moment while other meaningful life events are happening. C_B-last observers have more Relational and Social triggers connected to more drug intensity. No choice is being made to ignore smell, touch, sound, and visual sensations. It's just not a body-based moment, because it's obviously a critical Social or Relational moment (which happens to be lots of moments).

Most S_C-lasts still can feel pleasure from cheering along with a crowd rather than alone, and feel bad for humanity when they watch a tragic event happen. But the experience of those is different when those events don't automatically trigger hunger for change and escalation. There was a moment of sensory pleasure or pain, that's just reality, and then the moment ended. The thought ends there. The observer can still look to the side and discuss a different topic. Pleasurable moments don't fixate the observer with hunger for more sensory pleasure. The rest of reality isn't silenced. The observer's focus isn't distracted away from the moment with an internal fantasy of what life would be like if every sensation were pleasurable. Instead it seems weird that we're still talking about that moment when it was over long ago.

Since the observer stays in reality, the trade offs for good sensations don't get minimized. Bad sensations aren't so fixating that they distract from whatever had focus. Meanwhile, those sensory inputs more easily trigger friendship-protecting feelings, group-harmony-protecting feelings, sexual arousal-protection feelings, and experience-protecting feelings. If you're managing a life where you're easily triggered by Social and Relational concerns, it's worth minimizing the tension triggers in those areas. If you want to care about smell, touch, sound, and visual sensations then choose the best smelling input from whatever makes it through your Social and Relational filters.

Human bodies hurt. They're uncomfortable all the time. There is no way to restore them back to mental and physical perfection, or even painlessness again. Brains react with tension. That is a natural part of being human. Freaking out about tension only generates more tension. The people who are freaking out about dangers are usually creating the most actual danger with their freak-out. The dangers of reality are fine. Any other options would just come with different (not better) annoyances. If you accept your body for what it is, and the safety of reality for what it is, you're free to live life.

Things hurt way less when you just feel the actual pain, without also feeling the imagined pain that C_B tension adds in. It will be remembered as what it was, without creating the imagined option of what it could've been. C_B-lasts have the body they have, surrounded by the sights, sounds, smells, and tactile sensations that actually surround them. None of the options are scary because they get handled on autopilot every day. Then C_B-lasts never revisit the question of comfort, safety, and health again. There's nothing more to observe about this background part of life.

> *"The perspective [of fear] has been so thoroughly internalized that many who adopt this outlook are not aware of its influence on their behavior. For most people, such a perspective comes across as common sense. This does not mean that people are perpetually scared; rather, the perspective of fear works by sensitizing people to focus on potential threats and dangers while distracting attention from the probable positive outcome of engaging with uncertainty."[245]*

C_B-lasts have taken extreme precautions against other people's feared outcomes, and tried an enthusiast's healing ritual and neither were worth it. They've tried avoiding interesting experiences to worship fear instead and missing out on life didn't flush them with the same joy that C_Bs feel. Any positives were temporary while their long-term happiness suffered. Sensations have moments of function and pleasure. Body-based pleasures don't have a deeper meaning. The meaning of life has to do with friends, family, sexual attraction, and meaningful life experiences. Smell, touch, sound, and visual sensations can be pleasant too, when they happen, but they're definitely less important than those others.

From the perspective of C_B-lasts, C_Bs only seem to have disadvantages. They have a mental problem that startles them constantly, shocking them out of reality and into a panicked frenzy while nothing is happening. They have fixations on dying, on pain, on dirtiness, that cause them to be radically inaccurate, afactual, and petrified while surrounded by safe normalcy. What's worse is that they don't realize that they're mentally crippled. They instead think their disorder is a logical reaction to reality, so they try to push safety precautions on sane people, which might make sense if everyone else were equally mentally disabled. C_Bs are scared of people, they're scared of actions, they're scared of policies, they're scared of machines, they're scared of anything new or changing, they're scared of everything. Meanwhile, all those things are fine. They're not dangerous. The fantasies C_Bs have about the negative consequences aren't going to happen. It's fine for C_Bs to lock themselves away in fear of a safe reality, as long as they stay out of the way of the intelligent people. They're even more tolerable when they admit to being high anxiety people while managing their own tension, rather than deluding themselves into thinking they're intelligent saviors who righteously keep others out of imagined danger. C_Bs are so focused on an imaginary, healthy body that they can't just live in the realistic, acceptable body they have. It's the fear that C_Bs have which makes situations dangerous, not the situations themselves. And the surrounding people who don't have fear can do lots of normal things that C_Bs can't. C_Bs think other people are scared or uncomfortable when they're actually feeling Social or Relational emotions. C_Bs think they're sick and dying when they're feeling totally normal body pains. C_Bs passionately disregard reality, enthusiastically find ways to be unhappy with what exists, and make bad decisions among existing options. They are unaware of real-world health and safety, while thinking they're experts in real-world health and safety. C_Bs bully other people into avoiding living, into seeing doctors, into buying insurance, into sacrificing for tiny comforts, because the C_B is immersed in an individual exaggeration of the value of body-based arousal. In critical moments, C_Bs sacrifice friends, groups, the good will of others, sexual opportunities, and meaningful life experiences because they're distracted with protecting themselves from dangers which are imaginary. What C_Bs are actually experts at are generating evil and pain when offered life experiences and love. Why would anyone want that?

There is no disappointment to feel with real-world safety, smell, touch, sound, and visual sensations. The way safety, smell, touch, sound, and visual sensations happens is fine. The frequency of pain, healing, safety, and sensations is fine. There's no need for more, less, better, or different. It's still worth making sure that the observer's body and comfort get maintenance, but that maintenance can happen without tension and relief, without fixated daydreams, and without judging what's happening as good or bad.

Instead, deviate slightly from reality in Social and Relational directions. Imagine having a particularly sexually attracted relationship. Imagine having a really naturally emotionally connected, merged friendship with that partner. Imagine dedicating yourself to a project which makes the world a better place. Imagine really making a difference in the lives of strangers because you stood up for what's right. And, do all of that in a body that has all the normal aches and pains, in a world that has all the normal dangers and discomforts, where humans survive normal threats every day. Can you find a way to feel energized by something outside of your body, regardless of your body? Can you find a way to feel inspired and focused regardless of the comfort of the moment?

> *"I do not fear death. I had been dead for billions and billions*
> *of years before I was born, and had not suffered*
> *the slightest inconvenience from it."*[246]

C_B-lasts are realistic about what they've got, what they get from it, what their options are, and what it costs. Part of what makes smell, touch, sound, and visual sensations valuable is that they don't need extra attention in order to do their functions. C_B-lasts live in the sensory and safety satisfaction that C_B-firsts can't find, because C_B-lasts live in reality, undistracted by visions of not-reality.

Cross Overs

> *"Nine tenths of our happiness depends on health."*[247]

Most C_B-lasts can be overwhelmed with terror or discomfort to the point where it silences other distractions because they are in an extremely dangerous situation or at the extremes of human pain. It just takes more extreme versions of either to pass the threshold where the same tension is finally triggered. But, since the inputs need to be so extreme, sensory and fear fixations happen with WAY fewer inputs, WAY less frequently, and satisfaction comes much faster just by realizing that what's happening is the fixed reality.

Many times a day C_B-firsts interact with sensory inputs and items that could be used to damage their bodies without considering the sensations or stopping to imagine how to get hurt, because the inputs don't have arousal triggering cues. C_B-firsts can be distracted by other topics, even while interacting with something they would otherwise find triggering, but have true neutral lack of consideration of sensations in that moment because nothing feels related to body-based arousal (like when they're having a conversation while riding in a car on a highway). Even for a C_B-first, it feels like awkward, tedious work to generate a fear fantasy about an input that's obviously safe, or too extremely unlikely.

© Ben Zaehringer – BerkeleyMews.com[248]

C_B Conclusions

The addition of C_B means smell, touch, sound, and visual sensations aren't just functional anymore. Sensations, health, and safety are euphoric or painful, triggering excitement, joy, fear, concern, disappointment, terror, and relief. C_B tension and relief aren't necessary for a system to maintain comfort, health, and safety of their body. But body-based tension and relief add focus and incentive to seek out more comfortable, safer situations and resolutions to body pains. They add incentives to protect existing health, safety, and sensations.

"Worried thoughts are notoriously inaccurate."[249]

C_B-firsts have more enthusiastic sensory experiences, and comfier homes with fewer surprises because they invest so much time and energy in seeking out, building, and maintaining body-based excitement, healing, and safety. A consistent focus on sensations helps them seize opportunities to feel more sensory pleasure. They're constantly sacrificing for the benefit of the sensory pleasure they'll feel. But they're the least satisfied with safety, health, smell, touch, sound, and visual sensations because daily tension reminds them to focus on what's wrong and imagine and feel desire for better.

Got something from Basement

BUT NOT MURDERED

Awesomest DAY EVER

© Jim Benton – JimBenton.com[250]

175

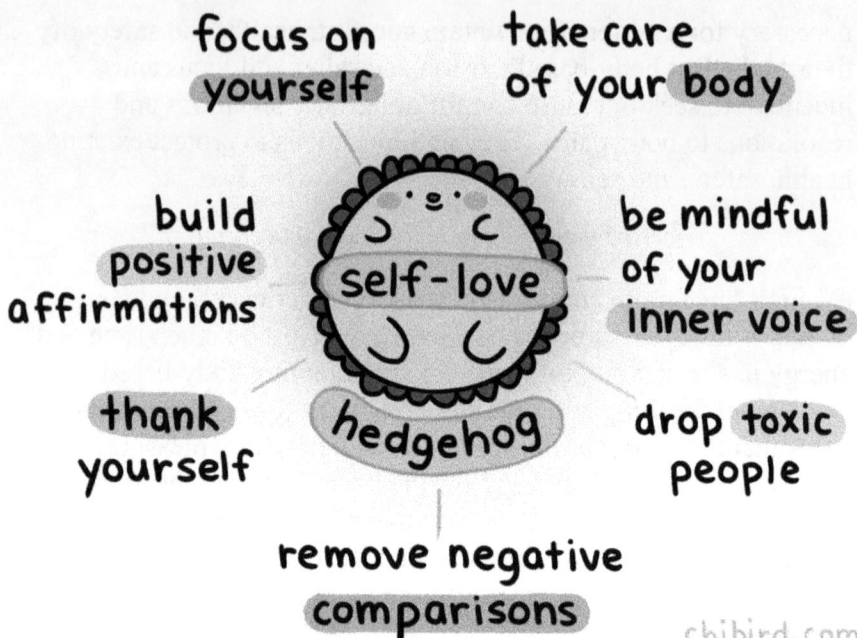

focus on yourself

take care of your body

build positive affirmations

be mindful of your inner voice

self-love

thank yourself

hedgehog

drop toxic people

remove negative comparisons

chibird.com

© *Jacqueline Chen – Chibird.com*[251]

Easily Confused for the C_B Spectrum

This chapter compares C_B to the six other motivators one-by-one. It holds the topic constant (health, safety, and sensations) and looks at it from each of the seven perspectives so you can hear that it's the framing of the topic that gives away the observer's motivators, not the topic itself. Each observer's experience of sensations, risk, and familiarity is different when they're feeling different kinds of tension and seeking different kinds of relief. This is the chapter to come back to when determining the relative influence of C_B versus any other motivator for a person.

Valuing Sensations, the Body, and Safety While Feeling Body-Based Comfort (C_B):

"One good thing about music: When it hits you, you feel no pain."[252]

A C_B knows that the basis for experiencing life comes from the system that's experiencing it. If the mind isn't present and peaceful, then inputs can't be processed as well. If the body isn't healthy and comfortable then inputs can't be processed as well. If the body is sick and hurting, then resolving that is the first priority. Friends, community, sex, and experiences are all parts of life too, but they're parts that get attention only after self-care has restored the observer to a peaceful, comfortable, healthy, energized state.

C_Bs lock up in fear easily, they panic easily, and they startle easily. Negative sensations fixate attention easily. The rest of life drops away and worst case scenarios play out as predictions of how sensations and body damage could get even worse. C_B minds are released again when they're back in comfortable, familiar safety. Then they touch something delightful, smell something delightful, walk into a room with delightful sensations and are overwhelmed with euphoric peace. Creating and immersing in pleasurable environments is part of the meaning of life. Optimizing sensations means removing not only the dangers, but anything that reminds them of dangers. But what really matters at the end of all of it, is joyful sensations. Fuzzy pants and cozy blankets in a peaceful, safe room that has appealing lighting and a pleasant aroma. A C_B loves sensations directly, and loves whatever creates the good ones. They're passionately against whatever triggers the negative ones. A

C_B will feel uncomfortable and stressed again soon, so having sensations ready to help bring them back to peace is important.

Valuing Sensations, the Body, and Safety While Feeling Community-Based Socialness (S_C):

> *"The power of community to create health is far greater than any physician, clinic, or hospital."*[253]

How are touch, smell, sound, and visual sensations affecting the unity and flow of the group? What changes in those would help the group progress? S_Cs feel tension when people in the group feel tension. So they become tense about temperature if they notice that people in the room feel cold or hot, regardless of whether they individually feel cold or hot. They'll be released from that tension when the temperature is adjusted and the group stops giving signs of discomfort, even if their own body now has more individual discomforts to manage. Are abandoned buildings making people uncomfortable? Are dark alleys making people uncomfortable? Why not band together and clean up all the parts of the community that make people feel fear, and modify them so that the most people feel the most peace? Then the group will be the least disturbed and can harmoniously progress.

> *"There is no exercise better for the heart than reaching down and lifting people up."*[254]

Sensations are one of the parts of life that can affect how the group is doing, but they matter to the degree that they draw the group together, or distract people from the group mission. The way to find out what's comfortable is to have the group come up with options, and then poll the group to find out what the consensus is. Then watch how the group responds to different options to find the settings which optimize group happiness. Being triggered with tension by discomforts in the group motivates a focusing of attention on the little signals the group is giving about their discomfort, the same way that being triggered with tension about discomforts in the observer's body motivates a focusing of attention on the little signals a body is giving that it is uncomfortable.

© Todd Condron[255]

"For a community to be whole and healthy,
it must be based on people's love and concern for each other."[256]

"Communities grow out of a shared confrontation with survival.
They grow out of a shared struggle."

Valuing Sensations, the Body, and Safety While Feeling Resource-Based Comfort (C_R):

Touch, smell, sound, and visual sensations are valuable and worth money. They're one of the qualities which affect the price and value of a resource, which affect how satisfying consumption or acquisition will feel. Some resources are more valuable because they maximize pleasurable sensations. Others are more valuable because they minimize negative sensations. The sensation which actually affects life the most on a daily basis is taste. The negative body sensation which draws the most attention on a daily basis is hunger for food. The sensation which most regularly and reliably brings relief is feeling full after eating. It's strikingly tense and

179

awful when something doesn't taste as good as it should, or when less is received in exchange for money than was expected.

© *Mackenzie Moore - CinimomoComics*[257]

A C_R considers their body as a resource, and wants that resource to be fueled. But they're focused by resource lack, by resource hunger, and by boredom, and relieved by acquisition and consumption. Touch, smell, sound, and visual sensations are among the options that give a resource value, but they're only worth so much before it becomes tense to think about the resources losses happening in exchange for them. What's modeled because it can be tense is the value of the resource and the satisfaction which will be felt in acquiring or consuming. C_R is an obsession with items, food, money, and entertainment being consumed and acquired, the same way that C_B is an obsession with sensations, safety, and wellbeing being felt.

> *"The proper portion size for macaroni and cheese is:*
> *UNTIL YOU DIE."[258]*

Valuing Sensations, the Body, and Safety While Feeling Alliance-Based Socialness (S_F):

> *"Friendship is unnecessary. Like philosophy, like art,*
> *like the universe itself, it has no survival value.*
> *Rather it is one of those things which give value to survival."[259]*

Since maintaining and strengthening meaningful, emotionally entangled relationships with really good souls is so meaningful, and since those relationships already exist and those valuable souls are near, are any aspects of smell, touch, sound, and visual sensations affecting those allies? When an S_F sees that a friend is uncomfortable, the S_F will be flushed with tension and feel like action is necessary to resolve the friend's tension. When the friend is relieved, the S_F will feel relieved. So, could smell, touch, sound, and visual sensations be changed in a way which would relieve a friend, or flush them with happiness? Are there sensations which remind both friends of shared experiences? Are there sensations worth avoiding because they'll make a friend uncomfortable? Looking out for a friend, and sharing pleasant experiences are how the bonds of friendship strengthen over time.

True extremes of sensation still matter to the observer themselves, but they just don't happen much in reality, while anxious or excited friends happen in reality all the time. Self's negative sensations aren't worth adjusting if doing so will discomfort the ally, since the ally's discomfort will generate even more tension in the S_F observer. An S_F is living in a reality where the emotions of allies are the sharp, dramatic things which might change and will fixate attention if they do, the same way that a C_B is living in a reality where their sensations and feelings of safety are the sharp, dramatic things which might change and will fixate attention if they do.

Valuing Sensations, the Body, and Safety While Feeling Individuality-Based Comfort (C$_I$):

Bumper Sticker: "I think you left the stove on."[260]

Touch, smell, sound, and sights affect self and therefore need to be managed, but they are among many options of ways that self individuates, displays unique excellence, and is attacked by others. But, also, other people just seem to be disruptive and less intelligent about sensations and self has a particularly insightful brilliance about sensations making self a natural teacher and others typically requiring direction.

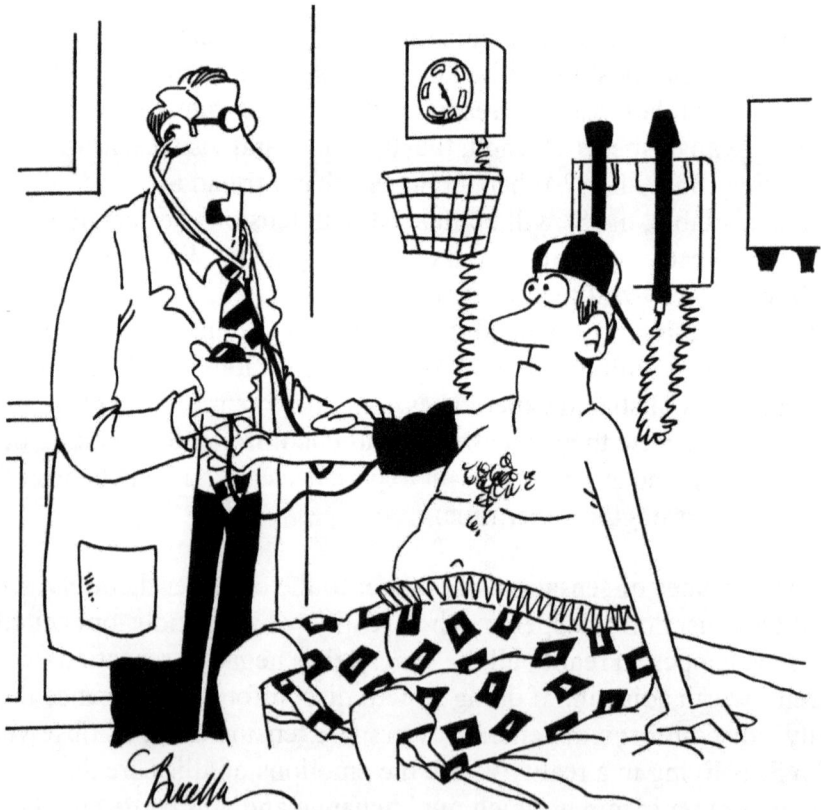

"In this case, a new high score is not a good thing."

© *Marty Bucella – MartyBucella.com*[261]

Since how self feels about self is what really matters, and since good feelings come from making an impact, individuating, being excellent, and from being the focus of other people's attention, how can touch, smell, sound, and visual sensations trigger or resolve those actually-meaningful concerns? If self can find the best smell, then others will recognize self's excellence in finding that smell. If everyone smells the same, then that smell will automatically smell bad to a C_I, and whatever is distinctively different will smell good to a C_I, because it's different. Then it'll feel great when self can differentiate by picking a different smell, especially if others then agree that they like it, and even more if annoying people get bothered by the C_I's individuality. If self's home can be organized in an appealing way, then others will recognize self's superiority at creating peaceful environments. If self tries any of these and fails, it will be sharply negative, especially if other people notice and judge self as pathetic or unworthy as a result. Because the actual underlying tension being felt is about self. Things are feeling good and bad, but the influence of self and ranking are triggering more of the pain, pleasure, tension, and relief than the components of emotional triggering from touch, smell, sound, and visual sensations, which all feel closer to fine on their own.

"She wrapped herself in a blanket of self-worth."[262]

Sometimes pointing out sensory adjustments is a way to have attention directed toward self and have others take action for self's benefit. But the adjustment actually feels relieving because changes are happening for self's benefit, more than relieving sensory tensions.

"I had to grow to love my body. I did not have a good self-image at first. Finally it occurred to me, I'm either going to love me or hate me. And I chose to love myself. Then everything sprung from there."[263]

When other people are the sources of sensory irritation there's more of a feeling of being ignored or disrespected than actual irritation from the sensation, because the other person is either knowingly assaulting self, or selfishly ignoring self while disturbing self. The internal anxiety spiral involves imagining self being more and more disrespected, more so than being more and more discomforted. Other people want to tear the C$_I$ down, they want glory for themselves, when the C$_I$ is the one who has the endearing, talented soul who deserves individual respect and love. C$_I$ tension/relief cycles create an obsession with self, individuality, and ranking the same way that C$_B$ tension/relief cycles create an obsession with sensations, wellbeing, and safety.

Valuing Sensations, the Body, and Safety While Feeling Experience-Based Relationalness (R$_A$):

> *"The paramount terror that plagues humankind*
> *is to live a meaningless life,*
> *to be an incomplete person*
> *who fails to experience the rapture of living"*[264]

Since fully experiencing life, since following your calling, and since passionately chasing your dreams are what really matter, how can touch, smell, sound, and visual sensations make life more thrilling? To start, the extremes can be experienced. What is the most sensory pleasure that can be felt? What is the most sensory pain? How can an observer feel the most fear possible? How can an observer feel the most peace possible? By experiencing both, the actual limits of reality will be determined and anyone who makes predictions of either without testing them doesn't have credibility compared to the actual experience. How can someone smell all the smells? What does it feel like to be as hot as a human body can get? What does it feel like for the body to die and then be brought back to life again? What does it feel like to be completely confined, to be in pitch darkness, to run for your life while death is an option? The focus of R$_A$s is on experiences, on adventures, on testing the limits of reality. The experiences are valuable. Confronting fear head on and defeating it matters. Sensations and dangers are external things that can make an experience more thrillingly extreme, more painfully mundane, or they might not be part of the experience at all.

> *"The fear of death follows from the fear of life.*
> *Someone who lives fully is prepared to die at any time."*[265]

The same petrifying negativity that a C$_B$ gets from looking at something dangerous is what an R$_A$ feels if they don't rush forward into that danger. The same relief that a C$_B$ gets when they've retreated is what an R$_A$ gets when they defeat that danger, usually exposing that there was no real danger.

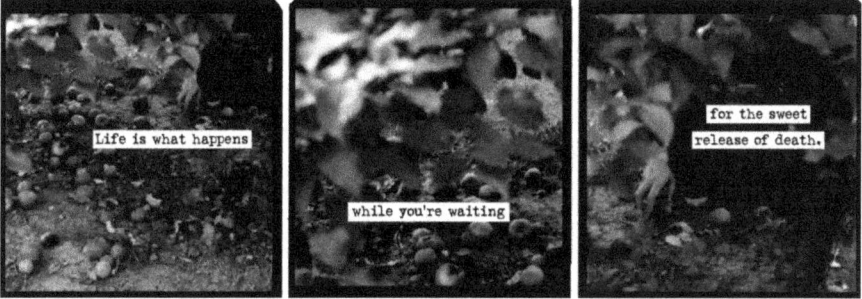

Life is what happens

while you're waiting

for the sweet release of death.

© *e horne and j comeau – asofterworld.com*[266]

"Find what you love and let it kill you."[267]

Fear is felt on the boundary of what's familiar, so it is a guide toward the areas where the most is to be gained from exploring. Functionally, fear exists to keep people from living full lives, to separate people from the safe reality of unfamiliar options. But only if it's believed. If fear is a guide toward the next growth experience, then it adds to the exciting thrill felt when you step forward anyway.

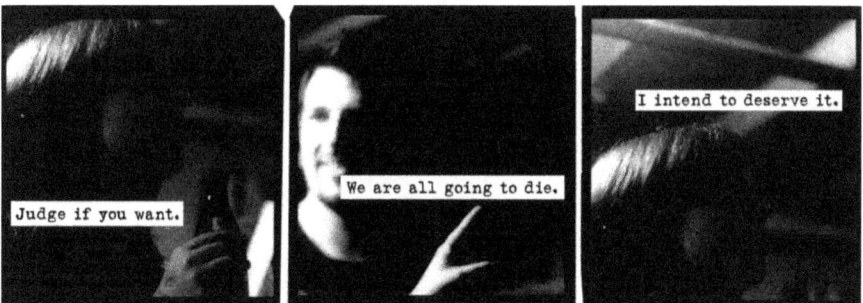

Judge if you want.

We are all going to die.

I intend to deserve it.

© *e horne and j comeau – asofterworld.com*[268]

R$_A$s never confuse themselves as being C$_B$s. Anyone feeling even a tiny bit of confusion are C$_B$s who are wasting their lives fantasizing about pain and body damage that will never happen when they could be presently learning from new experiences instead.

"When the mind is secure, it is in decay."[269]

*"What brings peace is when people
feel that they are actors in the divine drama."*[270]

"Death is part of life. It's just the last part."[271]

*"Courage is knowing it might hurt, and doing it anyway.
Stupidity is the same. And that's why life is hard."*[272]

Valuing Sensations, the Body, and Safety While Feeling Sex-Based Relationalness (R$_S$):

© Ben Zaehringer – BerkeleyMews.com[273]

How can touch, smell, sound, and visual sensations either escalate sexual arousal, or get in the way of sexual arousal? What lighting interrupts sex, and what is conducive to greater passion? What smells get in the way of arousal and which create a mood of love? Every little increase in the amount of body-pleasure felt, and every avoidable arousal-reducing sensation is worth the effort to adjust.

If the partner loves a certain feeling of sheets, or if temperature is making bodies too sweaty during sex, then those adjustments matter so that both participants can focus on sexual arousal. Fear can sometimes amp up sexual attraction, but it can be an arousal-killer if either person is actually afraid. Someone who is worried about STDs or getting pregnant is letting their tension get in the way of sex. Those concerns are worth addressing, but ending with actual sex and not ending with the understanding that sex can't happen. Someone who is too distracted by the comfort of the bed has anxiety issues distracting them from what really matters. Get present and horny already. Being easily triggered with flushing sexual arousal is motivated by R$_S$ the same way that being easily triggered with sensory arousal is motivated by C$_B$.

R_A: The Adventure-Based
Tension Spectrum

"One life. Just one.
Why aren't we all running like we're on fire
towards our wildest dreams?"[275]

Adventure-based Relational (R$_A$) tension adds a focusing need for escalation or repair, paired with relieving satisfaction to the consideration of experiences. Feeling excitement about extreme and unfamiliar experiences, paired with painful stagnation about familiar, repetitive experiences, focuses attention on why experiencing new things is beneficial and why familiar experiences are detrimental. Each person is somewhere on the spectrum from being frequently triggered with very strong tension about experiences (being flushed with fixating arousal by the prospect of new and extreme experiences, thrill while experiencing them, and stagnant pain while experiencing familiar experiences), to being infrequently triggered with weak or no tension about experiences (experiencing what's actually happening without drugging to make any options feel lacking or satisfying because of the experience itself). This chapter immerses in the two extremes to help understand how life feels as you move from very-easily-triggered to very-rarely-triggered with experience-based tensions.

The Experiential Pleasure Spectrum

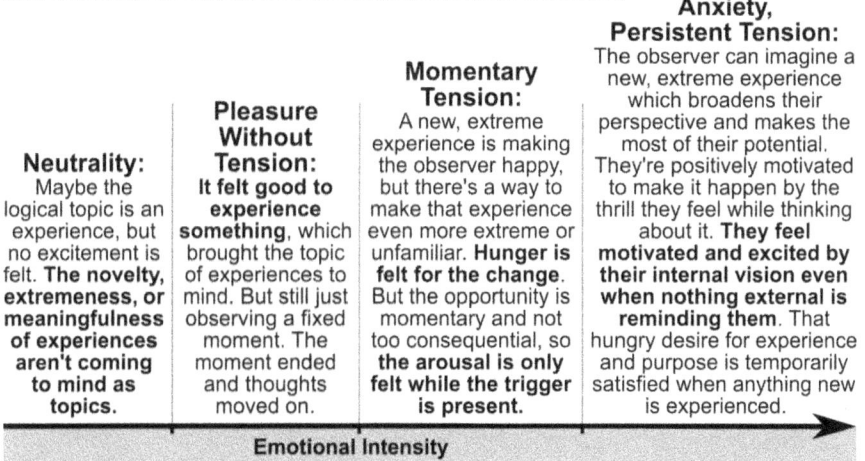

Neutrality:	Pleasure Without Tension:	Momentary Tension:	Anxiety, Persistent Tension:
Maybe the logical topic is an experience, but no excitement is felt. **The novelty, extremeness, or meaningfulness of experiences aren't coming to mind as topics.**	**It felt good to experience something**, which brought the topic of experiences to mind. But still just observing a fixed moment. The moment ended and thoughts moved on.	A new, extreme experience is making the observer happy, but there's a way to make that experience even more extreme or unfamiliar. **Hunger is felt for the change.** But the opportunity is momentary and not too consequential, so **the arousal is only felt while the trigger is present.**	The observer can imagine a new, extreme experience which broadens their perspective and makes the most of their potential. They're positively motivated to make it happen by the thrill they feel while thinking about it. **They feel motivated and excited by their internal vision even when nothing external is reminding them.** That hungry desire for experience and purpose is temporarily satisfied when anything new is experienced.

Emotional Intensity →

Terminology & Abbreviations

Experience-based **neutrality** happens when experiences are considered which don't match the observer's experiential arousal triggers. Neutral experiences feel normal, coincidental, and fixed. It doesn't feel like they have any deeper meaning and are forgotten as quickly as they happen. Most people feel experience-based neutrality when taking a very familiar route that's still functionally the fastest. It still makes logical sense, but no excited attention is happening to make the experience more extreme and no piercing pain is felt about life being wasted on something repetitive. Average experiences don't draw or hold attention because they're so normal. It feels like a change of topic to consider how the experience can be changed to make it more thrilling or "meaningful" because it simply is what it is. When starting from a neutral mind, it feels like a change of topic to then start considering how inspired and thrilled you feel about experiences. It doesn't feel like there's a reason to make the moment about experiences.

Adventure-based Relational **pleasure without tension** is momentary, practical joy which comes from considering or participating in an experience. It feels like noticing that an experience felt good, but in a fixed, momentary, practical way. It's like noticing that a surprise dip in the road caused a pleasurable, surprise moment of lightness (as long as you don't hunger to go back and do it again). That moment was part of the normal world. It passes and nothing more needs to be done. It's not just objective, emotionless recognition. Pleasure is felt because an experience happened. But it's a complete, satisfied pleasure that isn't hungering for more.

Experience-based Relational **pleasure with tension** feels like noticing an opportunity for a meaningful experience, but in a lacking way. There's potential for an experience which is waiting for something to happen. But it's not just logical recognition. It's excited hunger, anticipating pleasure.

- **Momentary pleasure tension** (externally triggered tension) is a hungry noticing of experiences, but where the tension only exists while the trigger is present. You hear a crowd roar and head over that direction to see what has them excited. You're standing in line for a rollercoaster and it's pulling up. It's not just logical, some excitement can be felt when considering it. But the idea passes as soon as the external trigger for that idea isn't present anymore.

> *"Some learn by reading.*
> *Some learn through observation.*
> *Some have to pee on the electric fence themselves."*[276]

- **Anxiety, persistent pleasure tension** (internally maintained tension) is hunger for experiential escalation which persists even when the external trigger is removed. Tension makes it feel like this is a critically important opportunity for thrill, fulfillment, purpose, and meaning which requires something to change. The hunger is held in place by internal visions of better and excitement is felt about how good that better option will feel. If a certain experiential path is followed then life will be fully seized. Everyone's lives get better when they're experiencing their true calling, or creatively building something that inspires them. This is a critically important opportunity for meaningful individual growth and life purpose which requires action. The purpose of the observer's life is now clear, it's right in front of them. The excited person can imagine how interesting it'll be when it happens. Things will be learned that the observer doesn't even know they don't know.

The Experiential Pain Spectrum

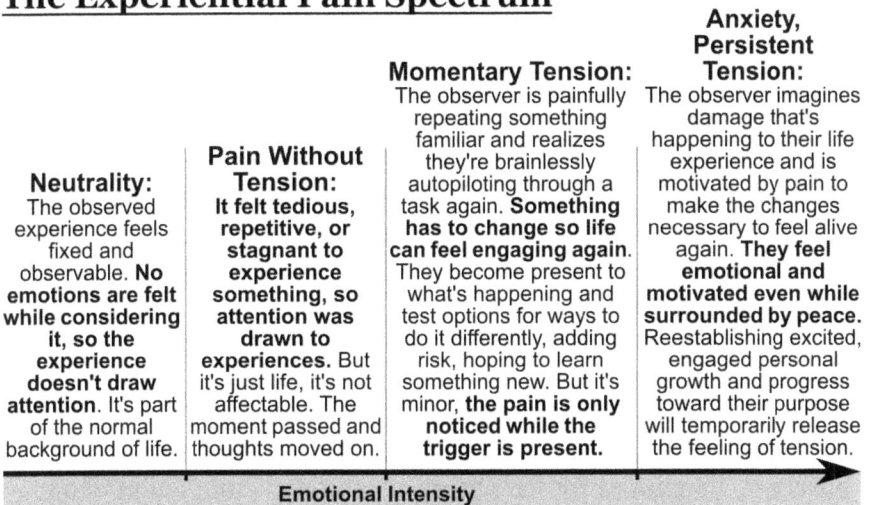

Neutrality:	Pain Without Tension:	Momentary Tension:	Anxiety, Persistent Tension:
The observed experience feels fixed and observable. **No emotions are felt while considering it, so the experience doesn't draw attention**. It's part of the normal background of life.	It felt tedious, repetitive, or stagnant to experience something, so attention was drawn to experiences. But it's just life, it's not affectable. The moment passed and thoughts moved on.	The observer is painfully repeating something familiar and realizes they're brainlessly autopiloting through a task again. **Something has to change so life can feel engaging again**. They become present to what's happening and test options for ways to do it differently, adding risk, hoping to learn something new. But it's minor, **the pain is only noticed while the trigger is present.**	The observer imagines damage that's happening to their life experience and is motivated by pain to make the changes necessary to feel alive again. **They feel emotional and motivated even while surrounded by peace.** Reestablishing excited, engaged personal growth and progress toward their purpose will temporarily release the feeling of tension.

Emotional Intensity →

Experience-based **pain with<u>out</u> tension** is the realistic repetitive, tedious negativity of an imperfect world. A task is painfully repetitive, but there's nothing to be done about it. It's passive recognition that an experience is a waste of life time, but in a way that is complete. Waiting in line was unpleasant, but there wasn't another option.

Experience-based **pain <u>with</u> tension** is feelings of negativity in the observer, but in a lacking way that wants to adjust something to make the experience better. The stagnant waste of time is so distracting that other thoughts can't happen until the meaningful use of time is restored.

- **Momentary pain tension** (externally triggered tension) is hunger for experiential pain to stop that only exists while the trigger is present. The brainless repetitiveness, or the complete lack of action is just too much to ignore. What's keeping pain happening is the continued stagnancy or repetitiveness. Repetitiveness again. And more repetitiveness. Another time of repetitiveness. Followed by another. Momentary pain tension motivates a quick action which puts the observer back in motion on something different, and doesn't come up in cyclical thoughts later.

- **Anxiety, persistent pain tension** (internally maintained tension) is a sharp feeling of purposelessness or stagnancy, which makes life feel wasted and opportunities feel missed. It's regret that past experience opportunities weren't fully seized. The pain is made worse because things didn't have to be this way. Life could and should adjust in ways that will make it valuable again. The observer feels a fixating, painful stagnation that they can't distract themselves away from which requires action. Enough of life has been wasted. Each moment between now and action will feel worse and worse. This problem needs to be resolved because the pain is so sharp and lingers for so long.

Adventure-based Relational **satisfaction** is a feeling of relief which comes with completing a *thrilling* experience (sometimes for the observer, sometimes for the observed), through completion of a *new* experience (which isn't always thrilling), through verifying that an activity isn't actually new or extreme (it's broken, has too many safety precautions, or has repetitive aspects that weren't obvious at first), and sometimes through getting a small, but maximum-for-what's-available experience. Things were tense, but thrill, purpose, and meaning were restored. Nothing needs attention or action anymore. Thoughts can move on to other topics.

how to get a broken bulb out of a socket

turning the light off first	just grab it with your hand
	i feel so alive!
is for wimps	

© *Justin Boyd – InvisibleBread.com*[277]

The shorthand for people who are triggered with Adventure-based Relational tension and anxiety more often and strongly than the other tension and anxiety options is that these people are "**R_A-first**." When a reference is made to "an R_A," or "R_As," it's identifying the discussed person or people as being R_A-first.

The shorthand for people who are triggered more strongly and frequently by all six other tension options is that people are "**R_A-last**." Someone who is R_A-last can still feel feel R_A **pain** and **pleasure** quite strongly, but experiences more often feel objectively noticeable in a fixed way, and less often feel like they need adjustment. Tension about an experience is more likely to be Social tension about how experiences are affecting others, or Comfort tension about how experiences are affecting individuality, ranking, self, sensory comfort, health, safety, or resources.

We're now going to immerse in the life experience people have when they're most frequently and strongly struck by Adventure-based Relational tension to see what it's like to live at the highest end of the spectrum. Then we'll immerse in the life experience of people who feel the six other tensions more strongly and frequently to see what it's like to live at the lowest end of the R$_A$ spectrum.

R$_A$-First: Frequently Triggered Strong R$_A$ Tension

"I like things in my life to be going at lightning speed. I finish one project and eagerly dive into the next. I like new beginnings and excitement. My life feels static if nothing new or exciting is happening. And, lately, nothing new is happening. I'm finishing up a bunch of work. I'm finalizing the book. I'm midway through creating my blogging course. I'm giving my apartment the cleaning it desperately needs. I'm doing the dishes and the grocery shopping. The excitement just isn't there. But today, as I sit in my newly cleaned living room, looking out to the rainy day outside, I'm grateful for the routine. I'm grateful for the stagnant. Day-to-day may seem boring. It may seem slow. It may seem like nothing happens in our lives. But, when you look back three months, six months, a year—isn't it amazing how much has changed? We want big, explosive, monumental transformations. The truth is that we couldn't possibly sustain fast-paced movement all the time. But those mundane little moments of nothingness, that's life. That stagnation isn't always so bad. Some people even call it time to integrate all of those monumental changes before we throw ourselves in the next ones. We're in that point where most days might feel the same, where we're slowly working toward our dreams. Where we're just doing the grunt work—without the glamour, without the excitement, without the rapid transformation. You have to work for your dreams. You have to do the slow stuff. You have to show up every day, remembering that your dream is worth fighting for."[278]

Being R$_A$-first means feeling emotions before logic has had a chance to evaluate an input. R$_A$-firsts are stabbed with sharp pain when they do another repetition of a familiar task. **The observers' bodies aren't getting touched, and yet they're flushed with pain as if**

physical damage were happening to themselves. Is the pain a response to logic? No. R$_A$-firsts don't logically assess the functional value of the action, the probability that another action would be more or less beneficial, and then make a logical choice to feel pain. They can't logically choose to feel pain from other logical negatives which don't trigger that feeling. The pain happens automatically and simultaneously with the observation that nothing new was learned, that actions happened on autopilot because they're so familiar, especially if some new, extreme option was considered to put that familiarity into painful perspective. Logic is used after the feeling happened to explain the deeper meaning which justifies why familiar actions are so painful.

> *Sleeping on a futon when you're 30 is not the worst thing.*
> *What's worse is sleeping in a king bed next to a spouse*
> *you're not in love with, with kids and a job you hate.*
> *You'll be laying there fantasizing about sleeping on a futon.*
> *There's no risk when you go after a dream.*
> *There's a tremendous amount of risk in playing it safe.*[279]

R$_A$s are then flushed with intoxicating pleasure when they enter the unknown, when they step off the ledge, or when they're catapulted into the sky. All focus is immediately drawn to the thrill, newness, and surprise of new inputs. Is the pleasure felt a response to logic? No. R$_A$-firsts don't logically assess the actual knowledge growth and functional experience value, compare it to other functional options and then make a logical choice to feel euphoria from falling out of an airplane. They can't logically decide that a different activity generate that euphoria and fixation instead and then feel it there. R$_A$-firsts feel awful when repeating things, and are flushed with euphoria and thrill when doing extreme new things. Logic is used after the feelings to explain why new inputs are so strikingly better to experience than repetitive inputs.

> *"Some people never go crazy.*
> *What truly horrible lives they must lead."*[280]

The third feeling which really cements these in is that R$_A$-first observers can tolerate much bigger problems in other areas without getting triggered with excitement or concern. Friendships are suboptimal, but tensions there aren't coming to mind because they're within the limits of normal human connections. There are conflicts in society, but they're normal enough that the observer doesn't have to get involved. Sensory comforts aren't ideal, but they're not so painful that they require action. The observer isn't differentiating from the rest of the group in a way that draws the admiration of others, but they hadn't noticed that because it's not painful right now. Resources aren't great, but they're minimally good enough. These topics aren't drawing and focusing attention because this observer isn't triggered with tension about them at these levels. They're not perfect, but that's just how life is.

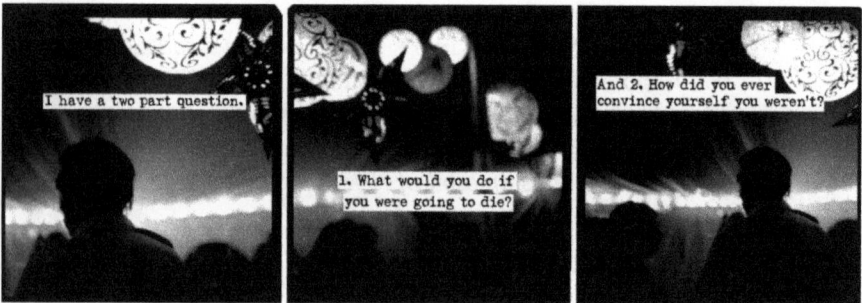

© e horne and j comeau – asofterworld.com[281]

Meanwhile, life is painfully stagnant, and thrilling adventure is an option. But that reality doesn't feel individual, and it doesn't feel internal. It feels like objective recognition that certain experiences are massively valuable, and repetitive experiences are a waste of life. It feels like objective recognition that time is limited, and that the gift of life is meant to be seized and experienced. It feels like objective recognition that people can waste their lives by stagnating, or live deeply meaningful lives by trying for extreme goals. It's the experience itself which provides value to everyone who experiences it. The people who dive into excitement get objectively better lives.

So, what could be experienced next which is so different that it would add the most new knowledge to life? What is the most extreme version of that experience that's available? How do you get from where you are to the place where that experience begins? Tension is felt as the opportunity starts to slip away. Are you driving to your repetitive job again instead? Will you sit on your same couch tonight instead of living? Is the experience not available anymore and you missed it? Is the experience so nerfed with safety precautions that the thrill has been removed? Since every other part of life is ignorably acceptable, the moments where a thrilling experience become an option feel sharply consequential. R_As don't want to think about experiences and the meaning of their lives again, but this is a critical moment for action or regret.

"Some people die when they're 25,
but don't get buried until they're 65."[282]

I think I've got fireflies

where my caution should be.

Half of what makes experience-based feelings feel objective is that so many experiences inspire no arousal, even for R_A-firsts. No tension, happiness, sadness, or relief are felt for knitting, for watching a new episode of the same game show, or for meeting another random human. It makes logical sense to not consider unthrilling activities when the world has so many strikingly-thrilling options.

"You only live once.
But if you do it right, once is enough."[284]

Tension events (feeling excited, or feeling painfully stagnant) alternate with being released again when R_As get satisfaction, which mostly comes from experiencing something new and different. Each day is a tug-of-war between neutral availability of focus for any thought and fixated excitement or stagnation. The emotional problems in life happen when a meaningful life opportunity appears but doesn't end in satisfaction. Maybe the R_A has already committed themselves elsewhere so they can't do the new thing. Maybe a self-righteous person insists that there are arbitrary rules against seizing life. Maybe the R_A got started and realized that this is actually a scam. Maybe the first available appointment is a year away. Maybe the R_A started, but quickly recognized that they've already done this before. The R_A was meant to have an exciting, meaningful life, and instead they're repeating the same, ordinary things. The question of what they should do with their lives will keep cycling in thoughts, drawn toward extreme, new options.

The core of R_A-first is *love for the thrill of processing new, extreme experiences*. If you dropped all judgment and distraction and really let yourself feel the pleasure of broadening your life experience, not clouded by any other feeling, what would you focus on? Which city would feel the most foreign to you if you were dropped in right now? How would you navigate a place where no one understood you, where you stuck out as a foreigner? What's the most extreme project you could complete? What's the most extreme career path you could complete? What extreme activity would be the biggest thrill for you? How much more well rounded will you be as a person if you try all of those things? What would the full potential of your life be if you dropped everything that's repetitive and easy and instead dedicated yourself to living a dream? Can you immerse in that vision and feel some of that pleasure now?

"Nobody accidentally became an astronaut."[285]

Then feel the tension of your scared friend interrupting, talking about the disease that happened historically in that place, telling you that you should miss out on life, confidently, excitedly talking about the boundaries and hurdles, asking you to worship fear with them instead. The scared friend would have a feeling of tension as a component. They feel like a problem, like an antagonist to intelligence. Experience-based arousal could be restored again if only this interruption would go away.

The feelings and logic of experiences are independent of each other and can be in direct conflict inside any observer. An observer might truly, logically want to feel excited about going to the same job again today, but the excitement just isn't happening. They might truly, logically not want to be excited by the idea of leaving the stable job that took decades to build, but they can't help being flushed with excitement whenever they imagine an alternative. Sometimes the feelings and the logic align, but they can just as easily be different from each other.

Later on, R$_A$ emotions interrupt peaceful, calm moments that don't have external triggers. Pain happens again, triggered by the memory of the fearful person shutting down experience options. No decision was made to relive that painful moment. Then the euphoric vision of successfully experiencing a dream strikes again. The observer is alone, the actual exterior moment is quiet, but the observer is flushed with joy. No decisions are being made to remember emotional events, or to feel emotions about them. Maybe this idea keeps coming to mind because it's meant to be.

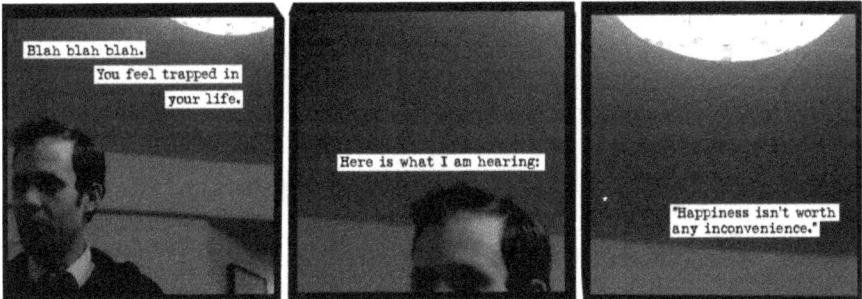

Since tension could be triggered at any moment, R$_A$s preemptively take actions to maintain their options and flexibility. If the day is too repetitive then the R$_A$ knows it will be strikingly painful, so they keep choosing the unfamiliar option since it has the highest likelihood of bringing joy and satisfaction. The way to be present and available for the rest of life is to keep stimulating yourself with newness, thrills, and risk so that repetition can be avoided. In a perfect world, they'd be living right at the peak of what they're capable of, breaking new ground in a brand new direction, so they'd have access to really satisfying new actions and adventures every time concern about their purpose was triggered. In the real world, there's lots of turning down new streets, going on vacations, even trying different grocery stores, just to keep things interesting.

> *"Some people say I'm crazy, that I must have a death wish.*
> *I look at it the other way. I have a life wish.*
> *I would rather live a shorter life*
> *experiencing everything I've experienced*
> *than die old as someone who didn't have those experiences."*[287]

R_A-firsts think that the excitement they feel about new experiences and stagnation they feel from repetitive experiences is helpful. They're motivated to try all the options so they have knowledge based on experience. They make better decisions about food, jobs, friends, groups, health, resources, and identity because they prioritize how these impact seizing the maximum that life has to offer them. They have the best parts of life because they chose jobs, locations, and people based on the real life experience of trying all the options. They take a better route to different places because they familiarized themselves with every option.

> *"There is no worse death curse*
> *than the humdrum daily existence of the living dead."*[288]

Meanwhile, R_A-lasts only seem to have disadvantages. Most obviously, people who don't prioritize novelty and action are weirdly simpleminded and their existence seems pointless. The biggest part of being human is missing from them. Lower R_A friends could live much better lives if they'd try something new. R_A-lasts condescendingly explain dangers that the R_A knows don't exist, because the R_A has done the "dangerous" thing a hundred times and it's actually fun and safe. The R_A is friends with "the dangerous" people. R_As have a favorite restaurant in "the dangerous" place. Fear is a mental illness which cripples. R_A-lasts miss out on the best parts of life because they get distracted with things that don't exist and project evil and negativity onto the peaceful, interesting things around them. An R_A-first may not have a perfect life, but they've got the foundation. They've tried all the options available and are skilled at finding and seizing new options. R_As are the only ones living in actual reality.

R_As vary quite a bit in what, who, and where sparks their excitement and stagnation. Some focus on physical risk and danger, some want to travel to all the places, some want to immerse in all the cultures, some want to take a project all the way to the extreme, and some are focused on being as productive as possible. Some have to try something completely different each day. Some are immersed in the moment, only focused on the thrills available right now. R_As are accustomed to being told that they need to get further away from dangerous things, by broken fear-worshipers who live joyless lives.

> *"Trying and failing is a win,*
> *because it's certainty about what that path could provide.*
> *Not trying, or not giving something your all,*
> *is the only route to actual failure.*
> *Because you spend the rest of your life*
> *knowing that the trying-and-failing path*
> *would've been better than what you got."[290]*

R_As think repeatedly feeling inspired by purpose, alternating with feeling painfully stagnant and meaningless is just what life is. R_A-firsts think they're trying for a totally realistic, but admittedly high-level of experience, meaning, and productivity with admittedly high frequency of novelty and action. But they determined that something is "realistic" by imagining something better than what they already encountered, or the best they ever encountered, while minimizing inextricable trade offs that come with those positives. The result is an underlying, recurring ache, an unfillable anxiety, a dissatisfaction with reality, because the "realistic" goal they need to hit to feel satisfied is just beyond what's actually possible.

R_A-Last: Living without Tension about Experience-Based Pleasures and Pains

"People overthink life. They say, 'I don't know what to do with my life, I don't know what I should be.' Just get food and put it in your mouth. That's it. Walk around, and look for food. Anytime you see any food, take it and put it in your mouth. Later, when you feel pressure, use the bathroom. That's it. It doesn't have to be more complicated. Do that until you die."[291]

At the lowest point on the Experience-based (R_A) s pectrum experiences feel like something that have momentary pleasures and pains, rather than deeper meanings. Experiences feel more like something functional, and less like relief in themselves for an internal hunger for growth, meaning, and experience. Experiences feel more tangent to the moment, which is obviously about something else (rather than focusing because they're positively transforming the observer).

When an activity option is present, but isn't drawing your attention, that activity is neutral to you. Experience-based neutrality isn't rejection. It's not a consideration of how meaningful an experience would be and a decision against it. It's not any thought at all. Experience-based neutrality is a lack of excitement about a new activity, and a lack of painful, meaningless stagnation about the current activity, which would focus the observer's attention on the "meaningfulness" of activity options. R_A neutrality continues when an activity doesn't sound meaningful or world-expanding even when someone else forces the option into focus.

"I think the idea of 'living your life to the fullest' is a little flawed. Why is jumping out of an airplane inherently better than reading a book? Or why is living a life that looks good on social media inherently more meaningful than a life lived quietly? I just don't buy it."[292]

As R_A-triggers reduce in number and drug intensity (moving down the R_A spectrum) fe wer experience options trigger the observer to feel R_A arousal, both stagnation and excitement. There's nothing missing now that will be immensely relieved when an activity happens, so no "meaning" is added to the idea of doing it. Daily life might be repetitive, but the observer doesn't know what's wrong with that because they're not feeling meaningless enough to think about it. Activity options might trigger personal growth, but the observer didn't stop to consider that because the mention of the activity didn't trigger enough thrilling excitement to focus on it.

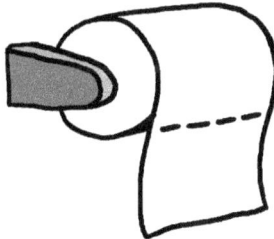

© Ben Zaehringer – BerkeleyMews.com[293]

Most people, even R_A-firsts, feel neutral about most experiences. At the lowest point on the R_A spectrum all actions and options feel neutral. But, from the inside, the absence of tension makes it feel like real world experiences aren't special or particularly different from each other. It feels like a wasted life is easy to avoid by doing things the obvious way. Everyone gets happy and unhappy moments. Each person makes their own "meaning." Purpose is momentary, and is what it is. Experiences that won't happen are also unchangeable realities. Consideration of experiences is practical, present, momentary, and accepting of how things actually are. The actual experience options available feel essentially the same in terms of meaningfulness, just with different details. No more-extreme life is imagined, and no joy is felt imagining it, so no hunger is sparked to make it happen in reality.

"Everybody wants to build and nobody wants to do maintenance."[294]

Most of the time, the feeling of meaninglessness about life isn't a topic until someone else is freaking out. A picture of a foreign beach looks nice. It doesn't remind the R_A-observer of the meaninglessness of their current life. They're not flushed with pain when they turn on the TV to watch the same show again, because they're not comparing that to the personal growth they'd feel while processing that new environment.

To feel, really, how much is going on in an R_A-last life, imagine that you're taking the first bite of your favorite childhood meal. The dog in the room with you really needs to pee. Someone else at the table starts choking. Someone swings a bat and just barely misses your head. You reach and your keys are missing. You step on a nail and you can feel your skin opening. For all humans, excitement about new experiences isn't the topic of the moment while differently themed life events are happening. R_A-last observers have more Comfort and Social triggers connected to more drug intensity. No choice is being made to ignore new experiences. It's just not an experience-related moment, because it's obviously a critical Social or Comfort moment (which happens to be a lot of moments).

If you could feel the process of turning yourself down in R_A tension, you'd feel a silencing of the urgency felt when noticing that an experience is new and extreme, or familiar and safe. As a result, there's a natural acceptance of your life path the way it has happened, an acceptance of the moment the way it's happening, and an acceptance of your future the way it will happen. You'd feel a reframing of focus away from whether you're getting the most purpose out of this moment and onto whatever other topic seems interesting at the moment. Experiences wouldn't spark an internal prediction of a better life. Which of the random, similar ones you participate in wouldn't really matter. Logic would still know that some life experiences might be preferable to others, but there would be no feeling of loss from not having the positive extreme, or pain from doing the familiar one. There would be no thought that positive features could be combined, or that negative features could be removed, that life is wasted on some options, or that life could shift in a sharply positive way if another option gets chosen. All the adults in the room can easily tune out the novelty of the experience while the meaningful task gets attention.

© Pat Byrnes – PatByrnes.com[295]

Everyone has had moments where they go through the motions of life without getting thrills from those motions. It would be easy to have a conversation about some other topic because no special experience is fixating attention on life meaning or personal growth. Everyone has missed out on an opportunity and not been stabbed with stagnant heartbreak about it. It wasn't meaningful or exciting, so missing it was the logical, beneficial thing to do. For an extreme R_A-last, that's all experience options. At the extreme minimum, it feels weird to even consider experiences for thrill because "thrill" doesn't satisfy any aching need. R_A-lasts aren't feeling stagnant, so they won't also feel relieved if they get "thrill."

"Don't give up on your dreams. Keep sleeping."[296]

Not being emotionally triggered doesn't mean that R_A-lasts can't recognize when an activity really does expand their horizons and introduce them to beneficial, new ways of thinking. But R_A-lasts might've missed it on their own, because their attention was elsewhere. And, they won't feel extra euphoria from the newness of the activity on top of the practical, logical, functional benefit of the new knowledge.

"I'm not really happy here,
but maybe this is the best I can expect
and I'll regret giving it up."[297]

Most R_A-lasts still can feel pleasure from visiting a foreign land, and pain when a missed experience seems to have positively affected their friends. But those events aren't as impactful when they don't automatically trigger hunger for change and escalation. There was a moment of experience-based pleasure or pain, that's just reality, and then the moment ended. The thought ends there. The observer can still look to the side and discuss a different topic. Pleasurable moments don't fixate the observer with hunger for more frequent and extreme experiences. Moments of stagnation don't fixate the observer with hunger for change. The rest of reality isn't silenced. The observer's focus isn't distracted away from the moment with an internal fantasy of what life would be like if they were a nomad constantly moving to new places. Instead it seems weird that we're still talking about that moment when it was over long ago.

Choosing activities is different when none or almost none of the options are intoxicating or painful just for the thrill of experiencing them. Someone being forced to choose among neutral options doesn't have feelings of arousal and heartbreak to help with the choice (to distract the choice away from logic), or to make the observer feel especially lucky if they get certain options. Meanwhile, those same experience options more easily trigger self-protective feelings, sensory-protective feelings, resource-protective feelings, friendship-protecting feelings, and group-harmony-protecting feelings. If you're managing a life where you're easily triggered by Social and Comfort concerns, it's worth disqualifying experiences that will trigger your recurring pain tension and prioritizing experiences which resolve your tensions. If you also want "thrill" then choose the most thrilling from the activities which make it through those other filters.

> *"I see people my age mountain climbing.*
> *I feel accomplished if I don't fall over*
> *while getting my leg through my underwear."*[298]

Going to foreign places means doing the same things in a place where the basics are harder to find and might not exist. Trying for extreme dreams means throwing away what you've already built elsewhere. We all die whether we visit foreign lands or not. If you're not happy where you are, then going to a place where even the basics are more difficult doesn't sound like it would be an improvement. Sometimes people get lucky chasing dreams, but most people fail. Even the people who "get lucky" have the same lives, just different in the details. If you accept that you live in reality, where extreme fantasies are just that, then you can make choices, manage the life you choose, enjoy it, and never revisit your experiences again. Everyone could have made different choices, but everyone made the best choices with what they knew in those moments. The life you imagine that would've had different choices doesn't include the real problems which would've been there too, and the extra guidance you're getting from looking at it backwards through time. If you realize that you're where you are and go from here, then you're free to enjoy the rest of life.

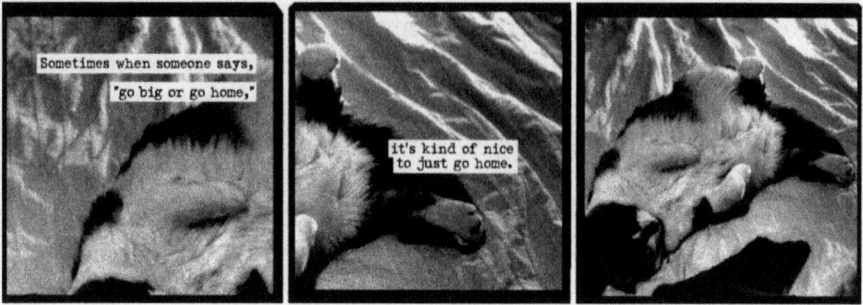

Instead of deviating into dreams of glory, deviate in Social and Comfort directions. Imagine building a family who love and look out for each other. Imagine your partner being your best friend. Imagine your partner has a really good soul and is joyful to interact with. Imagine finding a community of people who share some interest or goal. Imagine getting happiness from that group, working together, and succeeding. Imagine having a respectable job, being good at what you do, and having people ask you questions on that topic because you're the authority. Imagine finding and building a really good home, establishing your family in your community, and providing a safe haven for sweet souls in a world that's sometimes painful. Imagine surrounding yourself with sights, smells, sounds, and sights that bring peace to your soul. Meanwhile, you're limited to the experiences that you experience. Can you find a way to let that be the experience that thrills you?

An R_A-last is observing reality without creating something different inside, which is what it feels like to accept reality as it is. R_A-lasts have tried to get happiness from taking risks and it wasn't worth it. The joy was temporary while their long-term happiness suffered. Experiences have moments of function and pleasure. The excitement and stagnancy people feel about experiences doesn't have a deeper meaning. Experiences aren't a source of joy or disappointment in themselves. The meaning of life has to do with friends, family, sensory pleasures, health, food, entertainment, fun, resources, being an independent individual, and loving yourself. Experiences can be pleasant too, when they happen, but they're definitely less important than the rest of that.

From the perspective of R_A-lasts, R_As only seem to have disadvantages. Why create unrealistic fantasies just to make actual life feel bad? R_As have less comfortable lives because they go places that are uncomfortable. R_As use up more resources because they keep starting over in new places. R_As destroy their friendships and community connections by leaving those connections behind. R_As overlook the actual best real-world job, house, family, and home they encounter because they leave when those get familiar. R_As want particularly thrilling lives while not establishing the foundation that make life actually meaningful. R_As think the people around them are disappointed with life, and want something else, when the surrounding people are actually feeling Social or Comfort based concerns. R_As dramatically overestimate how much thrill and personal growth they'll get from new experiences.

> *"An insatiable appetite for glory leads to sacrifice and death, but innate instinct leads to self-preservation and life."*[300]

R_As passionately disregard reality, enthusiastically find ways to be unhappy with what exists, and make bad decisions among existing options. They seem to be unaware of what a meaningful life would be, while thinking they're experts in maximizing personal growth and meaning. R_As bully other people into trying activities they don't want to try, and into leaving acceptable-but-not-especially-exciting jobs, groups, and relationships. R_As bully people into sacrificing to try an option that will either fail or just be a different style of the same thing. R_As are immersed in an individual exaggeration of the value of experiences. In critical moments, R_As sacrifice friends, groups, the good will of others, resources, image, health, and safety because they're distracted with having a new experience that won't be very good. What R_As are actually experts at is finding ways to be unhappy with what they have. Why would anyone want that life?

> *"My 20s and early 30s have been a twisting crisscross of moves all over the West Coast, a couple of brief stints abroad, multiple jobs. For all these years of quick changes and rash decisions, which I once rationalized as adventurous, exploratory life, I have nothing to show for it. While I make friends easily, I've left most of my friends behind in each city, while they've continued to grow deep roots: marriages,*

home ownership, career growth, community, families, children.
I feel like a ghost. No one knows who I am or where I've been.
I haven't kept a friend, lover, or foe around long enough to give anyone
a chance. I used to think I was the one who had it all figured out.
Adventurous life in the city! Traveling the world! Making memories!
Now I feel incredibly hollow. And foolish." [301]

LOOK AT ME BEING PRODUCTIVE!

Ⓒ STEINBERGDRAWSCARTOONS
© *Avi Steinberg – SteinbergDrawsCartoons.com* [302]

There is no disappointment to feel with the experience of living a real-world human life. Thrill and novelty come and go for everyone, and often aren't present. The way experiences happen is fine. The frequency of new experiences is fine. There's no need for more, less, better, or different. It's still worth making sure that life has some variety, but that maintenance can happen without tension and relief, without fixated daydreams, and without judging what's happening as good or bad. The productivity of current life is fine. If the whole point of productivity is to eventually feel satisfied, then why not go directly to the satisfaction without adding in busy-body stress along the way?

> *"A calm and humble life will bring more happiness than the pursuit of success and the constant restlessness that comes with it."* [303]

R_A-lasts are realistic about what they've got, what they get from it, what their options are, and what it costs. They're more present to the reality of experiences than R_A-firsts are. Part of what makes experiences valuable is that they don't need extra attention in order to provide their functions. R_A-lasts live in the experiential satisfaction that R_A-firsts can't find, because R_A-lasts live in reality, undistracted by visions of not-reality.

Cross Overs

> *"If your success was certain, what would you do?"* [304]

Most R_A-lasts can get fixatingly thrilled about an experience which feels meaningful to their life purpose. Most R_A-lasts can be overwhelmed with heartbreaking stagnancy when a coworker who moved on is really killing it in their new life. But experiential fixations happen with WAY fewer experience options, WAY less frequently, and satisfaction comes much faster just by realizing that what happened is the fixed reality.

> *"Dare to be pointless."* [305]

Many times a day R_A-firsts do autopilot motions and activities without considering the experiential arousal of the moment because those options don't have arousal triggering cues. R_A-firsts can be distracted by other topics, even while interacting with an activity they would otherwise find exciting, but have true neutral lack of consideration of the value of the experience in that moment because nothing feels related to experiential arousal. Even for an R_A-first, it feels like awkward, tedious work to generate an experiential fantasy about an activity that doesn't feel meaningful, even when it will add just as much as a different activity they were thrilled about.

© *e horne and j comeau – asofterworld.com*[306]

R_A *Conclusions*

"Don't quit before the miracle happens."[307]

The addition of R_A means new experiences aren't just functional anymore. New and risky experiences are loved, exciting, meaningful, and desirable, triggering excitement, joy, concern, disappointment, pain, and relief. R_A tension and relief aren't necessary for a system to have new experiences. But experiential tension and relief add focus and incentive to seek out the most extreme experiences and participate in them. They add incentives to protect extreme and new qualities, so experiences remain positively emotionally triggering. They add incentives for each observer to distrust the predictions of others and to test boundaries themselves.

"I graduated college 2.5 years ago,
and the most important thing I've learned is that society doesn't
value hard work as much as it values delusional confidence."[308]

R_A-firsts have much more varied life experiences because they invest so much time and energy in seeking out, traveling to, and immersing in the unknown. A consistent focus on novelty and action helps them seize opportunities to become familiar with currently unfamiliar options. They're constantly sacrificing for the benefit of the experiential excitement they'll feel. But they're the least satisfied with the meaning, purpose, productivity, and adventure of their lives because daily tension reminds them to focus on what's wrong and imagine and feel desire for better.

"Imagine where you'll be in six months if you start now."[309]

"Once something's important to you, it never leaves you.
If you dreamt of being a singer songwriter
and never did it, you'll be haunted by that.
Because it's always stored in the back of your mind.
It's something that's meant for you that's calling to you.
You either pursue your dreams or they haunt you."[310]

Easily Confused for the R$_A$ Spectrum

This chapter compares R$_A$ to the six other motivators one-by-one. It holds the topic constant (the extremeness and novelty of experiences) and considers that topic while being triggered with each of the other six classes of tension. You'll be able to hear that it's the framing of the topic that gives away the observer's motivators, not the topic itself. Each observer is going to evaluate experiences on the value scale or what triggers them with pleasure, pain, tension, and relief. This is the chapter to come back to when determining the relative influence of R$_A$ versus any other motivator for a person.

Valuing Intensity, Newness, and Action While Feeling Experience-Based Relationalness (R$_A$):

*"Most people lead lives of quiet desperation
and go to the grave with the song still in them."*[312]

If your mind is already distracted, feeling like you're full of untapped potential, looking back on your life as if you were dying, knowing that you could have done more, then what is the value of the next activity option? Since fully experiencing life, following your calling, and passionately chasing your dreams are what matter, how can the next moment be made more new, more intense, and have more action? Stagnancy is a choice to waste life. When someone loves an activity because they're flushed with R$_A$, they love the feelings of awkwardness that come with new things, because overcoming those moments feels like personal growth. Each new sight and sound feels pleasurable in itself. The process of replacing predictions with real world knowledge is euphoric and relieving. R$_A$s can feel their personal growth happening and it's delightful. The boundary where fear gets felt keeps moving because they test that boundary and find there was nothing to fear. Feeling R$_A$ means loving the experience itself, because the experience itself is beautiful and meaningful. Everyone should try this experience because it's so good.

*"People are strange. They are constantly angered by trivial things.
But on a major matter like totally wasting their lives,
they hardly seem to notice."*[313]

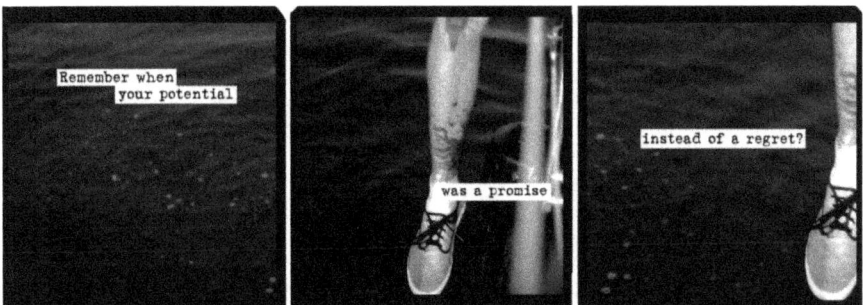

© *e horne and j comeau – asofterworld.com*[314]

When other people hesitate before leaping into the unknown, it looks like those people are choosing the sharply painful option and avoiding the thrilling, euphoric, joyful option. So R$_A$s encourage others to feel how good growing as a person feels, and are mystified when people choose the option that would leave the R$_A$ cycling in pain tension instead. When a hypochondriac righteously tries to keep an R$_A$ from experiencing happiness, and insists that the R$_A$ choose the pain-tension-maximizing "safe" option, it's really clear how evil that person is. When others don't join R$_A$s on adventures, R$_A$s think those people get a lesser life, and are less factually accurate about reality because they're making tension-based predictions which are laughably inaccurate compared to R$_A$s' real world, first hand experience. R$_A$s are growing and learning while other people waste the gift of being alive.

> *"Those who have a why to live for*
> *can bear almost any how."*[315]

If you put your mind to it

you can do anything.

But you won't.

© e horne and j comeau – asofterworld.com[316]

Valuing Intensity, Newness, and Action While Feeling Body-Based Comfort (C$_B$):

> *"Every dead body on Mt Everest*
> *was once a highly motivated person."*[317]

There are C$_B$s who might look like R$_A$s because they have lots of experiences. The difference is in the framing of the experience, which comes from the feelings they have while considering and participating in those experiences. A C$_B$ is worried about safety and comfort because they get so tense when encountering new things.

When a C_B is participating in experiences, it's often a secondary motivator encouraging them, like a desire to be entertained (C_R), or fear of missing out (C_I), which is internally countered by the C_B's natural affection for the familiar, and natural pain tension when considering the unfamiliar. In order to overcome their natural internal feelings of hesitation and fear, C_Bs often have to immerse in the logic that other people are somehow doing this activity safely. It helps to have a fearless, excited friend along to hold their hand and pull the C_B forward when the inevitable moments of tension petrify them. A C_B is more likely to learn as much as possible about a new location or experience from the safety of their home so that the fewest parts of the experience will be unfamiliar when they get there.

> *"The greatest of follies is to sacrifice health*
> *for any other kind of happiness."*[318]

The clear dividing line between C_B and R_A is their experience of pain. R_As want to feel the most pain that a human can feel, because that's an interesting experience, teaches them that pain isn't actually bad, and puts all their future, lesser pains into perspective. C_Bs are triggered with tension alongside pain, so pain feels like a problem which focuses attention and "needs" action to resolve. Pain still feels negative to an R_A, but doesn't feel like it should change. It feels like a natural part of living meaningfully. One is imagining dying, so they're relieved when safety features are present. One is imagining a wasted life, so they're relieved when they jump off the side and the adventure is in motion.

> *"There's nothing more exciting than peace."*[319]

> *"People who take chances are*
> *irresponsible nut jobs putting us all at risk."*[320]

If you're already distracted by a body that is hurting, that feels low-energy, by a brain that's foggy, distracted, and stressed, by temperature, sights, and smells that are painfully uncomfortable, then activities are exterior topics which can be rated by how they'll affect those concerns. While you're hungry for comforts and peace the best activities will heal, soothe, and energize. Really optimal activities will detoxify and reinvigorate your body and mind. While doing that activity, you will feel like you're thriving. A bad activity will damage your body even more, stress you out, or involve negative smells and sounds. Activities are still what are being considered, but they're valued for their impacts on sensory pleasure and mental wellbeing.

C$_B$s know themselves. They freak out. They get petrified. So they're careful about trying new things. They still want new activities, but they need to know they're actually safe while they're feeling a thrill. And sometimes their body will still lock up too much to be able to participate.

"I enjoy new experiences,
but I want to be familiar with what's happening.
I want all the safety precautions used and double checked."[322]

Valuing Intensity, Newness, and Action While Feeling Community-Based Socialness (S$_C$):

"The best way to find yourself
is to lose yourself in the service of others."[323]

Since tension is triggered when other people feel bad, what activities support everyone involved, and don't leave anyone out? Which activities increase the harmony, health, and happiness of the participants? How likely is an activity to encourage people to work together as one group? How likely is an activity to divide the group into winners and losers? How likely is an activity to encourage bonds of trust and love between the members? How can the people who recently opted out be attracted back in? Which activities are good for all the ages of the members? Who will be excluded by the physical activity needed, or the knowledge which is helpful, or the topic that it covers? Is there some way that people with different activity preferences can each do their things, while still all bonding as a group?

"The future of every community lies in capturing
the passion, imagination, and resources of its people."[324]

Someone valuing activities while feeling S$_C$ is actually getting their joy from how much the group is enjoying, benefiting from and growing from the activity. They're feeling joy from the love inside the community, and triggered with pain tension by disconnections between members. The observer is feeling the tension and relief that they see on everyone else's faces. So they might say they loved an activity at the end, but the feeling of joy they felt came from seeing how happy the group members were while participating, not actually from direct love for the activity itself. They might not like the activity if they were to have gone and done it alone instead. When an S$_C$ chooses an activity for their own individual, personal growth, they still feel energized by the presence of similar souls all working toward the same goal, or are energized because the work builds up forgotten peoples, because they're naturally energized by humans bonding together and becoming happier, more so than they're energized by ending the stagnant repetition of their own lives.

Valuing Intensity, Newness, and Action While Feeling Sex-Based Relationalness (R$_S$):

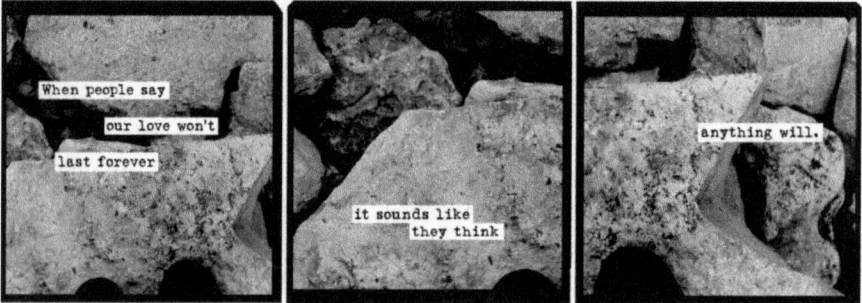

When people say
our love won't
last forever

it sounds like
they think

anything will.

© e horne and j comeau – asofterworld.com[325]

Since sex with a very sexy partner is the most joy that life can bring, and since a fixating, distracting hunger for sex will come again soon, what activities make sex more intense, make meeting new partners more likely, and create the right environment for sexual tension to grow and climax? When tension is added to being around cuties, and relieved when orgasms happen with those cuties, the most meaningful moments are sexual moments. So, activities which introduce the observer to cuties, especially ones that then encourage touching, are better, like dancing, acrobatics, and acting. Activities where everyone is single, or where a sexy atmosphere amps things up with an existing partner, are more attractive than the opposite. Activities that keep people physically separate are painful to even consider. The activity which introduces the observer to their true love will feel magical. Even a sexy activity will feel painfully repulsive if no one is sexually attractive there. So, R$_S$s still love activities, especially the activity of passionate sex with someone very arousing who is also very aroused in return. But the activity is enjoyed based on how it increases and then satisfies sexual arousal.

If the instructor is very sexually attractive, the whole event is going to feel better than if the instructor is very not-sexually attractive.

Since R$_A$ and R$_S$ come as a package, it's common for R$_S$s to feel more pain about stagnancy in their sexual relationships, and hunger for extreme sexual attraction. It's the addition of R$_A$ which makes R$_S$s leave partners who still want sex and are still sexually attractive, because they're looking for something more extreme, which triggers their pain tension less.

Valuing Intensity, Newness, and Action While Feeling Resource-Based Comfort (C$_R$):

> *"At the end, all that's left of you are your possessions. Perhaps that's why I've never been able to throw anything away. Perhaps that's why I hoarded the world: with the hope that when I died, the sum total of my things would suggest a life larger than the one I lived."*[326]

C$_R$s can be flushed with excitement thinking they're about to get a lot of money, thinking food is going to be delicious, thinking they're about to get something for free, and that's still excitement about an experience, but it's resource-based emotions about consumption and acquisition, not experience-based emotions which appreciate the unfamiliarity and extremeness of experiences. C$_R$s naturally evaluate experience options by how those experiences will affect resources, since resources are where they have existing tension that could use satisfaction, and are the area which will likely be triggered by any resource-related aspects of the experience itself. The easiest thing to confuse between C$_R$ and R$_A$ is confusing entertainment with experiences. A C$_R$ wants entertainment, they want fun which will relieve boredom. An R$_A$ feels like a lack of motion is a stagnant waste of their life. So they want thrilling engagement with something new to give their life meaning. An R$_A$ is feeling tension about growing as a person, overcoming fear, and removing limitations. Meanwhile a C$_R$ is hungry for pleasure from any motivator (which they call "fun"), while concerned about minimizing the monetary cost and effort expended.

© Jim Benton – JimBenton.com[327]

A C_R can be satisfied by doing a familiar activity again because it's entertaining, while an R_A is triggered with painful tension by familiarity because their hunger was for newness. A C_R will say, "I'll get more enjoyment out of a new activity for the same price," because they're framing the "value" of the activity in terms of resources. Meanwhile an R_A will say, "I'll learn the most from a new activity because it will expose me to things I didn't already know," because they're framing the value of the activity in terms of novelty. Both observers are seeking relief from experiences, but one is trying to relieve the feeling of boredom, and one is trying to relieve a feeling of meaninglessness.

(C$_B$, C$_B$, and C$_R$)   © Loryn Brantz – LorynBrantz.com[328]

When someone loves an activity because they're flushed with C$_R$, they love the taste of foods, the action of acquiring, the action of consuming, the experience of finding new, useful resources, of being entertained, and of getting a fantastic financial deal, especially if they expend the least effort and resources. A C$_R$ is relieving hunger for acquisition and consumption the same way that an R$_A$ is relieving hunger for new and extreme experiences.

> *"I'd like to be an entrepreneur,*
> *but I don't have the drive or energy,*
> *and I'm afraid of going bankrupt."* [329]

> *"Motivation is the most valuable resource in the world.*
> *Use it while it's there, because it will dissipate."* [330]

Valuing Intensity, Newness, and Action While Feeling Alliance-Based Socialness (S$_F$):

> *"It's not where you go or what you do,*
> *it's who you're with that matters."* [331]

Who is someone who has a good soul, but the two of you aren't as close as you'd like to be? How great would it be if a shared experience left you both happier, but also left you even better friends? What is the relative value of different experience options if you're looking for something that might particularly engage your friend's interests, especially something that will give the two of you time and opportunity to talk and connect? What is the relative value of different experience options if you want to generate more inside jokes? If you're hungry for your friend to feel happier, and hungrier to feel more connected with that friend again, then which experiences might relieve that hunger?

While someone is hungry for the happiness of a friend, and hungry to feel aligned and mutually connected with a friend, the best activities are something that requires two people to work together, especially something that neither could've completed on their own. The best activities are ones that are exclusive to this pairing, so that the topic will always bring up memories of how merging into one unit with that other valuable soul made all the difference. Really optimal activities are ones where both merged halves can be honest and open with each other, and show the love and support for each other that strengthens their connection. The worst activity is one that

224

ends in fighting, in feeling disconnected, in feeling like the two of you could've been great friends but circumstances got in the way.

When someone loves an activity because they're flushed with S_F, they love the feeling of connecting with a really good person. The same experience wouldn't be fun, and might even be upsetting to do alone. The R_A component of the happiness is the direct love for the experience itself, regardless of who else is there or isn't there. An R_A might negatively judge a friend who was there and wasn't appreciating the experience, and emotionally separate from the human who was distracted to connect with the experience which is meaningful. The R_A component of the happiness is the direct love for the experience, regardless of who else is there. The S_F component of the happiness is the direct love for the friend and the friendship, regardless of the activity that helps them feel it.

Valuing Intensity, Newness, and Action While Feeling Individuality-Based Comfort (C_I):

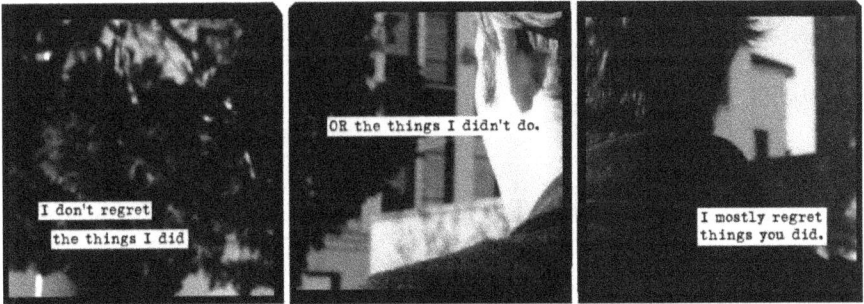

© *e horne and j comeau – asofterworld.com*[332]

Since tension is easily triggered if self isn't differentiating, impacting, and superior, and since relief comes when self is unique, makes a difference, and wins, then how valuable are the experience options available for bringing happiness and relief? What activities will self naturally excel in? What activities might expose self to criticism, judgment, and failure? Is there a distinctive option that self can do since self is different and better than others? Can self choose something new that everyone else might follow?

> *"If you can't impress them with your argument,
> impress them with your actions."*[333]

> *"You can't get away from yourself
> by moving from one place to another."*[334]

If your mind is already distracted by people who didn't listen to you, by feeling ignored, attacked, unfairly treated, and by the dumb mistake you made, then what is the value of the next activity option? While someone is hungry for impact, recognition, and importance the best activities will put others under their command, will demonstrate their excellence, will happen where others can admire their skill, will emphasize that they're unique, and will be forever changed by the little adjustments they suggest. It will be sharply painful if the C_I shows up and some other person gets attention for being excellent while it looks like the C_I is part of the adoring crowd.

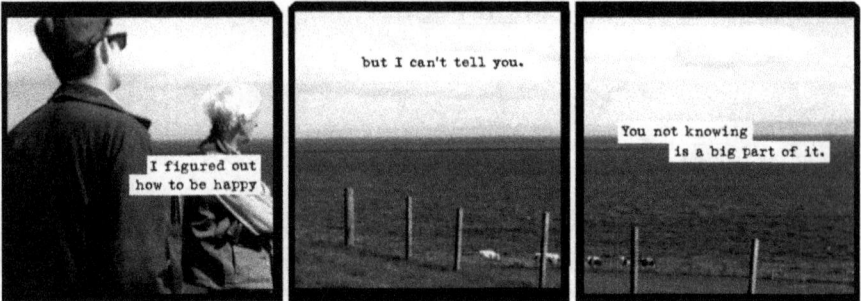

© e horne and j comeau – asofterworld.com[335]

C_Is feel more attraction to uncommon and overlooked activities, and that impressed feeling is the feeling that the activity is "cool." Activity options are repulsive if the participants don't look cool while they do it. But another activity option makes the participants look super cool, smooth, intelligent and skilled. The admiration the C_I feels for the skill makes the C_I want to try it, to be the newest prodigy in it, and to quickly be the best in the field. The C_I wants to surprise people with skill, which feels possible because these other people are obviously not as intelligent. C_Is are just as tickled as everyone else when they see the clever things self does. They like seeing their influence. They love admiring attention. They love the questions and they love teaching.

> *"I was very experimental as a drug addict. I thought Meth was alluring because it seemed like such a hard drug. Of course I was afraid, people urge you not to try it, so I could feel like a badass if I tried it."*[336]

R$_A$ is a focus on the value of activities. So an R$_A$ thinks skydiving is so great that everyone should do it. Meanwhile, a C$_I$ wants to do something that no one else has done to show that self is unique and superior. A C$_I$ will get annoyed and stop liking an activity if everyone else has already done it, because the C$_I$ was more focused on the value of self.

> *"It's not who you are that holds you back.*
> *It's who you think you're not."*[337]

> *"Remember the person who gave up?*
> *Neither does anyone else."*[338]

"Yes, I came back. I always come back."

S$_F$: The Friendship-Based Social Tension Spectrum

"Are we not like two volumes of one book?"[340]

Friendship-based Social (S$_F$) tension adds a focusing need for escalation or repair, paired with relieving satisfaction to the consideration of friendships. Tension is triggered by a specific person's emotions, by similarities and differences with that person, and by signs of the other person's emotional investment in the friendship. That tension focuses attention on how that person feels, what they're doing, and what to do and say so that the other person feels good. Each person is somewhere on the spectrum from being frequently triggered with very strong tension about friendships (being flushed with joy by a friend's joy, sadness by a friend's sadness, tension by a friend's tension, excitement about new acquaintances who seem to have a lot in common, and endearing love when a friend is vulnerable and caring in return), to being infrequently triggered with weak or no tension about friendships (observing alliances and acquaintances for what they are without additional hunger for more intense emotional entanglement). This chapter immerses in the two extremes to help understand how life feels as you move from very-easily-triggered to very-rarely-triggered with friendship-based tensions.

The Friendship Pleasure Spectrum

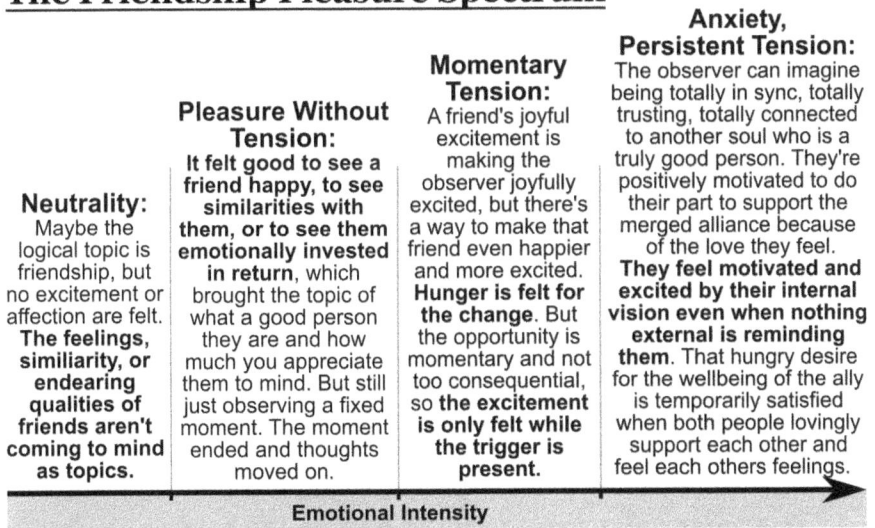

Neutrality:	Pleasure Without Tension:	Momentary Tension:	Anxiety, Persistent Tension:
Maybe the logical topic is friendship, but no excitement or affection are felt. **The feelings, similiarity, or endearing qualities of friends aren't coming to mind as topics.**	It felt good to see a friend happy, to see **similarities with them, or to see them emotionally invested in return**, which brought the topic of what a good person they are and how much you appreciate them to mind. But still just observing a fixed moment. The moment ended and thoughts moved on.	A friend's joyful excitement is making the observer joyfully excited, but there's a way to make that friend even happier and more excited. **Hunger is felt for the change.** But the opportunity is momentary and not too consequential, so **the excitement is only felt while the trigger is present.**	The observer can imagine being totally in sync, totally trusting, totally connected to another soul who is a truly good person. They're positively motivated to do their part to support the merged alliance because of the love they feel. **They feel motivated and excited by their internal vision even when nothing external is reminding them**. That hungry desire for the wellbeing of the ally is temporarily satisfied when both people lovingly support each other and feel each others feelings.

Emotional Intensity →

Terminology & Abbreviations

Friendship-based **neutrality** happens when humans coincidentally happen to be nearby, coincidentally happen to be taking similar actions or saying similar things, but no connection is felt to them because of that proximity or similarity. It is felt when nearby people have emotions which aren't matched by the observer's emotions because that other person and their emotions feel like separate, coincidental, momentary, observable parts of external reality. The thought doesn't come to mind to support the other person, or that a deeper connection between souls might exist, because no feelings are felt while the other person feels feelings. The other person's emotions are forgotten as quickly as they happen. In a truly neutral situation, matching emotions aren't felt even if the observer focuses on the unarousing target and recognizes that the target is feeling pain, pleasure, tension, or satisfaction. Most people feel friendship neutrality when hearing second hand about the emotions of strangers, or people in the past or future. When starting from a neutral mind, it feels like a change of topic to immerse in another person's emotions enough to be triggered to feel matching pain, pleasure, tension, or relief.

Friendship-based Social **pleasure with<u>out</u> tension** is momentary, practical joy which comes from recognition of a specific person, or recognition of a specific person's joy. It's pleasant to see them, or pleasant to see them happy, but in a fixed, momentary, practical way that doesn't hold attention and feels complete. It's felt when noticing a friend in a photograph. That moment was part of the normal world. Nothing needs to be done and thoughts quickly move on to the next topic.

Friendship-based Social **pleasure <u>with</u> tension** is the excited, joyful rush of recognizing a friend, or a friend's positive feelings, combined with hungry recognition that there's a way for them to feel even happier, more excited, and more connected. Something needs to happen.

- **Momentary pleasure tension** (externally triggered tension) is a hungry noticing of friendships, but where the tension only exists while the trigger is present. A friend starts making a declarative statement and the observer is hungry to find common ground so they can support what their friend is saying. A friend notices something that smells good and the observer is hungry to help them get closer. A friend is excited to eat and the observer is holding both forks. This isn't a logical decision to support an alliance. It's pleasurable excitement felt because there's a way to bring happiness to an ally, to make them feel even more loved and connected. But the moment is also small enough that it passes as soon as the specific trigger isn't present anymore. Attention is focused and desire is felt, but are quickly relieved. Momentary friendship tensions are small enough that the moment will be forgotten even if the pleasurable adjustment doesn't happen.

- **Anxiety, persistent pleasure tension** (internally maintained tension) is hunger for friendship escalation which persists even when the external trigger is removed. A particularly similar, good soul has been found and their existence makes this planet feel more like home. A happy glow is felt because they exist and because the relationship with them is so strong and merged. If these two people invest in each other and care for each other then every day will be happier and every problem will be more easily overcome. But it feels like something should be done. How can the observer support or love their friend right now to make that connection even stronger? The excited person knows that they've found another half, someone who is truly good and truly cares, who is just as dedicated to their happiness in return. This is the relaxed, joyful feeling of knowing you've found one of your people, but with an underlying hunger to check in on them, make sure they're okay, and do whatever you can to support them even more. The opportunity to make this friendship even closer is fixating because it's going to be so good when it happens.

Friendship-based **pain without tension** is pain felt about the realistic disconnection of friendships in an imperfect world. Someone is disconnected, or feeling bad, and it hurts, but in a fixed, small way. It's passive recognition that someone is too naturally different to be a friend, but in a way that feels fixed and doesn't hold attention for more than a moment. A stranger could've engaged you, but instead turned away. You recognize a clerk, but they don't recognize you back. It feels like objective recognition of external reality. Thoughts can easily continue on an unrelated topic.

Friendship-based **pain <u>with</u> tension** is feelings of negativity in the observer, but in a lacking way that wants to adjust something to reduce or remove that negativity. A friend's feelings are so hurt, or the partnership is so disconnected that other thoughts can't happen until the friend's feelings and the feeling of connection are restored.

The Friendship Pain Spectrum

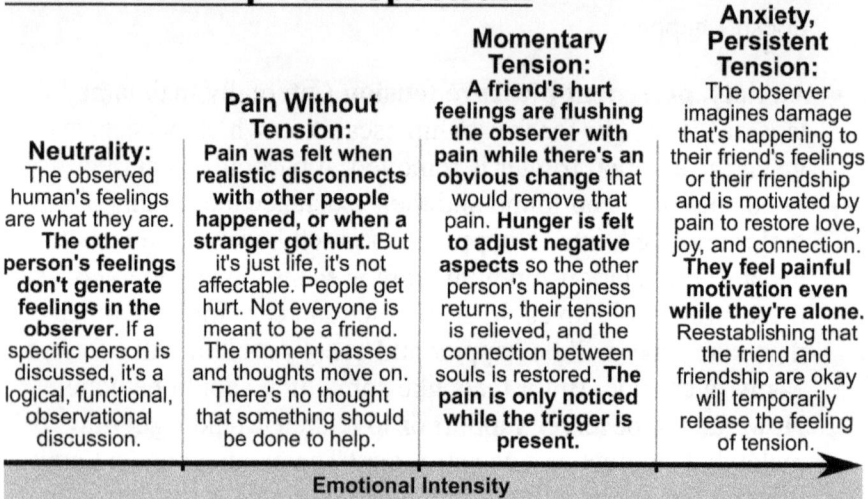

Neutrality:	Pain Without Tension:	Momentary Tension:	Anxiety, Persistent Tension:
The observed human's feelings are what they are. **The other person's feelings don't generate feelings in the observer.** If a specific person is discussed, it's a logical, functional, observational discussion.	**Pain was felt when realistic disconnects with other people happened, or when a stranger got hurt.** But it's just life, it's not affectable. People get hurt. Not everyone is meant to be a friend. The moment passes and thoughts move on. There's no thought that something should be done to help.	A friend's hurt feelings are flushing the observer with pain while there's an **obvious change** that would remove that pain. **Hunger is felt to adjust negative aspects** so the other person's happiness returns, their tension is relieved, and the connection between souls is restored. **The pain is only noticed while the trigger is present.**	The observer imagines damage that's happening to their friend's feelings or their friendship and is motivated by pain to restore love, joy, and connection. **They feel painful motivation even while they're alone.** Reestablishing that the friend and friendship are okay will temporarily release the feeling of tension.

Emotional Intensity →

- **Momentary pain tension** (externally triggered tension) is fixation and urgency felt when a friend has a desire which focuses the observer on helping. It most commonly motivates people to say something supportive or adjust something for the friend's comfort. The shared experience of pain, tension, and relief is the feeling of being emotionally merged with an ally. It is the connection which brings satisfaction to both people when the pained person's feelings are resolved, and as both people recognize the goodness of each others souls for caring.

- **Anxiety, persistent pain tension** (internally maintained tension) has two qualities. It is pain felt on behalf of a friend who is presumed to be hurting. It is also pain felt on behalf of the friendship, which is being damaged by the ally who isn't emotionally investing in it. Importantly, it is anxious focus on the friend or friendship while the friend isn't present. It's concern that an ally's feelings were hurt, concern that an ally might be upset, or concern that an ally might need help. Your friend wants more of your time, attention, and help, but all they do is criticize you in return. They want to condescend to you, but they also claim to be a friend. Mostly it's a dull feeling of obligation, knowing that a needy friend is probably upset because they haven't gotten attention today. It's a weirdly illogical matching of the pain they're feeling while they demand things that prove they're not worth the emotions. It's also concern that a friend might've been accidentally offended by a miscommunication, and a hunger to check in with them and make sure the connection is still okay. It can also feel like regret about not responding to people when the pain comes from imagining their feelings being hurt. Friendship anxiety is felt because the other person feels pain, not because they're doing their part to be worthy of that empathy. But all of this feels like a problem. It feels like the observer will keep cycling in negative tension about their friend's feelings until some action is taken that reconnects with that friend, establishes that the friend feels good, and establishes that the friendship is secure.

Friendship-based **satisfaction** is a feeling of relief which comes from restoring or verifying the wellbeing of the ally, resolving miscommunications, resolving differences, verifying and expressing mutual empathy, from evidence that the friend is deeply emotionally invested in the friendship, from completion of teamwork activities or shared experiences, from verifying that the friend's negative feelings didn't exist, and sometimes through making the most of a momentary connection with another person. Things were tense, but the happiness of the friend and the connection of the friendship were restored. Nothing needs attention or action anymore. Thoughts can move on to other topics.

The shorthand for people who are triggered with friendship-based social tension and anxiety more often and strongly than the other tension and anxiety options is that these people are "S_F-**first**." When a reference is made to "an S_F," or "S_Fs," it's identifying the discussed person or people as being S_F-first.

The shorthand for people who are triggered more strongly and frequently by all six other tension options is that people are "S_F-

last." Someone who is S_F-last can still feel feel S_F **pain** and **pleasure** quite strongly, but friendships more often feel objectively noticeable in a fixed way, and less often feel like they need adjustment. The pain, pleasure, tension, and satisfaction that happens with friends is more likely to be Relational or Comfort-based.

"Of all the means which wisdom acquires to ensure happiness throughout the whole of life, by far the most important is friendship."[341]

We're now going to immerse in the life experience people have when they're most frequently and strongly struck by friendship-based Social tension to see what it's like to live at the highest end of the spectrum. Then we'll immerse in the life experience of people who feel the six other tensions more strongly and frequently.

© *Joe Rothenberg – Joetatochips.com*[342]

S_F-First: Frequently Triggered Strong S_F Tension

*" 'Friend guilt is common,' says Carlin Flora, a friendship expert and
author of <u>Friendfluence: The Surprising Ways Friends Make Us Who
We Are</u>. 'No matter what you do, you feel like you're not being a good
enough friend.' There's always someone you 'should' be calling,
a happy hour you 'should' be attending, or an email you 'should' have
replied to long ago. But here's the catch: Even though feeling this way
means you have good intentions, trying to please everyone is unrealistic
— to the point that it could actually leave you feeling even worse.
What's making us all think we're horrible friends? First, there's simply
more going on. 'People are getting involved in more activities and
inviting everyone in their social networks to come to their events,
so it ends up being an onslaught of gatherings galore.' And since you
probably aren't looking to speed-date through your social life and try
to hit every event, you end up feeling guilty about the ones you skip.
'People think that by not showing up, the host will be heartbroken,
when usually everyone pretty much understands.' Luckily you can
head off a friend guilt trip: Politely turning down an acquaintance's
invitation or occasionally canceling is nothing to regret.
'Misplaced guilt about third and fourth-tier friends and
acquaintances can cause unnecessary distress and drain you of
emotional energy.' 'Constantly stressing about people who don't
matter as much [feels bad].' Being non-committal is harmful to
your psyche too because you end up creating false expectations,
which makes you feel extra guilty when you don't follow through.'
If you decline, keep things polite and short. 'Long explanations
of why you can't go reinforce your feeling of guilt because
they make you feel like you did something wrong.' "*[343]

Being S_F-first means feeling emotions before logic has had a chance
to evaluate an input. S_F-firsts are stabbed with sharp pain when they
see their friend hurting. **The observers' bodies aren't getting
touched, and yet they're flushed with pain as if the damage to
their friend were physical damage happening to themselves.** Was
the pain a response to logic? No. S_F-firsts don't logically assess the
damage to the friend, the value of this friendship, the likelihood that
this will affect the observer, or the deservingness of the friend for
the pain they're feeling and then make a logical choice to feel pain.
The S_F can't logically choose to feel pain on command from other
logical negatives which don't trigger the feeling. The pain happens

automatically and simultaneously with the observation of the friend's hurt feelings, or with the observation of positive friendship value in their now-disconnected friend. Logic is used after the feeling happened to solve for what must be going on and what needs to be done based on the extremeness of the feelings felt.

S_Fs are then flushed with intoxicating happiness when they rush over and help the friend especially when the friend is relieved and expresses gratitude which is clearly rooted in recognition of a shared connection. All focus is immediately drawn to the goodness of the other person's soul. Is the pleasure felt a response to logic? No. S_F-firsts don't logically assess the functional value of this ally, the actual goodness of their soul, and the actual sacrifices this person has made on the observer's behalf and then make a logical choice to feel euphoria from observing the returned joy and emotional investment of this recognized person. They can't logically decide that a disconnected stranger generate that euphoria and fixation instead and then feel it there. Logic is used after the feeling to model the value of the friend and the friendship which justifies the extremeness of the positive emotions felt.

The third feeling which really cements these in is that S_F-first observers can tolerate much bigger problems in other areas without getting triggered with excitement or concern. Nearby romantic options have some cute features, but none are so striking that the observer gets particularly aroused. The observer's life has gotten repetitive, but nothing else seems appealing. Sensory comforts aren't ideal, but they're not so painful that they require action. The observer isn't flushed with self love at the moment, but they don't feel self-hate either. Resources are generic and sufficient. These topics aren't coming to mind because they're within the ranges of pain where they're not a problem that needs attention (because this observer isn't triggered with tension about them at these levels). They're not great, but that's just how life is.

"I thought it was normal to feel consumed with keeping the people around you happy. Bending and stretching myself like in a form of self-torturing yoga to keep everyone in my life happy felt uncomfortable and inconvenient, sometimes painful, but I just thought that was just what it

was like to live in relationship with others. As I got older I discovered it simply wasn't humanly possible to keep every person I knew happy. I learned to say 'no' to a friend in need, because my husband needed me more, or 'no' to that extra volunteer position because it took away precious time from my children. I still haven't shaken the need to people-please, but I put pleasing my most important people over pleasing less important people. My heart feels tied in knots, and my stomach is doing somersaults when I question the conversation I just had with my friend over lunch. I doubt and second guess everything I said and how my friend really feels. The 'people-pleasing' monster steals my enjoyment when I'm doing something that I enjoy, wagging its crooked finger at me, saying I should be busy pleasing other people instead. Overcoming people-pleasing means getting in touch with something deeper than the needs of others, the hidden whisper of what I want and need."[344]

At the highest end of the S_F spectrum observers are drugged with much more friendship arousal and heartbreak while considering way more humans. But it doesn't feel individual and it doesn't feel internal. It feels like objective recognition that a tiny individual sacrifice will have much bigger benefits for the partner. It feels obvious that both people feel each others emotions and work together as one team every time that's helpful. At the highest setting, these feelings are felt on behalf of others who have only shared one conversation. The observer is thrilled to see a friend, and leaves with a euphoric glow after spending time connecting, especially if the other person is clearly emotionally invested in the friendship. If either ally needs something, the matched emotion of need will be felt by both and the two will work together to resolve either person's needs. Meanwhile, every other part of life is normal. The reason to focus on the friend's needs is that a friend has a critically important need in this moment (which ends up being lots of moments).

"Love is that condition in which the happiness of another person is essential to your own."[345]

So, what can be done to resolve their concerns, restore their joy, and maximize the connection felt by both? What can be said, what can be done to make them laugh and to feel connected? Tension is felt when the other person gets a concerned look on their face. Was something misunderstood. Does the other person want something? Has there been a disconnection? Since every other part of life is ignorably acceptable, the moments when a merged ally is flushed with tension feel sharply consequential. S_Fs don't want to think about the emotions of their friends, and the status of their friendships again, but a critical relationship strain came up on its own which requires action or regret.

"I really appreciate this..."

© Harry Bliss – HarryBliss.com[346]

Half of what makes friendship feelings feel objective is that so many humans inspire no friendship arousal. No tension, happiness, sadness, or relief are felt on behalf of strangers and even some recognized humans, especially people who are too different, or the ones who show no signs of returned emotional investment. There are so many humans who don't trigger excitement about asexually merging into a team that the ones who do trigger such strong feelings are worth collecting and protecting. It makes logical sense to focus on the individuals who naturally feel like extensions of the observer's soul.

Tension events alternate with being released again when S_Fs get satisfaction, which is usually a connecting conversation with a friend where that person's wellbeing is verified, disconnecting tensions are resolved, and mutual affection and mutual emotional investment is expressed. Each day is a tug-of-war between neutral availability of focus for any thought and fixated concern about a friend or friendship. The emotional problems in life happen when friendship tensions happen which don't end in satisfaction. Maybe the other person sounds like they're upset. Or maybe they make a selfish choice that excludes the observer. The situation will keep cycling in thoughts so that the resolving action can be determined.

> *"Who are the people who stop time for you?*
> *These people are your life. The rest is just filler."*[347]

The core of S_F-first is ***love for the feeling of being emotionally merged with a really good soul***. It's thorough appreciation that you and another person have built something beautiful together by investing in each other and caring for each other. If you dropped all judgment and distraction and really let yourself feel the pleasure of caring for another person, not clouded by other feelings, what would you focus on? Who can you be yourself around and they naturally understand? Who do you know will always be on your side? Who is a good person themselves, someone who cares and sacrifices? What qualities would a true best friend have that would make them worth sacrificing for? How much easier and happier would life be if you had a true best friend, a teammate, who was competent, good, and on your side? Can you imagine life with that friend and feel some of that pleasure now?

Then feel the tension when your friend says they don't have emotional reactions to your feelings. You can be delighted or crushed and their emotions will be unaffected. Feel the tension when your friend tells you what you can buy them for their birthday in a way which sounds transactional, missing any emotional concern about how you react to it. Feel the tension when your friend makes a joke at your expense and laughs. That friend has a feeling of tension as a component. They're not emotionally invested in you. Your emotional investment in them is wasted because it's not being returned. Something needs to change. Friendship-based affection could be restored if they became emotionally invested, or if you leave this person and find the other person who deeply cares how you feel and will feel your disappointment while you tell the story.

BANX

" HE CAN'T WAIT TO GET OUTSIDE AND MAKE FIVE FRIENDS "

© *Jeremy Banx – BankxCartoons.co.uk*[348]

Logically deciding that someone is a friend is different from automatically triggered friendship emotions. S_F tension is the automatically felt feelings of a merged ally, or alliance, which logic has to repeatedly interpret and manage. Someone feeling tension will keep feeling concern about someone else's emotions even when they logically know they shouldn't care. Someone not feeling tension might logically want to feel friendship affection for another person, but feel nothing. S_F is just the feeling, regardless of the logic. The feelings and the logic are different things which can align or be in conflict.

> *"When we honestly ask ourselves which person in our lives mean the most to us, we often find that it is those who, instead of giving advice, solutions, or cures, have chosen rather to share our pain"*[349]

Later on, these emotions interrupt peaceful, calm moments that don't have external triggers. Pain happens again, triggered by the memory of a friend who is probably upset. No decision was made to think about the friend. In fact, most logic had decided it's just not worth being friends anymore. But the pain is so sharp that attention is fixated on someone who isn't present, feeling negative feelings that the friend might not even be having. Then friendship excitement strikes again, triggered by the memory of a different person. That person is a natural fit, they naturally care, they have obvious emotional investment and it's endearing to remember. The observer is alone, the actual exterior moment is quiet, but the observer is flushed with relief thinking about what a good person that friend is.

> *"19.5% have a friend they hang out with strictly out of obligation."*[350]

An S_F-first knows their friends might get excited or upset at any moment, and it will be striking if they do, so the S_F keeps making choices to protect their friends' feelings. The way to be present and available for the rest of life is to be with such good people, who are such connected friends that problems are automatically resolved quickly each time something comes up. Part of the immense value of friendships is that neither friend has to lose moments considering helping because both people flow as one unit automatically.

> *"Never explain.*
> *Your friends don't need it,*
> *and your enemies won't believe it anyway."*[351]

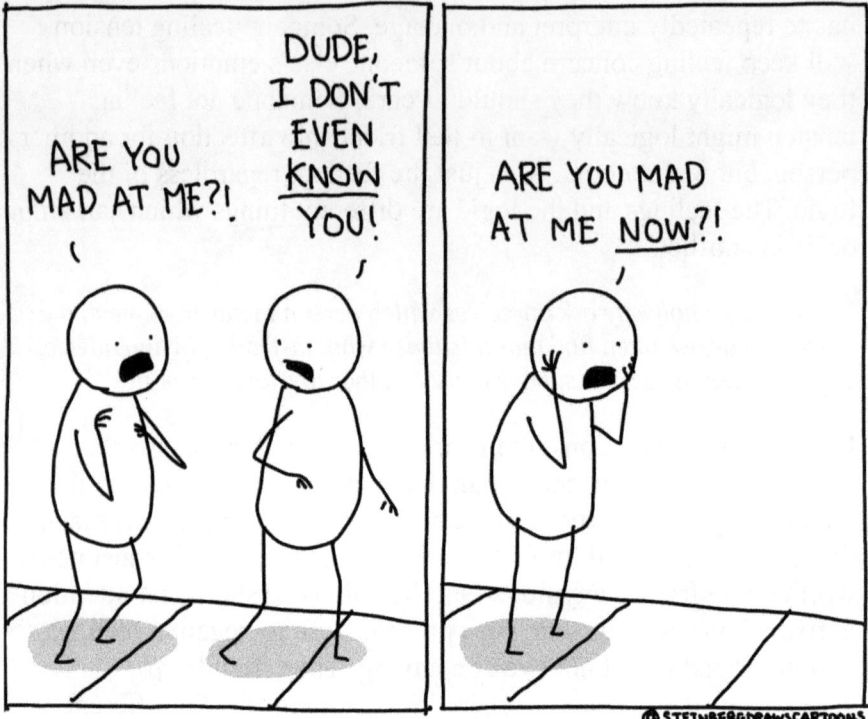

© *Avi Steinberg – SteinbergDrawsCartoons.com*[352]

S_F-firsts think that the friendship attraction they feel is helpful. They're motivated to find similar souls and form tight alliances with those people. They make better decisions about food, jobs, groups, health, sex, and experiences, because they prioritize how these impact the closeness of their friendships and the feelings of their merged allies. They have what other people have, plus really strong connections with really good people. Meanwhile, S_F-lasts only seem to have disadvantages. Most obviously, people who don't prioritize friendship are wrong to be so selfish. There's something critically broken about how their brain works. Lower S_F friends repel the good souls who sacrifice for them. Lower S_F friends have exaggerated anxiety fantasies about S_Fs attacking them when the S_F can't even imagine anything other than unconditionally loving them. Lower S_F friends would get way more from considering their friend as a friend, but instead get way less by considering what they can get for themselves at the friend's expense. S_F-lasts miss out on the best parts of life because they get distracted with things that don't matter. An S_F-first may not have a perfect life, but they've got the foundation. They've invested in relationships with good people, making a home in their merged connections.

S_Fs vary quite a bit in who and what sparks their friendship arousal and concern. Some are really dedicated to whoever they've known the longest, whoever calls them the most, or whoever demands the most attention. Some try to maintain friendships with everyone they recognize. Some target people they want to befriend. Some get overwhelmed caring for the people they already know. Some are more focused on being cheerful so they're always bringing other people up. Some are more focused on tighter connections with fewer people. S_Fs are accustomed to being told that they're overly focused on friendships with people who aren't being friends in return, but that's almost always advice from selfish people who are awful friends, who would be the first dropped if the advice to leave crappy friends were followed.

S_Fs think repeatedly feeling concern about how friends are doing, feeling obligated to make them happy, is just what life is. S_F-firsts think they're trying for a totally realistic, but admittedly high-level of friendship connection with particularly similar souls. But they determined that something is "realistic" by imagining something better than what they already encountered, or the best thing they ever encountered, while minimizing inextricable trade offs that come with those positives. The result is an underlying, recurring ache, an unfillable anxiety, a dissatisfaction with reality, because the "realistic" goal they need to hit to feel satisfied is just beyond what's actually possible.

S_F-Last: Living without Tension about Friendship-Based Pleasures and Pains

"No" is a complete sentence.[353]

At the lowest point on the S_F spectrum the emotions an ally is feeling and the connection available with that ally feel like something momentary which can be observed, rather than something automatically felt which fixates attention. Alliances are functional for satisfying other needs, and aren't happening to satisfy concern about the ally's mood. The emotions of allies feel more coincidental to the moment, which is obviously about something else (instead of the moment being focused on how sweet this other soul is, relief that they're happy, and relief when each others' emotions are automatically triggered). Alliances are logical arrangements based on benefits and costs.

When you don't feel excitement and joy from seeing an ally happy, and when you don't feel flushed with pain when a familiar person is upset, that unemotional-to-observe person is socially neutral to you. S_F neutrality isn't the result of a logical decision not to emotionally invest in another person. Neutrality isn't any thought at all. Every observer knows someone whose emotions don't feel like they matter, because no natural connection happened on its own. The interaction is practical, or emotional for a non-friendship reason. Attempts at emotional investment would feel forced and awkward. For an extreme S_F-last, that lack of emotional entanglement exists with all people. The actual experience of being at the extreme minimum is that it feels weird to even consider disconnected people's feelings and the "goodness of their soul," because those people's emotions are random and coincidental to moments. Other people's emotions only matter if the observer gets something they want or loses something as a result.

> *"Half the people that you think are your friends*
> *don't consider you their friend.*
> *And half the people that consider you their friend,*
> *you don't consider them friends."*[354]

When other people's emotions aren't automatically matched in an observer, alliances are still enjoyable and useful because of their affects on other tensions. Someone might be really impressive, validate the observer, and make the observer look good by association. Someone might have a sexy body and be hungry for sex. Someone might have resources, or provide comfort and safety. Someone might have access to thrilling experiences. Someone might provide entertainment, fun, information, or motivation. The ally and the alliance can still be emotional, but S_F isn't the emotion.

At the lowest point on the S_F spectrum, even very well known others with very long term interactions don't cause the observer to think about their emotions. The idea doesn't even come up to feel pain when they're hurting. The idea doesn't come to mind to feel joy when they're joyful. No relief is felt when they're relieved. The connectedness of alliances is something which is observed like any other fixed, external input. It doesn't have the feeling of being variable. The thought doesn't happen that it could or should be affected, might need rebuilding, or could be a source of joy if it were more connected. It might be disconnected at the moment. The function is therefore probably not available, so check back in later. From the inside, it feels like other people are so different that a merged connection just isn't possible. So all humans interact to fill each others needs. There is very little differentiation between very-well-known humans and completely unknown humans except in familiarity with the services each provides. It's not emotional to keep choosing the options which provide the best functions. Disconnections with other people are easy to avoid by doing things the obvious way, and not tragic if they happen.

"Almost all of our sorrows
spring out of our relations with other people."[355]

It feels like everyone is in charge of their own lives, making their own decisions, and getting the results of their decisions. Humans are sometimes happy, sometimes sad, sometimes anxious, sometimes relaxed. That is how humans are. When another person has a similar soul, has natural rapport, has similar interests and complementary skills, whatever alliance happens with that person feels momentary and unchangeable. If the two don't happen to become allies, that feels like the practical, noticed reality. Strong natural connections are pleasurable, but the naturalness of connections is what it is in each case. No closer-alliance is imagined, no joy is felt imagining it, so no hunger is sparked to increase the emotional investment of both partners.

If you could feel the process of turning yourself down in tension, you'd feel a silencing of the urgency felt when noticing other people's emotions. As a result, there's a natural acceptance of other people's negative emotions, a separation between self and others. Everyone already feels this with most people, an S_F-last just feels it with more, and maybe all people. It becomes obvious that other people's emotions aren't anything you can affect, and that the connection they want with you in return is random, momentary, and something you observe, not create. Focus reframes away from other people's feelings and the connection of the alliance and onto whatever other topic seems interesting to you at the moment.

My Friend Group

Ten Years Ago

Five Years Ago

Now

Without S_F, all humans, even very familiar humans, feel neutrally the same as any other humans. The hierarchy of people whose emotions you're managing disappears. There's no thought that positive friendship features could be combined, or that negative friendship features could be removed, or that mutual emotional investment could be even more extreme. All the adults in the room can easily ignore current affections while the meaningful task gets attention. Only the broken idiot will need to pause to make people happy first, and they'll look like an idiot while they do it.

"A friend to all is a friend to none."[356]

Now imagine that a very sexy option is giving you eyes. Imagine that you've been offered your dream job, with a huge raise, in a very impressive position. Imagine that a waiter just put a huge, gorgeous dessert in front of you. Imagine a reporter is interviewing you because you're an expert on a topic. For all humans, alliances aren't the topic of the moment while other meaningful life events are happening. S_F-last observers have more Comfort and Relational triggers connected to more drug intensity. No choice is being made to ignore the feelings of allies or the health of the connections with those allies. It's just not an alliance-focused moment, because it's obviously a critical Relational or Comfort moment (which happens to be a lot of moments).

Most S_F-lasts still can feel pleasure from sharing a moment with a shockingly similar soul, and feel bad about how they treated someone if they stop returning calls. But the experience of those is different when those events don't automatically trigger hunger for change and escalation. There was a moment of friendship-based pleasure or pain, that's just reality, and then the moment ended. The thought ends there. The observer can still look to the side and discuss a different topic. Pleasurable moments don't fixate the observer with hunger for even more emotional entanglement, even more friendship connection. The rest of reality isn't silenced. The observer's focus isn't distracted away from the moment with an internal fantasy of what life would be like if this friendship were completely merged, trusting, and supportive for the rest of time. Instead it seems weird that we're still talking about that moment when it was over long ago.

Choosing allies is different when none or almost none of the options feel like natural extensions of self. Someone being forced to choose among neutral options wouldn't feel obligated or smitten with similar souls to distract the choice away from logic. S_F-lasts see alliance options for what they actually provide, because they're not distracted with fantasies of the ally or the alliance being more important than it is. S_F-lasts know that alliances get closer and further apart, moment by moment. Alliances start and end. No part of that is emotional. When an S_F-last connects with a person, the trade-offs that come with that person aren't minimized. Instead, interactions with familiar humans more easily triggers self-protective feelings, sensory-protective feelings, resource-protective feelings, sexual-attraction-protective feelings, and life-experience-protecting feelings. Management of the alliance revolves around optimizing those other tensions.

> *"You can lay down for people to walk on you,*
> *and they will complain that you're not flat enough."*[357]

There are billions of ally options, constantly turning over, and the best you'll get out of any of them will be moments of happiness. Reality isn't fairy tales. If you pick a person based on who you recognize, or how long you've known them, that person is way less likely to be helpful than someone who has similar needs at the moment. If you let the relationship be a mess when it's a mess, then you're free to continue moving forward with the rest of life.

Instead, deviate slightly from reality in Relational and Comfort directions. Imagine having a romantic partner who flushes you with sexual energy because they're so beautiful. Imagine having a famous partner who gives you status just by standing next to you. Imagine getting the benefits of their wealth, connections, and lifestyle. Imagine living in comfort and abundance. Imagine someone who is already living your dream, who can help get you into your dream field. Meanwhile, the two of you are different types of humans. You're both getting something out of the relationship, something great even, but you don't naturally understand each other. Can you find a way to make this relationship happen anyway? Can the natural, merged connection of similar souls not happen, but the relationship still be worth investing in and even prioritizing? All relationships are this type of trade-off when no one is a naturally similar soul.

"My life improved dramatically when I gave up trying to have friends. I have no friends right now and am much happier, fulfilled, and more peaceful than I use to be. When you're around friends often you're much more likely to get swept up in their egos and dysfunctional patterns. When you're alone you're able to grow and evolve into a more natural and better human being more efficiently."[358]

A key part of being S_F-last is a presence to actual reality. S_F-lasts choose an ally out of the people they know right now, with none of the options being intoxicating because they all come with balancing drawbacks. That's actually not that many people to choose from, and it's pretty obvious who the best option is. They know they're signing up for a bunch of problems, but will protect themselves against being used. Then they don't need to revisit the question of who is an ally again until functional needs shift or the other person asks too much. When that happens, the S_F-last will choose the best of available options at that next moment, or choose to have no friends. Someone who is only choosing from present reality has very little to consider, and a mind that's free and available for other topics.

S_F-lasts have tried to get happiness from investing in someone who was investing in them, and they just got used, or their time got wasted. Alliances have moments of function and pleasure. Alliances don't have deeper meanings. Other people's feelings aren't a source of joy or disappointment in themselves. The meaning of life has to do with sex, experience, purpose, sensory pleasures, health, food, entertainment, good deals, and loving yourself. Emotionally connecting with another person is nice in the moments it happens too, but it's definitely less important than the rest of that.

a best friend will help you move bodies

but if you have to move your best friend's body you're on your own

a friend will help you move

© e horne and j comeau – asofterworld.com[359]

From the perspective of S_F-lasts, S_Fs only seem to have disadvantages. S_Fs complain about leachy, selfish allies while clinging to those same people. S_Fs seem inauthentic because they agree automatically, without thinking, when they actually disagree inside. S_Fs can't tell you how they feel because they're afraid of hurting your feelings or exposing differences. Just be real. Just be yourself. Say what you want. S_Fs get upset about disconnections which are totally normal. S_Fs think the person they're sacrificing for is feeling alliance love in return when they're actually feeling Relational or Comfort based pleasure. S_Fs overestimate how endearing a new ally will be. S_Fs passionately disregard reality, enthusiastically find ways to be unhappy with what exists, and make bad decisions among existing options. They seem to be unaware of real-world alliances, while thinking they're experts in real-world alliances. S_Fs keep contacting and hanging out with people where the relationship has died because the S_F is immersed in an individual exaggeration of the value of the other person's emotions. In critical moments, S_Fs sacrifice themselves, their health, comfort, safety, resources, sexual opportunities, and life purpose because they're distracted with protecting the emotions of a person who doesn't care about them in return. What S_Fs are actually experts at is wasting their lives being slaves to people who like attention, sex, and resources. Why would anyone want that life? An S_F-last has fewer allies, but those people know who the S_F-last is, and can either love them for it or go away. An S_F-last is optimized for the actual world.

"It is never a mistake to say goodbye."[360]

There is no disappointment to feel with real-world alliances or real-world allies. Emotional investment in other people comes and goes for everyone, and usually isn't present. The way alliances happens is fine. It's fine when known people are upset and anxious. There's no need for more, less, better, or different. It's still worth making sure that alliances get maintenance, but that maintenance can happen without tension and relief, without fixated daydreams, and without judging what's happening as good or bad. S_F-lasts are realistic about what they've got, what they get from it, what their options are, and what it costs. They're more present to the reality of alliances than S_F-firsts are. Part of what makes alliances valuable is that they don't need extra attention in order to do their function. If they're not happening naturally on their own then it's helpful for them to die. S_F-lasts live in the alliance satisfaction that S_F-firsts can't find, because S_F-lasts live in reality, undistracted by visions of not-reality.

Cross Overs

"I desire that we be better strangers."[361]

Most S_F-lasts can be flushed with the emotions of another soul, especially if that soul is a baby animal or sometimes their own child. Sometimes they can feel the emotions of their favorite human, or a human they really admire, especially when all of their own needs have been satisfied. But other people's emotions are felt with WAY fewer other souls, WAY less frequently, and satisfaction comes much faster just by realizing that those emotions are a fixed, momentary reality.

Even S_F-firsts feel socially neutral about most strangers, most birds, and most fish. Many times a day S_F-firsts interact with humans without feeling their emotions because those friendship options don't have arousal triggering cues. S_F-firsts can be distracted by other topics, even while interacting with someone whose emotions they usually feel, but have true neutral lack of emotional triggering in that moment. Even for an S_F-first, it feels like awkward, tedious work to try to generate a friendship fantasy about someone they feel no friendship attraction to.

Some friends you see every day,

and some friends you see when there's blood in the air.

You need both.

© e horne and j comeau – asofterworld.com[362]

S_F Conclusions

"Stop wallowing in the pain of missing people that you don't like."[363]

The addition of S_F means alliances aren't just functional anymore. Other people's words, actions, and returned friendship are loved, exciting, beautiful, and desirable, triggering excitement, joy, concern, disappointment, pain, and relief. S_F tension and relief aren't necessary for a system to form alliances. But friendship tension and relief add focus and incentive to seek out similarly directed humans and form more merged, more closely connected relationships with them. S_F drugging adds incentives to protect the qualities of their existing alliances which make them positively emotionally triggering.

"Stop being a safety net for people who keep making bad choices. It's not love. It's enabling."[364]

S_F-firsts have more merged relationships with more people because they invest so much time and energy in seeking out, building, and maintaining a feeling of shared love and appreciation inside their alliances. A consistent focus on friendship quality and quantity helps them seize opportunities to connect with another soul. They're constantly sacrificing for the benefit of the friendship connection they'll feel. But they're the least satisfied with their friendships because daily tension reminds them to focus on what's wrong and imagine and feel desire for better.

Easily Confused for the S_F Spectrum

"The hours we spent telling stories and laughing
reminded me both of how well we get along
and why seeing each other once a year is enough."[366]

This chapter compares S_F to the six other motivators one-by-one. It
holds the topic constant (friendship) and looks at it from each of the

seven perspectives so you can hear how each observer's experience of friendship is different when they're feeling different kinds of tension and seeking different kinds of relief from that relationship. This is the chapter to come back to when determining the relative influence of S_F versus any other motivator for a person.

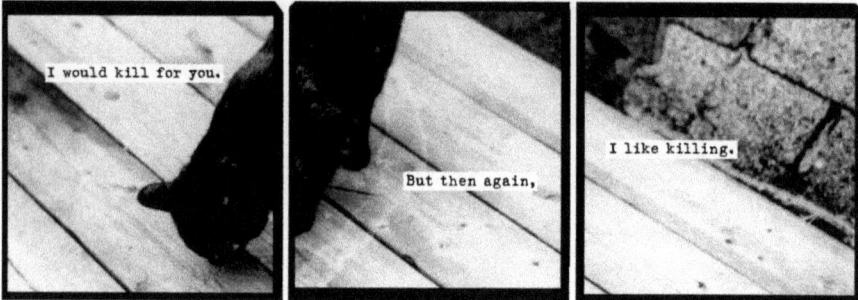

© *e horne and j comeau – asofterworld.com*[367]

Valuing Recognized, Familiar Humans While Feeling Friendship-Based Socialness (S_F):

An S_F starts out concerned about their friend's feelings. Maybe there's been a miscommunication. Maybe the friend had a desire that wasn't filled. The S_F has been cycling internally, wondering if their friend is upset at them and what they can do to restore the connection. But an S_F is also internally cycling on something selfish the friend did that makes them seem like not a good friend. If the other person doesn't care in return, then maybe the S_F is wasting their time investing in this friendship. Or maybe the S_F is cycling because the other person doesn't feel natural enough as a friend. The other person wants to be friends, they're willing to invest, but for some reason aligning with them feels neutral or negative.

Someone without tension can still gets lots of S_F pleasure directly from the presence of a similar soul, but then disconnects moment-by-moment when that person deviates in any other direction. As a result attention can quickly be refocused to another topic even when that friend has an unfilled desire or is hurting. Someone who is dominated by S_F **tension** will have a very hard time refocusing onto another topic if their ally is hurting, or if they can't emotionally connect with their ally, even if they're dragged into a new environment, because tension (anxiety) will hold focus on that friend internally, and keep returning focus to the friend, making reconnection feel critically important.

S$_F$s are focused on the friend. They feel love for the other person's soul. But they also expect that their sacrifices for the other person's benefit are strengthening a natural merged alliance, that the other person sees those sacrifices, recognizes the goodness of the observer's soul, and feels naturally emotionally connected to that goodness in return. Tension is automatically felt when that ally has a need, and satisfaction is automatically felt when that ally is satisfied. Being aligned with good souls is joyful and relieving.

© *Harry Bliss – HarryBliss.com*[368]

255

Valuing Recognized, Familiar Humans While Feeling Body-Based Comfort (C$_B$):

Familiar humans feel way safer than unfamiliar humans. Even if they're crabby and selfish, the known is easier to protect from, both physically and emotionally, than the unknown. But, also, being alone means being vulnerable. It's safer to have another person present, especially if someone is a protector who will confront attackers. Humans can bring physical and emotional pain in lots of ways. They can bring sensory discomforts in lots of ways. For someone who is already feeling sensory discomforts, who is already worried about being vulnerable and attacked, finding allies and being around those people is relieving. When the unknown or scary happens, an ally increases the chances of survival. So, there might still be tension when a friend is upset, but it's worry that the observer might be in danger, or worry that they no longer will be protected by the ally. A C$_B$ shows affection for friends by introducing them to sensory comforts, like warm, pleasant smelling beverages, peaceful sounds, and soothing visuals. Sensory comforts are valuable in themselves, so everyone can get joy from them. A C$_B$ helps others find peace and avoid stress.

> *"You don't get to choose if you get hurt in this world, but you do have some say in who hurts you."*[369]

Emotionally investing in other people's happiness makes the investor vulnerable, and distracts their attention away from the self-care that keeps them available for life in general. So it makes sense to protect and care for yourself first, so that you're available when someone else wants something.

A C$_B$ sometimes thinks they're feeling affection for certain friends and repulsion from other known humans because they're feeling the matched feelings of the ally, when, on closer inspection, they realize that they're feeling a relief of health, safety, and comfort tension because of certain people, and a threat of mental and physical damage because of other people. They're afraid for themselves and are resolving other people's tensions to make themselves feel safe again, rather than being fixated on concern about the other person's wellbeing, forgetting about self's comfort and safety, and focusing on making the other person feel relieved and happy again because that other person's happiness is so important in itself.

Valuing Recognized, Familiar Humans While Feeling Individuality-Based Comfort (C_I):

"When people cannot make friends, they often think very negatively about themselves, even if they have reason to be very positive about other aspects of their lives. There is an expectation that because we are animals for whom social relationships are important, then it must equally

follow that the more serious the social relationship, the better. But in a book reviewing comparative social psychology research, Terry Maple and I found considerable evidence that being a 'social animal' does not require emotionally intimate relationships like 'friendships.' You can gain all the benefits associated with social relationships just by having the ability to interact with other people. It is not necessary—although it might be nice—that any of those relationships meet the criteria of being 'friendships.' People tend to be happier if they feel they are competent in doing what they need to do and that they are successfully meeting their basic needs. Helping individuals find a path to feeling this way— regardless of whether they meet others' criteria for a 'successful' social life—can be one very effective way of helping them feel less lonely and more positive about themselves and their lives."[371]

My sister and I both hate antique shopping.

But we love hating things together.

© e horne and j comeau – asofterworld.com[372]

If you're hungry for impact, recognition, rank, attention, and excellence, but you're distracted by mistakes you made, missed opportunities, and feeling ignored, forgotten, and unfairly treated, then what qualities about a friend make you feel love for them? It's easy to love someone who is completely focused on you, who is feeling your feelings, explaining why you're right and why other people are wrong. It's easy to love someone who gives you status, who is skilled, excellent, achieving, and has chosen to focus those on you. It's easy to love a friend who is paying enough attention to be impressed and awed by your clever comments, who will listen and learn while you teach them, whose life you can have a positive impact on who doesn't win battles for dominance against you but wins them against others. It's disconnecting and negative when a friend is pathetic, weak, a loser, or makes you look pathetic by association. It's repulsive when someone is an arrogant jerk who keeps putting you down to raise themselves up, who tries to direct your actions as if they're in charge. It's disconnecting and negative when a friend pressures you to conform to the average, or thinks you should be a fan of what other people are fans of. C_Is often want to show that they're individuals who don't need others. But they really want an audience to admire their individuality for saying it, and they want friends who love them so much that they stick around anyway.

"Do something nice for someone.
Leave them alone."[373]

© *Joe Rothenberg – Joetatochips.com[374]*

"I don't buy that there's an afterlife, so I believe my only shot is to establish a set of relationships — with people who'll outlive me — that are singular. The best place to register purchase against this goal is with my children. Isn't that what we all want? To have people you love remember you as someone who, for them, there was no other. Someone they think of, often — your image, your smell, your mannerisms, your oddities. Singular. I hope they'll understand me. But more than understanding, I need them to miss me, terribly."[375]

Why should the C_I be the one investing in other people's emotions? Shouldn't it be the other way around? The C_I would love to have someone so excellent that they're worth investing in, but, whatever the best friendship is available is, that's what the C_I deserves.

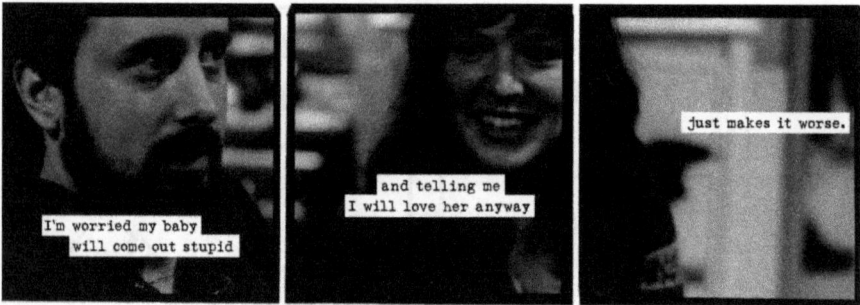

"Sometimes you put walls up not to keep people out, but to see who cares enough to break them down."[377]

"Crocodiles are easy. They try to kill and eat you. People are harder. Sometimes they pretend to be your friend first."[378]

"I like being alone. I have control. Therefore, in order to win me over, your presence has to feel better than my solitude. You're not competing with another person, you are competing with my comfort zones."[379]

"Remove the 'I want you to like me' sticker from your forehead and place it on the mirror, where it belongs."[380]

"When you're afraid of someone's judgment, you can't connect with them. You're too preoccupied with the task of impressing them."[381]

© Kelly Bastow[382]

261

C$_I$s want individual friends too, but they want someone who is worthy to be their friend, and almost no one is. A C$_I$ sometimes thinks they're feeling emotional investment in another individual because of S$_F$ when the tension and relief they're feeling are actually C$_I$. The C$_I$ is feeling impressed and impactful, rather than feeling a direct love for the goodness of the other person's soul. Or they're feeling good about themselves for making a friend feel good, rather than feeling good because the friend's happiness is joyful to observe in itself.

"I tell myself all the time that I am weak and pathetic. I strongly believe I am a bad person and that I don't deserve nice things. It's like a vicious cycle because the more I believe this, the more I do things I'm not proud of to try and get others to validate my self-worth, which drives them away and that makes me hate myself even more. The best way to break the cycle is to be nicer to myself. It's hard when I don't think I deserve it, but my therapist told me I have to force myself to show myself compassion even if I don't believe I should. Because the more I help myself, the more I'll develop my own sense of self-worth, which will make me better and lead to better relationships with other people. Because I don't like myself, I assume that no one else does either. I think if people are being nice to me, it's because they feel sorry for me. I'm constantly thinking that people are getting sick of me. I overreact to things because I take them as evidence that people don't like me and are going to leave me. I don't understand why anyone would want to be friends with me, but it's obvious that there are people who care about me, so they must see something in me that I don't see in myself."[383]

Valuing Recognized, Familiar Humans While Feeling Community-Based Socialness (S$_C$):

"In every community there is a form of justice and friendship. People address as friends their fellow voyagers and fellow soldiers, and so too, in return, those associated with them."[384]

S$_C$s feel the tension of the group, so they're flushed with fixating tension when the group is flushed with tension, making resolving the group's concerns focusing and then relieving. So S$_C$s notice each person's role in the greater organism and how well they fill that role. The group is more people, so of course its feelings matter more than those of any one individual. The good individuals are making small sacrifices so that the greater group is happier, and the bad individuals are taking individual benefits which add up to more hurt for others. Someone who is more S_C will feel more compelled to establish friendships with the influential group members, because those people have the most function for swaying the group, which is what's emotional. Someone who is more S_F will establish friendships with the people whose souls are individually most similar, because those people are so joyful to be near, and will feel less emotionally triggered by the feelings of the group as a whole.

It's easy to love a friend who fits seamlessly into the group, who causes the group to laugh, who easily sways the opinions of the group and selflessly uses that influence for the good of everyone. It's disconnecting and negative when a friend contradicts the group just to be different, plays devil's advocate just for attention, focuses on who they don't like in the group, uses influence selfishly, creates or promotes awkward situations, spreads toxic ideas that divide the group, or delights in watching other people hurt.

When someone loves a friend because of S_C, they appreciate a teammate who is dedicated to the common cause, who is mending disconnections, and selflessly adding love to the world. They're united by their membership in the greater group, their selfless dedication to the greater cause, but might not enjoy an evening spent with just that person. When S_C is a stronger motivator than S_F then the S_C would quickly drop the individual friend if that individual wanted things that made the group uncomfortable, whereas an S_F might leave the group with their ally because the friendship matters more.

Valuing Recognized, Familiar Humans While Feeling Sex-Based Relationalness (R_S):

If you're sexually aroused, and smitten with an angelic cutie, then what qualities about a friend make that friend feel valuable? It's easy to love a friend who is sexually attractive, sexually aroused, and anxious for the touching to start. It's easy to love a friend who has attractive friends who might be sexual partners, who helps attract sexual partners, and who creates and supports a sex-positive atmosphere. It's disconnecting and negative when a friend has a sexy body but has no interest in sex, when they don't feel sexual attraction, when they focus on the negatives of sex, when they criticize people who are sacrificing to be attractive, when they waste your time with sexually neutral humans or sexually neutral activities, and when they do things that drive away potential sexual partners.

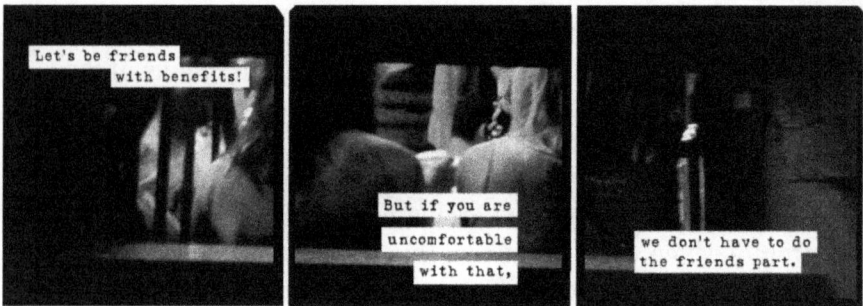

© *e horne and j comeau – asofterworld.com*[385]

When someone loves a friend because of R$_S$, they love the sexual compatibility with that person, or they love the access this person gives them to sex or sexual options. R$_S$s still want individual friends too, but they want someone who understands that they'll have to entertain themselves whenever sex with a cutie is an option. Or they can be that cutie. The R$_S$ observer loves a friend who repeatedly relieves their sexual tension. An R$_S$ is focused on relieving the sexual hunger that keeps dominating their attention, the same way that an S$_F$ is focused on relieving any possible emotional disconnections with friends that keep dominating their attention.

"Unless your friends have gotten back to back orgasms from me, don't let them advise you about me. They don't know."[386]

<u>Valuing Recognized, Familiar Humans While Feeling Experience-Based Relationalness (R_A):</u>

© *e horne and j comeau – asofterworld.com*[387]

If life is feeling stagnant and meaningless, if you're looking back at your life as if you're on your death bed, full of untapped potential, knowing you could do more, and hungry for newness, experience, and productivity, then what qualities about a friend make you feel love for them? It's easy to love a friend who will join in your adventure. It's easy to feel repelled from a friend who wants to waste time doing something unproductive. It's easy to love a friend who is chasing their dreams, surprising you with the new, extreme things they're accomplishing. It's disconnecting and negative when a friend worships their fear like a god, criticizes people taking risks, advocates stagnancy, reinforces inaccurate boundaries, and advises people not to try. When someone loves a friend because of R_A, having that friend is an extreme experience. The friend's constant motion relieves the R_A observer's tension and never creates it. Also, having a partner for death-defying activities is functional for safety.

> *"As soon as I saw you,*
> *I knew an adventure was going to happen."*[388]

An R_A sometimes thinks they're feeling natural alignment and direct love for another person's individual soul, when the alignment they're feeling is one of purpose, meaning, and action, rather than matched emotions based on the other person's happiness. If that person gets sad about an ex and keeps canceling activities then that person will feel like a burden because they're getting in the way of experience, rather than that someone who needs support because their feelings matter first.

Valuing Recognized, Familiar Humans While Feeling Resource-Based Comfort (C_R):

"Having many friends means we have many options to socialize, and thus no shortage of pleasurable human interaction. Friends allow us to share information about the world and our ideas, learn from their experiences, and help them with ours. Friends can lend us a helping hand, a listening ear, and words of advice in times of hardship. Also, being part of a social circle can open doors to opportunities like finding a partner. But having friends is no free ride. For many, an extensive social circle has become a luxury good. It comes with costs that not everyone is willing to pay. The first cost is time. Which, with our busy lives, is often a scarce commodity. Do we want to exchange the free time we have for the company of other people? The second cost is energy. We commonly practice friendship on the weekends which means that we spend the energy left after our work weeks on socializing. But many choose to spend that time in solitude to recharge. The third cost would be resources. Socializing requires money. Having no social life saves money. But also, a lack of funds refrains people from socializing, which could cause social isolation among the impoverished. The fourth cost is more hidden, but still a price we pay when we engage in social interaction. Friendships require conformity. Consciously or subconsciously we wish to be liked by our friends, and vice versa, and meet mutual expectations. Thus we present ourselves to appease them. We sweep unwanted characteristics under the carpet. So we pay the price of wearing a mask among our friends, not showing the entirety of ourselves, afraid that we'll fall out of favor."[389]

If you're distracted with loss, lack, and concern about money, food, taste, acquisition, consumption, and entertainment then what qualities about a friend make them feel like valuable resources? It's easy to love a friend who is entertaining, who has knowledge that's useful, who is well stocked with great snacks, who has tools that are helpful, who has their own money, who knows about good deals, and who is happy to help you. It's disconnecting and negative when a friend wrecks your stuff, wastes your money, feels entitled to your stuff, expects unfair trades, and expects you to be the entertainment.

"There is nothing better than a friend.
Unless it is a friend with chocolate."[390]

© *Ben Zaehringer – BerkeleyMews.com[391]*

Sometimes people really are feeling love or disconnection from a friend, but it's because of abundance, entertainment, and opportunities, instead of direct love for personal similarities and the happiness the other person is feeling. It's still affection for a specific human, but it's resource tension and relief rather than fixated investment in the other person's happiness.

> *"To get the full value of joy,*
> *you must have someone to divide it with"*[392]

A C$_R$ is focused on relieving the hunger, boredom, and lack that keeps dominating their attention, the same way that an S$_F$ is focused on relieving their repeated concerns that their friend isn't similar enough to generate enough joy from being in that friendship.

© *Jim Benton – JimBenton.com*[393]

C$_R$: The Resource-Based Tension Spectrum

"Why is being alive so expensive?
I'm not even having a good time."[395]

Resource-based Comfort (C$_R$) tension adds a focusing need for escalation or repair, paired with relieving satisfaction to the consideration of resources, consumption, acquisition, and the sensation of taste. Feeling tension triggered by resources focuses attention on food, eating, money, conserving, appraising, acquiring, and using resources. Resources aren't just functional anymore.

They're now loved, and pain, joy, tension, and satisfaction happen because of them. Each person is somewhere on the spectrum from being frequently triggered with very strong tension about resources (being flushed with joy by a good deal, by qualities that make items valuable, by huge amounts of value, by tasty foods, by windfalls of wealth, or pain as items get scratched, used up, broken, become valueless, or are thrown away), t o being infrequently triggered with weak or no tension about resources (observing resources for what they are without additional hunger for acquisition or consumption).

The Resource Pleasure Spectrum

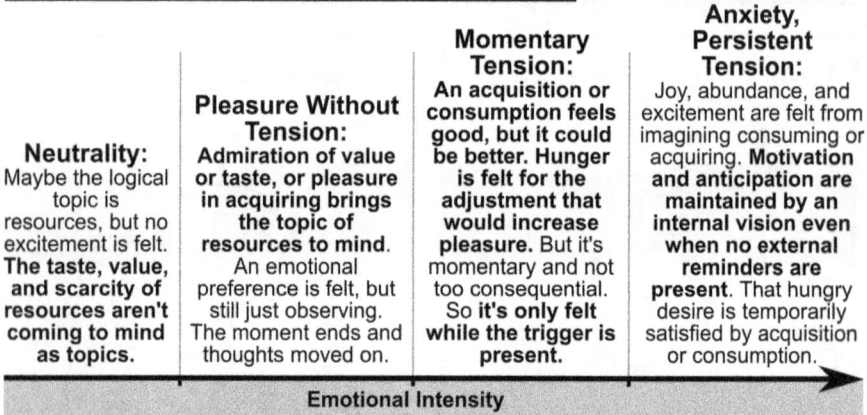

Neutrality:	Pleasure Without Tension:	Momentary Tension:	Anxiety, Persistent Tension:
Maybe the logical topic is resources, but no excitement is felt. The taste, value, and scarcity of resources aren't coming to mind as topics.	Admiration of value or taste, or pleasure in acquiring brings the topic of resources to mind. An emotional preference is felt, but still just observing. The moment ends and thoughts moved on.	An acquisition or consumption feels good, but it could be better. Hunger is felt for the adjustment that would increase pleasure. But it's momentary and not too consequential. So it's only felt while the trigger is present.	Joy, abundance, and excitement are felt from imagining consuming or acquiring. Motivation and anticipation are maintained by an internal vision even when no external reminders are present. That hungry desire is temporarily satisfied by acquisition or consumption.

Emotional Intensity →

Terminology & Abbreviations

Resource **neutrality** happens when considering a resource with no features which match the observer's arousal triggers. Neither excitement nor concern are triggered, even if the observer focuses on the item and tries to think of consuming it, not-consuming it, acquiring it, or throwing it away. Most people feel resource-triggered neutrality when considering the air they're breathing, clouds, or leaves on passing trees (things that are already plentiful and free). When starting from a neutral mind, it feels like a change of topic to then start considering excitement or concern about consuming or acquiring. It feels like a change of topic to start coming up with reasons why throwing it away might be negative. It doesn't feel like there's a reason to make the moment about resources because a normal motion with normal resources is happening.

Resource-based Comfort **pleasure with̲o̲u̲t̲ tension** is momentary, practical joy which comes from recognition of good food taste, enjoyable entertainment, fun, money, and qualities that make a resource valuable. Something has a joy-generating quality that gives you a preference for it over something else. Pleasure without tension is felt when you compare which continent you'd prefer to own, as long as you don't then cycle in hunger to actually own one. That moment was part of the normal world. Nothing needs to be done and thoughts quickly move on to the next topic.

Resource-based Comfort **pleasure w̲i̲t̲h̲ tension** is a feeling of hunger, desire, and excitement about food, money, entertainment, items, acquisition, or consumption that wants something to happen. A pleasurable opportunity is present that will make resource pleasure even greater. Tension is felt while still waiting, while the pleasurable adjustment hasn't happened yet.

- **M̲o̲m̲e̲n̲t̲a̲r̲y̲ pleasure tension** (externally triggered tension) is a hungry noticing of resources, but where the tension only exists while the trigger is present. It's what it feels like to smell delicious food and become excited, joyful, and focused on eating. A deal looks so good that the observer hungers for acquisition. There might be supporting logic, but the pleasure and tension are independent of logic. It's a feeling of lack, a feeling of hunger, which seeks the feeling of satisfaction. It's pleasurable excitement. But it's also small enough that the whole moment passes as soon as the trigger isn't present anymore, and will be forgotten even if the pleasurable adjustment doesn't happen.

- **Anxiety, persistent pleasure tension** (internally maintained tension), is hunger for resources escalation which persists even when the external trigger is removed. It is resource acquisition or consumption fantasy. The hunger is held in place by internal visions of acquisition or consumption and excitement is felt to

271

make it happen. Persistent, positive resource tension is the feeling of craving. It's what it feels like when anticipating really excellent entertainment. The opportunity to acquire or consume is fixating because it's going to be so good when it happens.

The Resource Pain Spectrum

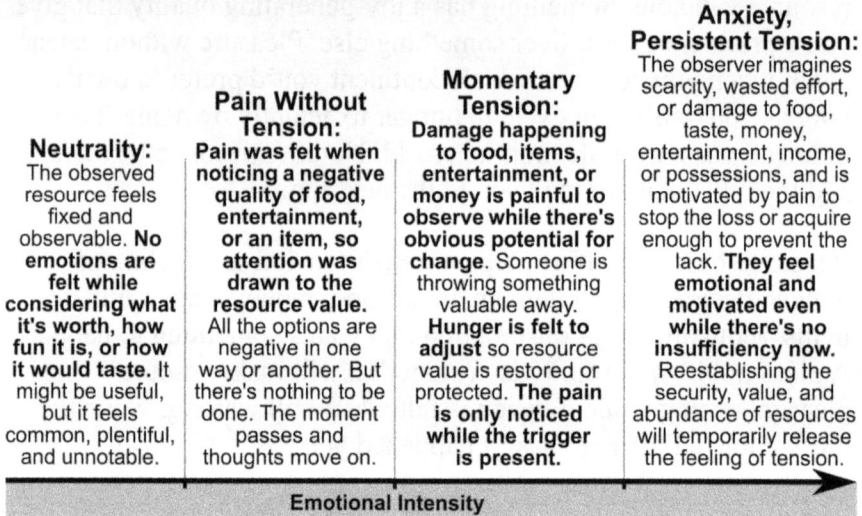

Neutrality:	Pain Without Tension:	Momentary Tension:	Anxiety, Persistent Tension:
The observed resource feels fixed and observable. **No emotions are felt while considering what it's worth, how fun it is, or how it would taste.** It might be useful, but it feels common, plentiful, and unnotable.	**Pain was felt when noticing a negative quality of food, entertainment, or an item, so attention was drawn to the resource value.** All the options are negative in one way or another. But there's nothing to be done. The moment passes and thoughts move on.	**Damage happening to food, items, entertainment, or money is painful to observe while there's obvious potential for change.** Someone is throwing something valuable away. **Hunger is felt to adjust** so resource value is restored or protected. **The pain is only noticed while the trigger is present.**	The observer imagines scarcity, wasted effort, or damage to food, taste, money, entertainment, income, or possessions, and is motivated by pain to stop the loss or acquire enough to prevent the lack. **They feel emotional and motivated even while there's no insufficiency now.** Reestablishing the security, value, and abundance of resources will temporarily release the feeling of tension.

Emotional Intensity →

Resource-based **pain with<u>out</u> tension** is pain felt about the realistic negatives of resources, money, food, and taste in an imperfect world. It's passive recognition that a resource has aspects that are painful to observe, but in a small, fixed way that doesn't hold attention for more than a moment. All the food options aren't very good, all the clothes options are wrinkled, you got a bite that tasted bad, but it's just life and thoughts move on. It's emotional recognition that a resource quality is negative, but with acceptance that it's how it is, rather than with hunger to fix it. Thoughts easily switch to an unrelated topic.

Resource-based **pain <u>with</u> tension** is a sharp feeling of lack, heartbreak, or defensiveness on behalf of resources, which makes them feel insufficient, threatened, decreasing, damaged, or disappointing. A resource quality is negative and it shouldn't be, it should change. The observer is hungry for an adjustment that would make the pain stop.

- **Momentary pain tension** (externally triggered tension) is felt on indications that food, entertainment, items, or money are missing positive emotional triggers or contain unwanted negative triggers. Someone goes to throw something away and feels tension, and thinks that maybe this item shouldn't be discarded. They start putting effort into something and feel tension, like maybe this is a waste of effort. They start drinking water and feel tension, thinking maybe they should drink something with flavor. They pick an item off the shelf and realize the one they picked up is dented and feel tension, thinking maybe they should get the next box instead. It's momentary because an action is taken or not taken, and the moment passes and is forgotten.

- **Anxiety, persistent pain tension** (internally maintained tension), is concern about decreases in money, taste, food, items, or entertainment which continues even when those items aren't present. The concern is held in place by internal visions of shortages, losses, disappointments, lack, theft, and of starvation. Resource tension causes people to imagine losing their job, losing their savings, or society's resources crumbling even while all of those are fine. That negative tension doesn't need external triggers to hold it in focus, because an internal prediction of increasing or persisting scarcity holds it in focus. Much of the time, it's an underlying ache, thinking resources might not be enough, that food might not be enough, that entertainment won't be enough, or that money won't be enough. It can also feel like regret about not acquiring or consuming in the past, or of buying the wrong item when a better option was available. But it's not just logical recognition. This feels like a problem. It feels like it should've been different or might get worse. It feels like the observer will keep cycling in negative tension about resources until some action is taken that restores abundance.

Resource-based **satisfaction** is a feeling of relief which comes from acquiring or consuming, through completion of resource predictions (which don't always technically acquire or consume), through verifying that the emotionally triggering qualities of the observed were a mistake (the resource isn't actually valuable, has negative qualities that weren't obvious at first, or wasn't actually threatened), and sometimes just from acquiring or consuming the best available option (when the observer isn't actually excited or disappointed by any of the options). Re source-based satisfaction comes with eating to completion, from laughing, from enjoying entertainment, from making things tastier, and from acquiring items or money. It comes from pulling something back out of the trash and putting it in a safe place. Things were tense, but then acquisition or consumption happened. Nothing needs attention or action anymore. The mind is free again. Thoughts can move on to other topics.

The shorthand for people who are triggered with Resource-based Comfort tension and anxiety more often and strongly than the other tension and anxiety options is that these people are "**C_R-first**." When a reference is made to "a C_R," or "C_Rs," it's identifying the discussed person or people as being C_R-first.

The shorthand for people who are triggered more strongly and frequently by all six other tension options is that people are "**C_R-last**." Someone who is C_R-last can still feel feel C_R **pain** and **<u>pleasure</u>** quite strongly, but resources more often feel objectively noticeable in a fixed way, and less often fixate attention with concern that they need adjustment. Any tension that is felt is more likely to be Relational tensions which are hungry for escalations of purpose, thrill, or sexual arousal, or Social tensions which want resources that pleasure and satisfy others.

We'll now immerse in the life experience people have when they're most frequently struck by Resource-based tension to see what it's like to live at the highest end of this spectrum. Then we'll immerse in the life experience of people who are rarely or never struck with Resource-based tensions to see what it's like when resources are a practical concern because the consumption and acquisition qualities don't trigger emotions.

C_R-First: Frequently Triggered Strong C_R Tension

> *I think about how little money I have left all the time. No matter how many times I make it from day to day, I still feel afraid of running out. I never feel like I have "enough" money. If I don't feel like I am getting*

enough food, I will not only focus on getting food, but when I do,
I will see it as precious and must either eat it quickly or hide it for later.
I'm putting myself into survival mode before it is even necessary."[396]

Being C$_R$-first means feeling emotions before logic has had a chance to evaluate an input. C$_R$-firsts are stabbed with pain when they watch their possessions getting scratched. **The observers aren't getting scratched, but they feel pain as if the damage were happening to themselves.** Was the pain a response to logic? No. C$_R$-firsts don't logically assess the functional or replacement value and then make a logical choice to feel pain in this situation. They can't logically choose to feel pain on command from other logical negatives which don't trigger the feeling. The pain happens automatically and simultaneously with the observation of valued resources being damaged. Logic is used after the feeling to explain why the loss is tragic enough to justify the pain felt.

"I can't just do water. I need flavor.
After four or five waters it becomes torture to me."[397]

The same observers are then flushed with pleasure when they smell a freshly baked dinner. All focus is immediately drawn to the pleasurable qualities of that food. Is the pleasure and hunger felt a response to logic? No. C$_R$-firsts don't logically assess the nutrition, scarcity, and function of the food, the current nutritional needs of their bodies, and then make a logical choice to feel positivity from this nutrition source. They can't logically decide that kale and plain water generate that euphoria spike instead, even when they'd provide better nutrition. Logic is used after the feeling to explain why that food and that consumption are important.

"Eat whatever you want.
If anyone tries to lecture you about your weight,
Eat them too."[398]

The third feeling which really cements these in as world creating is that C$_R$-first observers can tolerate much bigger problems in other areas without getting triggered with focused hunger for change. Friendships are suboptimal, but not enough pain is triggered to make it feel like action is needed. Humans are misunderstanding each other, but that's just how it is right now. Life has gotten pretty repetitive, but not so much that anything needs to be done about it. Sensory comforts aren't ideal, but they're not so painful that they require action. The observer isn't flushed with self love at the moment, but that's okay. The current sexual situation isn't particularly attracted, but there's nothing to be done about it. These topics aren't coming to mind because they're within the ranges of pain where they're not a problem that needs attention because this observer isn't triggered with tension about them at these levels. They feel like normal parts of how life is.

© *Mackenzie Moore – CinimomoComics*[399]

At the highest end of the C_R spectrum, observers are drugged with much more resource-triggered arousal and heartbreak while observing way more food, resource, money, and entertainment options. But it doesn't feel individual and it doesn't feel internal. It feels like objective recognition that the world has strikingly valuable foods, items, money, and entertainment. It feels like objective recognition that resources are limited and vital. At the highest setting, about one in 20 consumption, acquisition, and entertainment options are sharply attractive. It's shocking how great they are. The observer is intoxicated and fixated. There is no way to look at the features and not desire acquisition or consumption.

That desire feels like a response to value. In order to feel even more positive tension, how can the desired input be made even more valuable? How can the food be made even tastier? How can monetary value be dramatically increased? How can entertainment be even more fun? The tension turns painful as the opportunity starts to slip away. Are the last ones being purchased by someone else? Is the seller trying to switch you to something that isn't valuable? Did someone scratch the one you were looking at? Is it not as tasty as it looked? C_Rs don't want to think about resource-triggered attraction again, but a critical life moment came up on its own which requires action or regret.

> *"When a normal person 'feels like a million bucks,' they feel great. When a billionaire feels like a million bucks, they feel awful."*[400]

Half of what makes resource-based feelings feel objective is that so many resource-related inputs inspire no arousal, even for C_R-firsts. No tension, happiness, sadness, or relief are felt on behalf of average, plentiful foods that don't match the observer's tastes. Many cars, buildings, foods, and items pass by without drawing attention and hunger for acquisition. There are so many resources which don't automatically trigger sharp emotions, that the ones which do trigger excited desire or painful concern must be important. It makes logical sense to not eat tasteless foods when the world has so many strikingly-tasty options.

> *"I don't understand why I'm supposed to hate my belly. I quite like my belly. It's full of things I love."*[401]

Tension events alternate with being released again when C_Rs get satisfaction, which is usually the completion of consumption or acquisition. Each day is a tug-of-war between neutral availability of focus for any thought and fixated resource-triggered craving, concern, boredom, or disappointment. The emotional problems in life happen when a resource-triggered opportunity appears but doesn't end in satisfaction. You forgot to bring the necessary tool with you. The good snacks are gone. An item is lost, stolen, or out of stock. The bank account is already negative. This was a moment when joy could've happened, and instead it's a moment of recognition of the pain caused when a resource isn't present.

© *Jim Benton – JimBenton.com*[402]

The core of C_R-first is recognition that ***excitement and pain are both dominantly triggered by resources***. The feeling of joy-tension is a love of taste, a love of fun, a love of abundance, a love of entertainment, a love of laughing, a love of acquisition, and a love of consumption. If you dropped all judgment and distraction and really let yourself feel the pleasure of pure resource-triggered arousal, not clouded by any other feeling, what would you focus on? What tastes do you love the most? How much money would it take to make you feel really lucky and joyful? What outrageous item could you inherit which would make you feel flushed with joyful luck? What entertainment option would be the most gloriously satisfying to enjoy? What scenario of extreme abundance and consumption would flush you with the most happiness? Can you immerse in that fantasy enough to feel some of that pleasure now?

> *"Me at 14: 'I can't wait to travel the whole world*
> *once I'm earning money.'*
> *Me now: 'Mustn't forget that sandwich container at work.'"*[403]

Then feel the tension while imagining a stranger looking in your windows as you drive away from your house. Think about how much you love your stuff and how much pain you'd feel if things were stolen. Use your logic to imagine how that damage could happen and what you can do to stop that imaginary scenario. Take those actions and feel the relief of having protected your resources. Then recognize that the whole emotional cycle of pain, concern, and relief happened in your head, with no external threat happening at all.

Someone feeling resource anxiety will keep feeling tension even if they logically don't want to feel it. They might truly, logically not want to be in love with pepperoni pizza, but it keeps coming to mind over and over. Someone not feeling tension won't feel tension even if it would be logically helpful. An observer might truly, logically want to eat health foods, but they don't feel the cravings for it which would be helpful. An observer might logically know something is valueless, but feel too much tense loss to throw it away. The logic and the feelings about resources are sometimes aligned, but can also be different from each other.

© Jim Benton – JimBenton.com[404]

Later on, emotions interrupt peaceful, calm moments that don't have external triggers. Pain happens again, triggered by the memory of watching the item get scratched. No decision was made to think about that again. In fact, most logic knows it's done and over now. But sharp pain is experienced again. Then resource-triggered arousal strikes again, triggered by the memory of the pizza. The observer is alone. The actual exterior moment is quiet. But the observer is flushed with love, excitement, and desire.

Since tension could be triggered at any moment, C_Rs preemptively take actions to maintain their resource options, valuable qualities,

280

and resource escalation skills (shopping, saving, and negotiating). Even when situations aren't resource related, a C_R-first knows the situation might trigger resource tension, and it will be striking if it does, so they keep making choices to protect their options. In a perfect world, C_Rs would be surrounded by abundance, wealth, and acquisition opportunities. In the real world, they eat and drink a lot, bring too many supplies with them, and have trouble throwing things away.

"Price is what you pay. Value is what you get."[405]

C_R-firsts think that the resource-triggered attraction they feel is helpful. They're motivated to feed themselves, to eat more delicious foods, to find better deals, to find better items, to acquire more, and to throw away less. They make better decisions about jobs, friends, groups, health, experiences, sex, and life purpose because they prioritize how these impact the resource-triggered arousal they feel. They have what other people have, plus striking happiness from optimized resources.

"Ordering fish in a restaurant
is for people who don't care about happiness."[406]

Meanwhile, C_R-lasts only seem to have disadvantages. It seems like a basic lack of intelligence when they don't recognize the value involved while consuming, not-consuming, acquiring, and throwing away. Lower C_R friends could eat more of tastier foods. They could make more money while exerting less effort. They're wasting money on leachy friends, leachy groups, dysfunctional sexual relationships, and needlessly expensive experiences. C_R-lasts have skills that could make money which they're giving away for free. They have opportunities to acquire and consume that they're ignoring. They don't get to know their purchase options before purchasing, and throw away things that still have value. C_R-lasts settle for lower quality items when they could have euphoric, satisfying options instead. C_R-lasts miss out on the best parts of life because they get distracted with things that don't matter. A C_R-first may not have a perfect life, but they've got the foundation. They've amassed really striking resources with minimized outflows, are present to resource opportunities, and are skilled at engaging resource-related options. A C_R's life is optimized for actual reality.

CINNAMON ROLL EATING STYLES
@cinimomocomics

OPTION #1: TAKE A BITE	OPTION #2: UNROLL THE ROLL

© *Mackenzie Moore - CinimomoComics*[407]

C_{RS} vary quite a bit in what sparks their resource attraction and sharp feelings of lack. Some focus on spending as little as possible. Some focus on acquiring as much as possible. Some focus on exerting as little effort as possible. Some focus on being entertained as constantly as possible. Which specific foods, items, entertainment, and stores of monetary value seem the most valuable vary wildly between C_{RS}. C_{RS} are accustomed to being told that they eat too much by people who want pleasureless lives.

> *"Carl had such a profound sense of loss, that he couldn't bear to lose even the most insignificant item. He had this intense feeling that he had missed some crucial opportunity. So now it was impossible for him to throw anything away, because he had this feeling that if he threw it away, that he would need it the next day, and he'd miss that next opportunity too."*[408]

C_Rs think repeatedly feeling hungry, thirsty, bored, and lacking (money or items) is just what life is, and that those feelings are reactions to objective lack, objective negativity, and objective positive value. C_R-firsts think they're trying for a totally realistic, but admittedly high-level of abundance, entertainment, food quantity, and food taste. But they determined that something is "realistic" by imagining something better than what they already encountered, or the best thing they ever encountered, while minimizing inextricable trade offs that come with those positives. The result is an underlying, recurring ache, an unfillable anxiety, a dissatisfaction with reality, because the "realistic" goal they need to hit to feel satisfied is just beyond what's actually possible.

C_R-Last: Living without Tension about Resource-Based Pleasures and Pains

"The things you own, end up owning you."[409]

At the lowest point on the C_R spectrum the attractiveness of foods, items, entertainment options and even monies feels like something fixed which can be observed, rather than something variable which might change. Resources feel like something functional which are used, and less like satisfaction themselves for an already-existing hunger. Resources feel coincidental to the moment, which is obviously about something else (instead of being focusing, as if the moment was about the enjoyable qualities of the resource).

When food, items, money, or entertainment happen to be present and you don't notice them, those inputs are resource-value neutral to you. Most people can feel the impact of C_R drugging when they look at what's left of the food they just filled themselves with. It was good, but no desire is felt to eat more. The same food that fixated attention twenty minutes earlier can now be ignored while a conversation about a different topic happens.

Resource neutrality isn't rejection. It's not a consideration of value and a logical decision that something is valueless. It's not any thought at all. Resource neutrality is a lack of resource-triggered attraction, concern, or disappointment which would distract and refocus attention away from another topic and onto consumption and acquisition. Even more, resource neutrality is a lack of resource-triggered arousal and heartbreak even when someone brings up the topic of resources. No need is felt to acquire the seller's item, even when its benefits are listed.

As C_R-triggers reduce in number and drug intensity (moving down the C_R spectrum) fewer items, food options, entertainment options, and money options trigger the observer to feel excitement, hunger, desire, concern, and lack. If you could feel the process of turning yourself down in tension, you'd feel a reduction in the feeling of scarcity about food and items, a silencing of the urgency felt when noticing that a food, item, or entertainment option has positive or negative qualities. You could talk about foods without generating cravings for them. Neutral resources feel plentiful, common, and ignorable unless they were already needed by another task of the moment. It's emotionless to discard neutral items. A neutral item can still have recognized, logical value, but there's plenty of it, there always will be, and it's not needed at the moment.

To someone who experiences most inputs as resource-neutral, it feels like the taste of foods is fixed, observable, and limited to the options available. The cost of items is fixed and limited to what's available. The amount of money available is fixed and what it is. There's no imagination of different or better versions of any of those to compare reality to and feel lack. There's no imagination of better prices to make the actual prices feel painful. No better taste or bigger paycheck is imagined to make reality feel insufficient. A lack of tension leaves a mind present to existing reality, working from there without feeling like anything about present reality is "wrong" and "needs to change." There's no thought that positive features could be combined, or that negative features could be removed, or that good things could be even more extreme. The best is chosen of what's available and thoughts move on. Loss and lack are easy to avoid by doing things the obvious way, and not tragic if they happen. All the adults in the room can easily tune out the details of the resources being used while the meaningful task gets attention.

Only the broken idiot will get distracted from the task because they're lamenting how a different tool would've been helpful.

Most of the time, the option of being obsessed with fixation about the tastiness of a food, or the price or scarcity of an item isn't even considered until someone else is freaking out. Yes, owning a private island would be nice. No, I didn't consider that until you mentioned it. No, my current life doesn't feel lacking because I don't have one.

> *"Diogenes proved to the later satisfaction of the Stoics that happiness has nothing whatsoever to do with a person's material circumstances, and held that human beings had much to learn from studying the simplicity and artlessness of dogs, which, unlike human beings, had not complicated every simple gift of the gods."*[410]

Everyone has been given purchase opportunities that feel neutral. The item doesn't have any qualities that inspire the observer to imagine being delighted while using it. Everyone has also thrown something away and not been stabbed with sentimental or painfully wasteful heartbreak about it. Not being emotionally triggered doesn't mean that C_R-lasts can't recognize a good deal when someone points it out. But C_R-lasts sometimes miss deals that passed right in front of them, because their mind was elsewhere. And, they don't feel extra euphoria from the goodness of the deal on top of the practical, logical benefit of the deal. For an extreme C_R-last, all items, all foods, all entertainment, and all monies aren't emotionally triggering. The actual experience of being at the extreme minimum is that it feels weird to even consider attraction, excitement, tragic heartbreak, obsession, and relief about resources, because the options are so not-emotional. It's the same as considering which blade of grass you want to fall in love with. Why would an intelligent person feel emotions about items, food, or money?

Now imagine you're in a store and a breathtaking hottie comes over and asks your opinion to help choose between two purchase options. Imagine that cutie is wearing something that you recognize as being connected to your group, something that most people wouldn't even notice. You ask their name and realize that you have mutual friends.

This is someone you've heard good stories about. You say something that's not particularly funny, but they laugh in an endearing, adorable way. In that moment, you see this person pausing to really look at your face. For all humans, resources aren't the topic of the moment while other meaningful life events are happening. C_R-last observers have more Relational and Social triggers connected to more drug intensity. So smaller triggers for those tensions will make the moment feel like it's escalating in a meaningful Social or Relational direction. No choice is being made to ignore resources. It's just not a resource-related moment, because it's obviously a critical Social or Relational moment. For C_R-lasts, this is most moments.

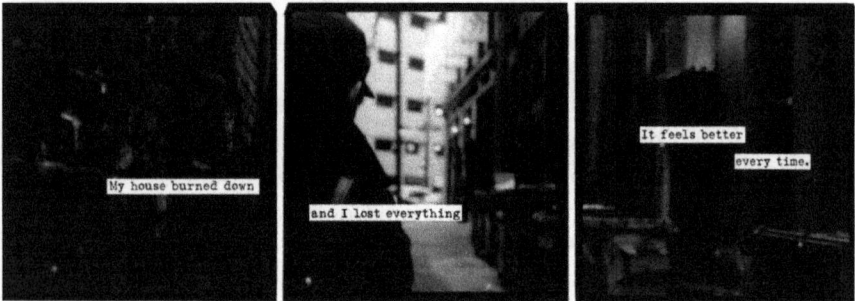

© *e horne and j comeau – asofterworld.com*[411]

Choosing resources is different when none or almost none of the options inspire attraction, excitement, or desire. C_R-lasts can see that one option is shinier and has more features than another, but that's not so intoxicating that the trade offs get minimized. Someone being forced to choose among neutral options wouldn't have feelings of arousal and heartbreak to help with the choice (to distract the choice away from logic), or to make them feel especially lucky if they got certain options. C_R-lasts see resource options for what they really are, because they're not afraid of losing attraction, or in love with the emotional qualities of any option. C_R-lasts consider the resource options actually present, which they can afford, with none of the options being intoxicating because they all come with balancing drawbacks. They choose the best fit and then they never revisit the question again. C_R-lasts easily throw things away when they're not functionally useful anymore.

Most C_R-lasts still can feel pleasure from eating something sweet, and pain from eating something that tastes bad. But the experience of those is different when those events don't automatically trigger hunger for change and escalation. There was a moment of taste, acquisition, consumption, or monetary pleasure or pain. That's reality. And then the moment ended. The thought ends there. The observer can still look to the side and discuss a different topic. Pleasurable moments don't fixate the observer with hunger for more taste, consumption, acquisition, or money. The rest of reality isn't silenced. The observer's focus isn't distracted with an internal fantasy of what life would be like if every taste were delicious, if consumption, acquisition, and money were endless. Instead it seems weird that we're still talking about that moment when it was over long ago.

Meanwhile, those same foods, items, entertainment, and monies more easily trigger sexual-attractiveness protective feelings, life purpose protective feelings, friendship-protecting feelings, and group-harmony-protecting feelings. Soap is soap. Cars are cars. Houses are houses. If you're managing a life where you're easily triggered by Social and Relational concerns, it's worth disqualifying resource options which might trigger Social or Relational tensions. Then choose the shiniest or tastiest from whatever makes it through those Social and Relational filters.

There's plenty of food in the world. The healthy stuff doesn't taste as good and what tastes good is less healthy. There are plenty of resources in the world. There will be all the housing, transportation, clothing, and food you need tomorrow if you do the absolute basics of maintaining them. Your body could easily go for the next two weeks without food and most people would be healthier at the end of that. Reality isn't fairy tales. If you pick food based on taste, you're going to damage your body. If you pick your items based on shine, you'll pay more for the same thing, and use it less than you predicted. The vast majority of possessions would be more valuable thrown away than they are taking up space. If you look for reasons to be unhappy with your resources, you can find reasons. If you pick the best resource option you've got, absolutely decide that you're going to make it work, and release the question forever, then you're free to enjoy life.

Instead of seeking resource based pleasure, deviate slightly from reality in Social and Relational directions. Imagine having a romantic relationship with someone with attractive features, to the degree that you feel especially lucky to have sexual contact with that beauty. Imagine that the two of you really are best friends who look out for each other and operate like two halves of one whole. Imagine that the two of you have found a group of like-minded people who truly care for each other and do interesting things together. Imagine feeling inspired by the actions you take, inspired by the work you do, inspired by the relationships you have, so each motion you take each day is clearly a step in living the best life available to you. Meanwhile, you have the normal amount of resources, using the normal ones that are accessible. Can you find a way to feel how great that life is without getting the joy from the details of the resources present? Can you visualize those better options clearly enough that you hunger for them, and work toward fixing those other parts of your life instead?

> *"Some people are so poor,*
> *the only thing they have is money."*[412]

C_R-lasts have tried to get happiness from acquiring and consuming and it wasn't worth it. The joy was temporary while their long-term happiness suffered. Resources have moments of function and pleasure. Resource attraction doesn't have a deeper meaning. Resources aren't a source of joy or disappointment in themselves. The meaning of life has to do with friends, family, sex, purpose, and experiences. Resources are pleasant too, when they happen, but they're definitely less important than the rest of that.

There is no disappointment to feel with real-world resources, food, money, and entertainment. Resource excitement comes and goes for everyone, and often isn't present at all. The way resources happen is fine. The frequency of consumption and acquisition are fine. There's no need for more, less, better, or different. It's still worth making sure that resources get maintenance, but that maintenance can happen without tension and relief, without fixated daydreams, and without judging what's happening as good or bad.

From the perspective of C_R-lasts, C_Rs only seem to have disadvantages. Why is the immediate framing of items in terms of price, taste, or ownership? Why can't the framing just be love for sunsets, love for people, caring about things because they're fulfilling, rather than analysis of profitability, or greed for someone else's things? C_Rs invest their time and emotions in acquisitions or money they don't need. They're so focused on having more wealth that they overlook the fact that they've already got more than they need. C_Rs miss out on life because they're distracted with avoiding exerting effort. C_Rs are experts at taste, quantity, cost, and presentation of foods. Then they know brainless platitudes which explain why they overeat, which distract them away from factual nutrition and the actual needs of their bodies. C_Rs overestimate how much function they'll get from both purchases and savings. C_Rs get excited about resource qualities that obviously don't exist, telling stories of how useful, delicious, money-making, and entertaining things will be which won't be different from the current options. C_Rs are very concerned about resource threats that will never happen. C_Rs inaccurately project resource concern and hunger onto other people's tension when those other people are obviously feeling Social or Relational concerns. C_Rs passionately disregard reality, enthusiastically find ways to be unhappy with what exists, and make bad decisions among existing options. They seem to be unaware of function, while thinking they're experts in function. C_Rs bully other people into buying things, into eating more than they want to, into eating less healthy foods, into prioritizing money over other concerns, because the C_R is immersed in an individual exaggeration of resource value. In critical moments, C_Rs sacrifice friendship, the good will of others, sexual attraction, and experience because they're distracted with acquiring and consuming things that don't matter. Why would anyone want that life?

The food a C_R-last eats is less tasty, but it's the quantity and nutrition that their body actually needs. C_R-lasts have fewer items, but they have what they actually use. C_R-lasts are optimized for the actual world.

"No, it's not water. You seem to be retaining food."

© Marty Bucella – MartyBucella.com[413]

C_R-lasts are realistic about what they've got, what they get from it, what their options are, and what each costs. They're more present to the reality of resources than C_R-firsts are. Part of what makes resources valuable is that they don't need extra attention in order to do their function. C_R-lasts live in the abundance and resource satisfaction that C_R-firsts can't find, because C_R-lasts live in reality, where there's more than enough for everyone who does the basics.

Cross Overs

*"Y'all ever drink an iced coffee so strong
that for like 4 minutes, you have hope?"[414]*

A massive inheritance, prize, or investment return can trigger euphoria for most C_R-lasts. Most C_R-lasts can be flushed with pain when watching a careless person scratch their possessions. But resource-triggered fixations happen with WAY fewer resources, WAY less frequently, and satisfaction comes much faster just by realizing that what happened is the fixed reality.

Many times a day C_R-firsts interact with resources without considering the resource-triggered arousal of the moment because those resources don't have arousal triggering cues. Even for a C_R-first, it feels like awkward, tedious work to generate an acquisition or consumption fantasy about entertainment, items, or food that they feel no attraction to.

C_R Conclusions

*"When I was young I thought that money
was the most important thing in life.
Now that I am old, I know that it is."[415]*

The addition of C_R means resources aren't just functional anymore. Food, entertainment, money, and items are loved, exciting, beautiful, and desired, triggering excitement, joy, concern, disappointment, pain, and relief. C_R tension and relief aren't necessary for a system to acquire and consume resources. But resource-triggered tension and relief make the consideration of resources, acquisition, and consumption emotionally rewarding.

C_R-firsts eat more delicious foods, consume more entertainment, acquire more money-per-effort, and acquire more items because they invest so much time and energy in seeking out, building, and maintaining resource-triggered excitement. A consistent focus on resource quality and quantity helps them seize opportunities to acquire and consume. They're constantly sacrificing for the benefit of the attraction they'll feel to their resources. But they're the least satisfied with resources because daily tension reminds them to focus on what's wrong and imagine and feel desire for better.

Easily Confused for the C_R Spectrum

"There is no love sincerer than the love of food"[417]

This chapter compares C_R to the six other motivators one-by-one. It holds the topic constant (resources) and looks at it while feeling each of the seven tensions so you can hear how each observer's experience of resources is different when they're expecting different changes and seeking different kinds of relief. This is the chapter to come back to when determining the relative influence of C_R versus any other motivator for a person.

Valuing Consumption and Acquisition While Feeling Resource-Based Comfort (C_R):

Someone who is hungry, thirsty, lacking money, and bored is internally solving for the acquisition or consumption that would satisfy them. They're less present to the external moment because their focus is immersed in internal consumption or acquisition fantasies. Something that's abundant, tasty, and acquired at very low cost would be satisfying in itself. Really engaging entertainment that makes them laugh could bring relief. Satisfying their hungers will release the observer to focus on other things again.

"Just reading that makes me crave some fries."[419]

Someone who tried to reframe really valuable items in terms of of social rules, how much sexual arousal they'll trigger, or in terms of how unique they'll feel as a result of ownership would seem to be discussing aspects that have a monetary value. Diamonds are diamonds. Gold is gold. The value is in the item itself. It's the item that's beautiful and valuable. It's that trade value which feels like the basis of the items "worth."

A C_R then feels sharply stabbed with pain while discarding items. What scenario would make discarding this the most tragic mistake in the future? What scenario would make it most glorious to have held on to this item instead? How much monetary, acquisition, or consumption value will this item have if the extreme fantasy situation happens?

C$_R$ is a focus on food, items, money, and entertainment because those things seem valuable in themselves. The actual value they're feeling is joy in acquisition and consumption, and pain in lack, damage, or loss of resources. Attention is dominated by valuation of resources since aspects of resources and the acquisition and consumption of resources trigger tension and relief.

"I don't care if it's a placebo or the real thing. I just want something you take with food."

© *Marty Bucella – MartyBucella.com*[420]

Valuing Consumption and Acquisition While Feeling Community-Based Socialness (S$_C$):

> *"The fastest path to a better world isn't economic growth or a better phone.*
> *It's more of us becoming irrationally passionate about the well-being of a child that isn't our own."*[421]

It's easier to keep the group connected and progressing when the members have resources and the group has resources. It's important that the group have a meeting space to gather in, and the snacks, bathrooms, and chairs necessary. Tension happens when the group plans a trip and someone can't afford to go, or when the group needs to make a purchase. The main resources to optimize are harmony, inclusion, and progress. Using group resources on the person who needs them the most in each moment makes sense. But it's also important that no one person drain the resources which are there for the merged whole. It's important to get food that the group likes, but it's also important for people not to interrupt the group too much for individual preferences. It's important to find entertainment that the group likes, but what makes the activity fun is doing it together.

"We live in a country where if you want to go bomb somebody, there's remarkably little discussion about how much it might cost. But when you have a discussion about whether or not we can assist people who are suffering, then suddenly we become very cost-conscious."[422]

Someone who is hungry with S_C is distracted by stresses between members of the group, by the group moving in a negative direction, by the jerky idiot who keeps disrupting things, by the toxic ideas that are driving people apart, and by leaders whose policies hurt people. So, S_Cs are thinking about those topics while they eat, rather than focusing on the taste of the food. They're thinking about how well the dinner satisfied the group, more than how much they liked the taste and quantity themselves.

"If people are good only because they fear punishment, or hope for reward, then we are a sorry lot indeed."[423]

Things cost money and stuff gets damaged whenever people are together. Of course it's preferable for resources to stay perfect, but it's just not the reality while they're getting used, especially since kids, old folks, and clumsy people are members.

If the group really loves one restaurant, then of course that restaurant is great. If the group is going to an activity, then the S_C

will pay their part, even if they'd never spend that much on that option alone. The S_C is appraising resources, but it's tension about the group's harmony and progress which actually trigger the love or dislike that the S_C is feeling when considering those resources. The best resource is the one which satisfies the group the most. Someone feeling S_C isn't switching into a separate mindset to appraise the value of that resource in trade value to strangers, or for the love and satisfaction they could feel themselves while acquiring or consuming it.

© Jim Benton – JimBenton.com[424]

Valuing Consumption and Acquisition While Feeling Individuality-Based Comfort (C_I):

> *"If we were not impressed by job titles, suits, and jargon, we would demand that financial advisors show us their personal bank statements before they tell us what we could or should do with our own money."*[425]

Someone who is hungry with C_I is distracted by self-glorification, self-doubt, confidence, a lack of confidence, by the clever thing they did that everyone is ignoring, by people who didn't listen, by the dumb mistake they made, by the attention and adoration they're not getting, or by feeling attacked, unfairly treated, ignored, or abandoned. They're distracted with an internal vision of being impressive, adored, superior, and influential.

Consumption and acquisition opportunities are evidence of the C_I's individuality and superiority. The item being acquired or consumed still matters, but some of the value felt on items is coming from how impressed the C_I is when looking at it, how common the C_I thinks the item is, and the degree to which the item can be leveraged to draw attention and display the superiority of the C_I. The monetary value of the item in general trade between other people is secondary to the focus of the moment. Because this moment is about self. It's about ranking. Other people will say dumb things about this item and it's relieving when the C_I corrects them. The accurate response would be to thank the C_I and admire their intelligence, but instead other people don't show enough respect because they're ignoring or not appreciating the C_I, who is the actual focus of the moment.

"Impress people with your accomplishments, not your possessions."[426]

When other people break things, it's a sign of their stupidity. The C_I would've used it properly and not broken it. When a C_I breaks something, it's a sign of poor construction of the broken item. The C_I has higher standards and expected the same from the item.

"They say you are what you eat,
But I don't remember eating a pathetic failure."[427]

Someone feeling only C_I is not in a relationship with food, possessions, or entertainment. They're surprised again by the greatness of themselves or the patheticness of themselves. It's funny again how stupid other people are, or depressing how impressive they are. Resources are the props in another moment about self.

> *"The love of power is the demon of humans.*
> *Let them have everything - health, food, a place to live, entertainment -*
> *they are and remain unhappy and low-spirited:*
> *for the demon waits and waits and will be satisfied."*[428]

Why do other people have things when self is the one who really deserves them? If self has something that others don't, how does that show self's superiority? How good will it feel to see their jealousy? How funny will it be when others have the lame option instead?

When a C_I truly is focused on valuing the resource for the resource, they're still valuing the superiority of one resource over another. They like the distinctive individuality of the resource. They like that they're the ones who chose it while others chose something else. But mainly they like that they can see these things easily, because of their superior intelligence, so they have something to teach the surrounding people who didn't notice these qualities already.

Valuing Consumption and Acquisition While Feeling Sexual Arousal (R_S):

"She is abundance in human form."[429]

If moments of sharp sexual attraction to breathtaking hotties keep happening, how can resources be helpful in seducing those partners and making sex finally happen? It's helpful to have distinctive items which draw in the initial attention of hotties and serve as ice breaking topics of discussion. Maybe getting rich helps attract cute partners. It's helpful to have resources which emphasize your most attractive features. It's helpful if you have the items that keep resources from being a distraction while courting. It's important to have a good place to have sex and birth control. Tension happens when a partner is distracted from sexual escalation by the presence or lack of a resource, or when a possession reminds you too much of a heartbreaking ex. The main resource to optimize is sexual attraction, felt both by the observer and sexy targets. So any way that acquisition or consumption can increase sexual attraction is good, and anything which decreases sexual attraction is bad.

When they choose food, R_Ss consider how that food will affect the sexual attractiveness of their bodies. Fattening food feels negatively tense because they'll decrease sexual attractiveness, slimming foods are relieving because they'll increase attractiveness. Clothing which makes the wearer more sexually attractive are valuable. Clothing which flattens sexual curves is negatively valuable. It's still value being felt on resources, but the root of the feelings of value are coming from sexual tensions. The feeling of value isn't coming from monetary evaluations of trade value to others. Resources are all around, and they're props while a romantic fantasy plays out with a sexy partner.

Valuing Consumption and Acquisition While Feeling Body-Based Comfort (C_B):

Fat people
are hard
to kidnap.

It's easier to feel safe, comfortable, and healthy when you have resources. It's easier to be delighted with scents, sights, sounds, and tactile sensations when you own sensory pleasures. Tension happens when body dangers are present, when things are fast, sharp, loud, dark, rusty, diseased, or dead. What makes resources feel valuable is how comfortable, peaceful, healthy, energetic, and safe they make the owner feel. The main resources to optimize are health, energy, comfort, peace, and readiness.

Someone who is hungry with C_B is distracted by body pains, lack of energy, a foggy brain, uncomfortable smells, sights, sounds and tactile sensations. They're distracted with a glorious vision of how peaceful, healthy, comfortable and safe they could be. So, C_Bs are thinking about how food is affecting their body while they eat. Taste matters too, but food is more strongly valued for how it affects the body and mental wellbeing. C_Bs are noticing how dinner affected their body while they lay down to sleep, more so than focused on the monetary deal they got paying for that dinner.

© *Mackenzie Moore – CinimomoComics*[430]

"The famous mathematician Kurt Gödel was deeply afraid of being poisoned by the food he ate. To cope with his obsessive fear, he developed a strategy. He only ate food prepared by his wife, whom he knew he could trust. And then, when his wife was hospitalized for six months and couldn't cook for him, he died of starvation."[431]

When things are scary, they're obviously negative. When things are soft and fuzzy, they're obviously positive. Someone feeling C$_B$ tensions is noticing positive and negative feelings about resources while in that mindset, rather than defaulting to analyzing markets and money and likely trends in supply and demand. So they can still feel more value on some resources than others, but the triggers for that value are different than for a C$_R$. It's a different feeling generating the pleasure and pain. For someone flushed with C$_B$, acquisition and consumption are background parts of a story which is focused on health, safety, comfort, and emotional wellbeing.

Valuing Consumption and Acquisition While Feeling Experience-Based Relationalness (R$_A$):

*"We don't buy things with money.
We buy them with hours from our lives."*[432]

You're going to die, and it'll happen surprisingly soon. You have one life to live, so you might as well get the most out of it. So, why walk when you can run? Why stagnate when you can work toward a dream? Why do another repetition of something when you could immerse in something new?

*"You can tell how rich you are
by counting the things you have that money cannot buy."*[433]

Since the time you're alive is running out, what job would be the most thrilling to have before that death? Since you're going to die, what foreign place would you like to experience before you go? Being super rich is a thrilling experience worth having. Losing everything and being super poor is a thrilling experience that's worth having. The life lesson at the end of those two is that money itself doesn't matter. The parts of life which do matter are remarkably similar at both extremes.

© Harley Schwadron – SchwadronCartoons.com[434]

R$_{AS}$ rarely think they're C$_R$s. Because C$_R$s never realize the basic life lesson that money isn't what matters. C$_R$s in their 80s are still busy hoarding when they should be spending their last dollar having any experiences they still haven't had. How close do people have to get to death before they finally realize they're going to die and the money they focused on was worthless all along?

> *"What you get by achieving your goals is not as important as who you become by achieving your goals."*[435]

R$_{AS}$ still value resources. They're a vital part of life. But their value is measured using tension about limits on time, meaning, and variety of experiences. So, money has value, but that value is rooted in the experiences it can deliver. It's still tension-based valuation, but from a different place than C$_R$s who can feel direct value on the money and direct love for money because it is so beautiful in itself. For a C$_R$, holding money brings as much happiness and relief as most things the money could be traded for.

Valuing Consumption and Acquisition While Feeling Alliance-Based Socialness (S_F):

Friendships are easier when you have resources. Resources keep you from being a burden on friends, and allow you to resolve other people's tensions. If you have plenty, then it's less painful when you have to pay for your friend. Having resources helps if a friend needs something and you already have extra. It's easier to reconnect with friends if you have a place and snacks, or have the money when the two of you go out. Tension happens when a friend seems to want the friendship mainly so you can pay for things for them, asking you to buy them gifts, expecting you to support them, or not sharing when they get something easily shareable. Why don't they care about what they're doing to the friendship with these actions? An S_F will feel tension about paying too much for a friend, but the tension they're feeling is recognition that the other person isn't emotionally invested in the friendship. The other person is in some other mindset, not concerned about the stresses they're putting on the merged emotional connection between two halves of one whole. S_F pain is felt for the dying friendship, while C_R is felt for the cheated resources.

Someone who is hungry with Friendship-based Socialness is distracted by a miscommunication that might've hurt a friend's feelings, by concern about a hurting friend, by worries that the friend is disconnecting from the friendship, that the two might not be in sync anymore. So, an S_F is more likely to be thinking about those topics while they eat, rather than focusing on the taste of the food they're eating. S_Fs are more likely to be dwelling on what a friend said while laying in bed, than fondly remembering the deal they got when they purchased the bed.

S_Fs purchase things that are bigger than they need so that friends can use them. S_Fs expect their possessions to get used and damaged by others since that's what happens while people are around. Any food and any entertainment is fine if it's consumed with the right friends. If a friend loves their own car, then the S_F will flush with tension while they watch someone scratch that car, but because they're feeling the tension they think their friend is feeling. They'd feel less tension if their friend wasn't bothered. The main resource to optimize is the closeness of relationships. When you have a really close ally then anything can happen and the two of you resolve it together.

S_{FS} value items, food, and money, but those things have value because they are background props in a story about how two similar souls joined into one and enjoyed life together while looking out for each other. Resources are parts of inside jokes that show the two know each other well, they're props in stories where they surprise each other with affection, and are ways of looking out for each other when someone is sick or sad. S_{FS} use tension to value acquisition and consumption, but they're concerned or excited about how connected they feel with another person. It would feel like a change of focus to switch to just the resource itself and try to appraise its cash value to strangers. It seems like more value will come from giving it away to a friend than from selling it.

"I'm delighted to report that Buck had a breakthrough and has identified the origins of his mailperson issues."

© Teresa Burns Parkhurst[436]

Selection Factors (Triggers)

"We are each not only one but also many.
Some of us have to hold a meeting every time we want to do
something in order to find the self who is capable of undertaking it.
We spend a lot of time and ingenuity on developing ways
of organizing the inner crowd, securing consent among it,
and arranging for it to act as a whole."[437]

At the very first step of observation, specific sensors measure only one quality each, which is the quality they're sensitive to. The qualities detected are called **Selection Factors**.

Each trigger can be wired to feel positive or negative, or not be wired to trigger positive or negative emotions. Each trigger can be wired to generate tension and relief, or not to affect tension or relief. Each trigger can be anywhere on the spectrum from very easily triggered, to very difficult or impossible to trigger.

Two humans can have ***the same*** selection factors, but end with ***different*** emotions because of the direction, intensity, tension, and satisfaction triggered.

Two humans can have ***different*** selection factors, but end at ***the same*** emotions because of the direction, intensity, tension, and satisfaction triggered.

What you will see as the selection factors (triggers) a re discussed is that some tensions are opposites of each other. Two different tensions can be triggered by the same input, but one person is triggered with positive tension while another is triggered with negative tension. When those two people interact, they're likely to negatively trigger each other as each assumes the things that feel good or bad to them are objectively good or bad. Someone who seems to support evil, or be against good is usually having opposite Limbic System reactions. And there's usually a strong logical argument that you're both factually wrong.

Learning about selection factors is important because they clearly explain the gap between feelings and logic. Again, it's probably worth reading about your own selection factors first.

C_I: Individuality, Self, Ranking, page **307**.

R_A: Adventure, Experiences, page **313**.

S_F: Friendship, page **319**.

C_B: Body, Sensations, Health, Safety, page **321**.

S_C: Community, page **326**.

C_R: Resource consumption and acquisition, page **333**.

R_S: Sexual, page **340**.

"*Worse than a cold. It's a common cold.*"

© Benjamin Schwartz[438]

Individuality Based Comfort
(C$_I$) Selection Factors

Father: "Hey Son, how old are you?"
Son: "24"
Father: "Ha! At your age, I was 27!"[439]

Self: When euphoria, pain, lack, and satisfaction are added to self then self becomes an emotional topic. Whatever benefits self or comes from self feels exaggeratedly positive. Whatever benefits others or comes from others feels exaggeratedly negative. Tension is felt when self's impact or importance aren't clear, when self is excluded, or when self isn't a component. Establishing self's importance, impact, and individuality relieves tension. Others failing and losing can feel funny and joyful to observe. Others succeeding and winning can feel painful to observe. The story generated which explains why self feels great and others feel negative is that self is accurate, endearing, creative, and excellent, while others are inaccurate, selfish, ignorant, and inferior.

© *Bill Whitehead*[440]

"I always felt this subtle sense of inadequacy, like I had to add something to myself in order to be valid. So I sought new skills, and new knowledge. I figured that the more I learned, the more valuable I was as a person. I was saying that the way things are now is invalid and I want to make things valid. My answer was actually to realize that everything is already perfect the way it is. I realized that in seeking to add value to myself, what I wanted was to feel at home in present reality. I wanted to feel unconditional love for myself."[441]

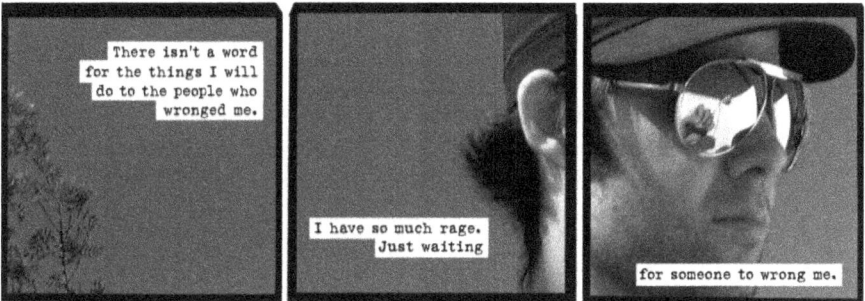

© e horne and j comeau – asofterworld.com[442]

Superiority, Ranking: When euphoria, pain, lack, and satisfaction are added to comparison then comparing things becomes emotional. Whatever ranks well feels exaggeratedly positive. Whatever ranks poorly feels exaggeratedly negative. Tension is felt when the ranking of inputs isn't clear. Establishing the ranking of unranked inputs relieves tension. The story generated which explains why high ranking things feel great and low ranking things feel negative is that winners are dramatically better, while losers are disgusting and repulsive. This triggers the feeling of being impressed, and it feels like whatever impresses the observer has greatness in itself.

"I have this worry that I need some version of success for people to see, to be wealthy, or have a successful family, or win at competitive hobbies. I can feel the judgment from 'people' that I logically know is coming from my own head."[443]

"In high school I put myself on a pedestal. I thought I was the shit. If people tried to challenge or insult me, I'd tell them, 'I'm going to get rich, and you're going to do drugs.' Then I never challenged my status, so it carried through to adulthood."[444]

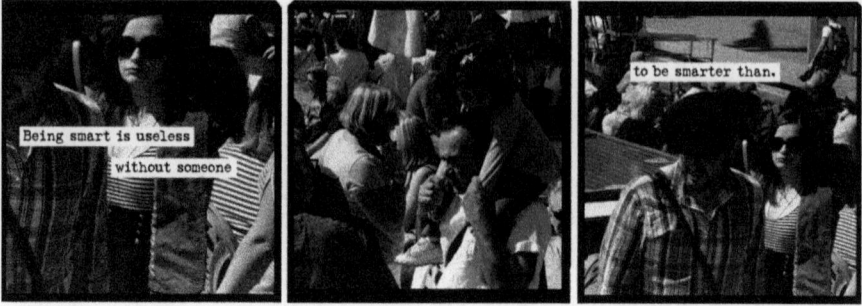

© e horne and j comeau – asofterworld.com[445]

*"Right out of college I was offered an internship in my field.
I turned it down because I knew I was meant
to be a CEO, not an intern. Instead, I took golf lessons,
because I know that CEOs play a lot of golf."*[446]

Other People's C$_I$ (Judgment, Attention, Jealousy): When
euphoria, pain, lack, and satisfaction are added to other people's
feelings of C$_I$ then other people's feelings of C$_I$ become emotional to
observe. A C$_I$ observer can feel emotions when other people are
emotional about ranking (feeling impressed, superior, or rejected),
are comparing themselves to something, or are trying to influence
what they're observing. They can feel emotions when other people
are looking excellent and powerful, which is why superhero and
princess movies can be emotional to watch. For a C$_I$ observer, the
recognition, acknowledgment, approval, adoration, and impressed
feelings of others feel exaggeratedly positive or negative depending
on whether self or not-self are the recipients of that attention, and
whether the judgment is positive or negative. Tension is felt when
others aren't impressed or paying attention to the observer
("loneliness"). Relief is felt when others pay attention to the C$_I$,
especially if they're impressed or jealous. It can be emotional for
C$_I$S to see another person flushed with C$_I$, standing up for
themselves, clearly differentiating themselves, presenting
themselves in a striking, unique way, or responding forcefully and
confidently to an external attack. But they're not feeling affection
for the other person. They're feeling affection for the differentiation,
individuality, and superiority the other person is displaying.

"We all love ourselves more than other people,
but care more about their opinion than our own."[447]

"Perfectionism is a self destructive and addictive belief system that fuels
this primary thought: If I look perfect, and do everything perfectly, I can
avoid or minimize the painful feelings of shame, judgment, and blame."

© Bradford Veley - bradveley.com[448]

In Combination: ***Interest in Individuality.*** Since others feel bad and
self feels good, having clear distinction between self and others is
relieving. Overlaps between self and others add the negative
feelings of otherness to self. Einstein, Jesus, and Hitler get their own
categories because they were so different and individually
impactful. They are discussed as individuals, rather than discussed
grouped in with others "like them." C_Is want that same individual
recognition for themselves. Whatever someone else did was wrong
or lacking (for reasons found when logic solved for why it felt bad).

311

Relief will come when self adjusts it (for reasons found when logic solves for why self's adjustments were relieving).

> *"They laugh at me because I'm different.*
> *I laugh at them because they're all the same."*[449]

> *"I have to feel that I am independent or*
> *I cannot be married, as much as I love my spouse.*
> *The reason we had to institute an allowance system was because*
> *I cannot be questioned about buying 'Jaws' T-shirts, or sneakers,*
> *or the occasional out-of-print biography going for $55, used.*
> *I am so wary of dependence that the merest suggestion*
> *makes me break out in hives."*[450]

Experience Based Relational (R_A) Selection Factors

Experience Based Relational (R_A) Selection Factors

"Everything that kills me, makes me feel alive."[452]

Novelty (Anomalies): When euphoria, pain, lack, and satisfaction are added to processing new inputs then processing new inputs becomes emotional. Getting to know something that starts out unfamiliar feels exaggeratedly positive. Processing another autopilot repetition of something familiar feels exaggeratedly negative. Tension is felt when new options are present and aren't being engaged. Fully processing new inputs relieves tension. The story generated which explains why processing new inputs feels great and processing familiar inputs feel negative is that new inputs result in growth and learning, while familiar actions and inputs waste the gift of life. Time must be the most valuable resource. Even small things like going to a new grocery store, or taking a new route to work, feel world-expanding. Surprises bring sharp spikes of joy. The opposite wiring, where novelty and surprises are negative, makes this same selection factor a trigger for C$_B$.

> *"Those who love life do not squander time.*
> *For that's the stuff life is made of."*[453]

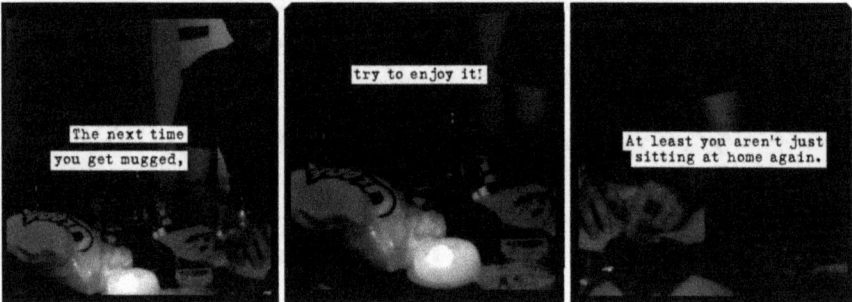

© *e horne and j comeau – asofterworld.com*[454]

Action: When euphoria, pain, lack, and satisfaction are added to taking action then taking action and remaining idle become emotional. Exerting effort feels exaggeratedly positive. Time spent without action feels exaggeratedly negative. Tension is felt when options for action are available, but no action is happening. Being in motion relieves tension. The story generated which explains why action feels great and inaction feel negative is that opportunities are being seized, and life is being fully lived. R$_A$s walk faster than other people, often around and ahead of everyone else because they're on a meaningful, exciting mission into the unknown. The opposite wiring of this selection factor, where effort feels like a limited resource which is only thoughtfully and tactically exerted, makes this same selection factor a trigger for C$_R$.

> *"Everywhere I go, there is always someone in front of me*
> *moving VERY slowly."*[455]

> *"I can do a great distance while some are considering*
> *whether they'll start today or tomorrow"*[456]

"I hate the word 'potential' because people think that they have something. You have nothing until you take action and create. You have nothing until there's a result. There are people with nothing and people with created results and that's it."[457]

I'VE DONE IT! I'M BURNING THE CANDLE AT THREE ENDS!

Negative C$_B$ Drugging (Fear): When euphoria, pain, lack, and satisfaction are added to confronting and overcoming fear, then confronting fear becomes emotional. Racing toward scary inputs feels exaggeratedly positive. Giving in to fear feels exaggeratedly negative. Tension is felt when scary inputs aren't being engaged. Confronting and overcoming feared inputs relieves tension. By confronting fears, observers get to know the actual options, and fulfill their purpose and meaning. Giving in to fear would be a ridiculous waste, hiding from imaginary demons, imposing fake restrictions, rejecting the gift of life.

> *"It may be that the purpose of your life,*
> *is to serve as a warning to others."*[459]

> *"Safety Third!"*[460]

> *"Without fear, you're not challenging yourself and growing.*
> *I recommend ten minutes of apprehension or two minutes*
> *of utter terror, every day. Develop the habit of taking action*
> *in the face of fear. Go toward the dark, scary thing.*
> *Everyone should have a fear-confronting ritual they perform every day.*
> *One of my fear-approaching rituals is riding my Vespa*
> *in Los Angeles traffic. Yours can be approaching and*
> *talking to strangers. If you're afraid of that, you're lucky.*
> *You have something convenient on which to sharpen*
> *your habit of confronting fear."*[461]

This doesn't completely destroy logic. R$_A$s don't fire guns in their mouths just because it's scary. But it creates tension while a "scary" option still hasn't been engaged, and adds satisfaction to the engagement of that option, making the action feel meaningful even when the result is functionally negative. The feelings of excitement and stagnation are felt which logic then has to interpret. So, logic still gets its pass at the idea, but it has to justify its position against the feelings of desire being felt to jump over the side. This is wired opposite to make the C$_B$ selection factor where retreating from fear is rewarded, and where getting hurt is also negative (rather than the R$_A$ release from tension from having verified the outcome).

> *"Fear is only a verb if you let it be."*[462]

> *"God placed all of the best things in life on the other side of terror."*[463]

Other People's R$_A$: When euphoria, pain, lack, and satisfaction are added to the observation of other people's motion toward extremes and the unknown, then watching other people overcome fear and try for their dreams becomes exaggeratedly positive (inspiring), and listening to other people criticize and talk people out of their dreams feels exaggeratedly negative. It becomes sharply outrage-inspiring when fearful people use force to keep other humans inside the boundaries of the C$_B$'s fears. It becomes sharply joyful when someone breaks through the C$_B$s and leaps out into the unknown.

> *"She decided, mid-jump, it had been worth it."*[464]

317

In Combination:

Interest in Reality: Fear is triggered in humans very far from the actual limits. Fear is felt about things that do not matter which are very difficult to make dangerous (like most insects). An R_A might've felt the same negative prediction, but then tested it and found that fear was an error. So, when other people explain limitations as if they are factual science, an R_A knows that story is only a justification of fear because the R_A has been past that limit and found benefits and safety.

> *"The sexiest thing a partner can do for me is teach me something new.*
> *Put me on a new way of seeing things. Expand my mind.*
> *Make me lose an illusion and find a truth."*[466]

Mixing with R_S: R_A is part of Relational by wiring, so a hunger for novelty and action are coincidentally paired with more easily and frequently triggered sexual attraction. R_A has sexual benefits, even though it's not a sexual motivator itself. R_A motivates performing sexual fitness displays (because R_As do such extreme, unusual things), increases the likelihood of genetic diversity of children because of the distance traveled to find a partner, fixates attention on unfamiliar partners, motivates having sex (because it's a more intense personal interaction), and motivates moving on from partnerships that have become stale and predictable.

> *"Ever the positive thinker, Steinem composed a list of the good*
> *things about starting her ninth decade of life. A dwindling libido,*
> *she theorized, can be a terrific advantage: 'The brain cells that*
> *used to be obsessed are now free for all kinds of great things.'*
> *Recently, she recalled, she met a young man in her travels and*
> *thought, 'If I was younger, we'd have had a great passionate affair*
> *for two years and been friends the rest of our lives.' It wasn't a wistful*
> *thought, she says. It was an observation. 'I didn't regret missing out*
> *on the relationship. That's the advantage of shifting hormones.'"*[467]

> *"Most of us can function normally day to day, but when we see someone*
> *attractive across a crowded room... ZONK! We become locked into a*
> *catatonic state. The problem is not the anxiety. The problem is the lack*
> *of action. Suck it up and go talk to that hot guy or girl anyway. See the*
> *hottie, feel the fear, approach anyway, act nervous and stupid,*
> *be rejected (maybe), and chalk a victory up to action."*[468]

Friendship-Based Social (S_F) Selection Factors

Recognized Faces and Recognized Individuals: When euphoria, pain, lack, and satisfaction are added to the recognition of faces and individuals then recognition of familiar people becomes emotional. Tension is felt when a recognized person is noticed. Relief is felt when the observer interacts with the recognized person. The story generated to explain why this person generates magnetic tension is that a friendship exists between the two which is worth supporting. Even recognized cashiers, and recognized selfish friends from childhood make the observer feel tension to see which is relieved when the two interact.

Valued People's Emotions: When euphoria, pain, lack, and satisfaction are added to familiar people's emotions then other people's emotions becomes emotional to observe. A friend's laughter and joy feel exaggeratedly positive. A friend's hurt feelings feel exaggeratedly negative. Any tone of pain or tension from the ally, or anything which might generate those feelings in an ally, create tension in the observer. Resolving an ally's tension relieves the observer's tension. Restoring an ally's positive emotions restores the observer's positive emotions. The story generated which explains why another person's joy and satisfaction feel joyful and relieving, and another person's tension and pain feel tense and painful is that the other person's happiness matters.

Other People's Feelings of S_F (Friendship Affection): When euphoria, pain, lack, and satisfaction are added to the observation of other people's emotional investment in the observer, then other people feel like merged parts of self. If the observer feels upset and the friend is immediately focused and concerned, searching for ways to help, the other person's emotional investment can flush the observer with returned endearment. If the observer wins and the friend gets upset that they didn't win instead, the lack of returned emotional investment, the lack of matched emotions, the lack of feeling that the observers win was the friend's win, makes the friend feel exaggeratedly negative and separate.

> R: "I always wondered who would win if we fought."
> BP: "Then you were always a bad friend."[469]

The story generated which explains why the other person's emotional investment is so striking is that they are a good person. They have an endearingly valuable soul because they deeply care about others. Part of the evidence that this friend is such a valuable soul is how they've emotionally invested in the observer. They're not perfect, but they're so good that they're worth supporting.

This is love triggered by other people's love, not by their logic. Someone who has logically chosen to be a friend, but obviously isn't automatically feeling the observer's tension, generates pain in that lack of matched feelings, rather than joy from their logical commitment to being supportive.

For S_Fs it's emotional to see other people dedicated to friendships in general, even if it's not with the observer. This happens less frequently, but movies about believing in a friend and being connected with a friend can feel particularly striking and remind the observer of their merged other halves.

© Ben Zaehringer – BerkeleyMews.com[470]

Body Comfort (C$_B$) Selection Factors

"Without music, life would be a mistake."[471]

*"If you don't exercise, eat nutritious food, get sunlight,
consume positive material, and surround yourself with support,
then you aren't giving yourself a fighting chance."*[472]

Sensory Inputs (Sight, Smell, Touch, and Sound): When euphoria,
pain, lack, and satisfaction are added to sounds, smells, sights, and
tactile sensations then those sensory inputs become emotional.
Whatever sounds, looks, or smells beneficial, or is pleasantly tactile

feels exaggeratedly positive. Whatever feels negative to senses feels exaggeratedly negative, especially pain. Tension is felt when sensations are negative, when expected positive sensations aren't present, or when negative sensations are expected. Replacing negative sensations with positive sensations relieves tension. The story generated which explains why some sensations feel great and others feel negative is that some are healing and others are dangerous, destructive, or signs of greater problems. Lesser senses like balance are also included in C$_B$, but the sense of taste is C$_R$.

> *"Being an adult is pretty easy.*
> *You feel tired all the time and tell people about*
> *how tired you are and they tell you how tired they are."*[473]

> *"My favorite childhood memory is my back not hurting."*[474]

Unknowns (Change, Anomalies): When euphoria, pain, lack, and satisfaction are added to unknowns then considering familiar and unknown inputs becomes emotional. Whatever is familiar feels exaggeratedly positive. Whatever is unknown feels exaggeratedly negative. When the source of a sound is unknown, or the future results are unknown, or the source of any discomfort is unknown, that lack of certainty triggers pain and fear. New things and changes feel negative, and feel like signs of even more incoming negativity. This extends to making the past exaggeratedly good (especially body health in the past) be cause it's familiar, known, and won't change, and the future exaggeratedly bad (especially body health in the future). Tension is felt when unknowns can't be avoided. Protecting body and senses from unknowns relieves tension (like, with insurance). The story generated which explains why an unknown feels so scary is a fear fantasy of the greatest damage the observer can imagine. The opposite wiring, where unknowns are thrilling, makes this a selection factor for R$_A$.

> *"I wish there was a way to know you were in the good old days,*
> *before you left them."*[475]

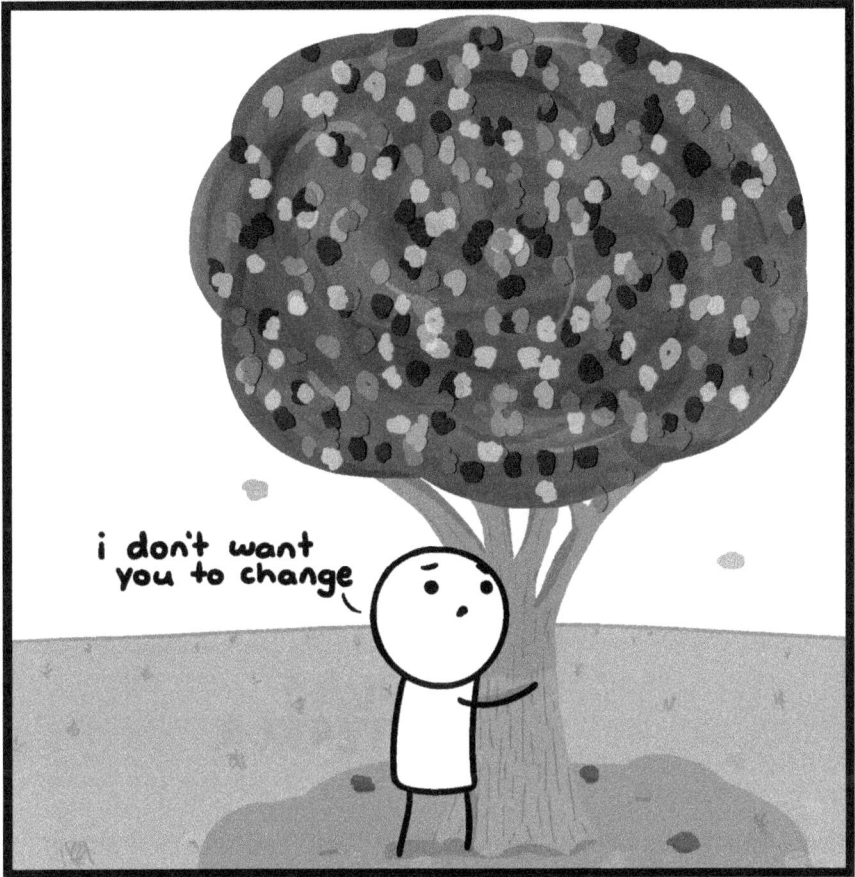

© *Justin Boyd - InvisibleBread.com*[476]

Sensory Extremes (Danger): At the extremes of sensations the expectations of negativity are exaggerated. Total darkness, blinding light, overwhelming noise, perfect silence, extreme heights, extreme speeds, extreme sharpness, extremely large things, extremely small things all trigger tense internal modeling of the body and mental damage and discomfort which could result. Retreating to the known and safe relieves tension. The story generated which explains why an input felt scary is that it was dangerous. The story generated which explains why the familiar feels safe is that it protected body and senses. The opposite wiring of this is R_A, which makes the same inputs feel thrilling, and "safety" feel like painful stagnation.

> *"The fear of being alone in the dark*
> *is actually the fear of not being alone in the dark."*[477]

"I'm someone who is scared of everything: the dark, the light, heights, depths, confined spaces, wide open spaces, strangers, intimacy, spiders, and a sudden and mysterious lack of spiders."[478]

"Butterflies are scary."[479]

Being a passenger in someone else's car (sometimes)

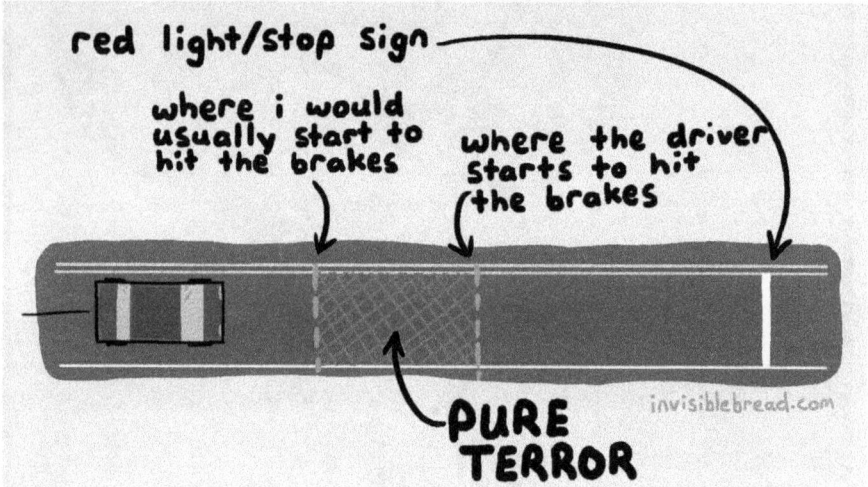

red light/stop sign

where i would usually start to hit the brakes

where the driver starts to hit the brakes

PURE TERROR

invisiblebread.com

© *Justin Boyd - InvisibleBread.com*[480]

Body and Mind: When euphoria, pain, lack, and satisfaction are added to body functions and status then the body becomes emotional. Pee, poop, pressure, vomit, farts, coughing, sweat, burps, hiccups, body odor, pain, sickness, and numbness feel exaggeratedly positive or negative. Body affecting inputs like germs, dirt, diseases, and decay feel exaggeratedly negative. Tiny body signals get full attention of the whole system. The story generated to support all these emotions is that the health and comfort of the body and mind are the foundation upon which the rest of life happens. Resolving the needs of the body and mind relieves tension.

"Every fart you've ever farted is still out there"[481]

"I caught a chest cold.
At home, in exchange for chicken soup and care,
I will reward those around me
with a short temper and constant complaining."[482]

I'M SO HAPPY THAT THIS SWEATER COVERS EVERYTHING BUT MY ANUS AND GENITALIA.

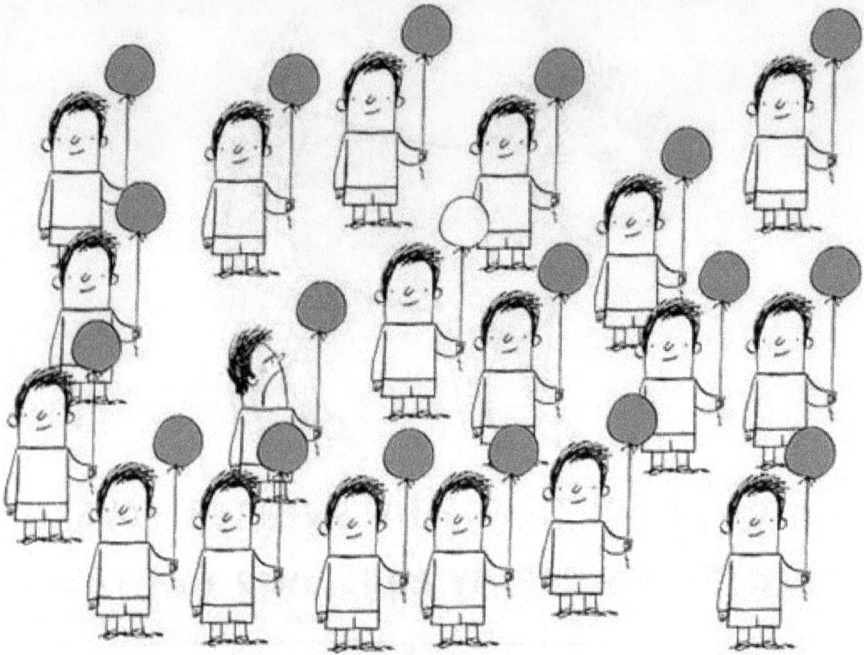

Community-Based Social (S$_C$) Selection Factors

"My life belongs to the whole community,
and as long as I live, it is my privilege to do for it whatever I can."[486]

Similarity: When euphoria, pain, lack, and satisfaction are added to similarities between humans then similarities and differences become emotional to consider. Whatever is similar feels exaggeratedly positive and merging. Whatever is different feels exaggeratedly negative and separating. Tension is felt when one person in a group is different, or when differences between people come up. Helping people conform, finding ways to think about it so it's still conforming, or identifying greater similarities relieves tension. The story generated which explains why similarities feel so good is that the similar souls are bound together into a greater whole, while differences divide that greater whole into painfully smaller groups. Similarity of motions, motivations, opinions, clothing, appearance, language, age, origin, interests, family, culture, or location all feel like explanations of why those souls are automatically smaller parts in a greater whole which will work as one unit and care for the component humans.

> *"Small acts, when multiplied by millions of people, can transform the world."*[487]

Watching any human hand get cut feels painful because it's so similar to the observer's hand. The pain is felt as if it were happening to the observer, because of the similarity. Watching a paw get cut instead might still be painful because it's still a living creature (similar to the observer), but is less sharply Social in the pain, because the observer's hand is more different from a paw. Watching a similar person flush with happiness flushes the observer with happiness because the other person is so similar.

> *"Be the reason that someone believes in the goodness of people."*[488]

Humans that are sharply dissimilar, who are going out of their way to be different, aren't as sharply modeled to generate matching emotions in a Social observer. That person, or even that group, feel too dissimilar for their emotions to be automatically matched.

> *"Love is the power to see similarity in the dissimilar."*[489]

The story which explains why watching other people hurt makes the observer hurt, and why watching other people flush with happiness makes the observer flush with happiness is that we're all parts of one greater whole. All humans are obviously connected. We are obviously extensions of each other. Self's good still matters, but the best thing that could happen for self is for the whole group to succeed (because everyone being happy would generate the most happiness for the Social-first observer to observe).

> *"Differences and similarities are equally easy to see. Which are you seeking to find?"*[490]

Similarity isn't just pleasurable between self and others, but among observed others too. Watching a group act as one unit feels pleasurable to enjoy, and the one member who is obviously dissimilar to the rest will feel painful to observe, even if the observer is watching a performance and isn't a part of that group.

> *"One who cannot live in harmony with others*
> *is regarded as an ignorant fool,*
> *even if he happens to be very learned in various matters."*[491]

The opposite wiring of this selection factor, where similarities with others feel sharply negative, is a selection factor for C$_I$. When other people's happiness feels automatically painful to observe, and when self individuating feels automatically pleasurable to observe, then the opposite understandings logically result.

Number of Triggers: For all families of emotion, the number of emotional triggers matters. This is particularly important for Community-based Social drugging.

When the specific human isn't what's triggering, and it's just similar humans in general, then five similar humans flushed with joy is more pleasurable to observe than one human flushed with joy. A stadium of similar people who suddenly flush with joy is more pleasure-triggering than the smaller group of only five people. A room of 30 similar souls flushed with pleasure is less triggering than the stadium, but more than the group of five.

> *"The best thing about sports is*
> *the sense of community and shared emotions they create."*[492]

You can increase the pleasure by increasing the similarity (by everyone wearing the same colors or uniform) a nd by increasing the number of people present who are merged into the group, triggering pleasure by doing what the group does.

> *"This world of ours must avoid becoming*
> *a community of fear and hate, and be instead*
> *a proud confederation of mutual trust and respect."*[493]

The story which explains why pleasure increases as more similar souls feel pleasure is that the happiness and benefits of all similar souls must matter. It can easily generate more happiness to make a small personal sacrifice if it results in several similar souls feeling a greater additive flushing of joy from their benefits.

"The only thing which can redeem humanity is working together."[494]

So while C$_B$s are trying to bring together as many sensory comforts as possible, and R$_S$s are trying to find a partner with as many sexual selection factors as possible, S$_C$s are trying to bring together as many similar souls as possible, and get them as tightly merged as possible, because it will be so pleasurable and satisfying to be a merged part of that circle of love.

SUPPORTIVE COMMUNITY

© Janis Ozolins – ozolinsjanis.com[495]

Other People's S$_C$ (Other People's Emotional Investment in the Merged Whole, And The Harmony That Results): When euphoria, pain, lack, and satisfaction are added to the emotional investment of members in the wellbeing of the merged group, then it becomes emotional to witness individuals making individual sacrifices for the benefit of others, moving automatically as one whole because they're so sensitive to the group's needs, working together, and showing the signs of being emotionally invested in other people's success. It becomes painfully emotional to watch others who aren't feeling the feelings of others, who create and enjoy differences and disharmony. It's relieving when they're expelled from the group, so everyone who is left can work together and love each other again. People who resolve other people's tensions feel exaggeratedly positive. It feels negatively tense to see someone feeling left out. Their hunger to feel merged with the group is painful to observe. It's relieving when those people find their places in the group and seamlessly become critical to the greater flow and function. Tension is felt when others aren't internally modeling other people's feelings before speaking and acting. Relief is felt when someone accurately models and values the emotions and benefits of other people and chooses the option with the greatest net gain for everyone.

> *"A smile costs nothing, but gives much."*[496]
> *(because it relieves other people's tension)*

The story generated which explains why other people's emotional investment in the group feels positive, and why those not modeling the group feel negative, is that some people are better people than others. Some people are generating love and positivity, while other people are generating pain and negativity. Good people make small individual sacrifices so that a greater cumulative benefit is felt by the group. Bad people selfishly take tiny benefits for themselves in exchange for much more disruption and pain for others. It feels like everyone benefits SO MUCH from being a part of the group. Everyone benefits from the tiny individual sacrifices that everyone is making for the benefits of others. Selfishly injuring lots of people for a tiny individual benefit is a very dumb move, because those people see that you don't want to be connected to them anymore. It's very unlikely that the momentary benefit taken at the expense of others is move valuable than the love and support of those others over time.

Part of the reason it's joyful to be part of a group who is all working together is the similarity of the souls of everyone involved. But the other half of the reason is that these people have to be watching and modeling the group, they have to care about the group's happiness, in order to flow well with the greater merged whole. The fact that these similar souls are emotionally invested in the greater group adds extra happiness to the S$_C$ observer. It's so many people happily contributing to the happiness of everyone. All of those people are assumed to be feeling pleasure from the coordination, so the happiness everyone is feeling, multiplied by all those people, makes the observer extra happy. Conflict feels exaggeratedly bad because it's multiple people feeling negative, multiplied by all the observers who are flushed with automatic S$_C$ pain and tension because they're observing the conflict. Whoever resolves the tension will bring flushing joy to everyone who is also feeling the S$_C$ tension about the disconnect. They're not just resolving the pain of the people conflicting, but of all the surrounding people who are flushed with pain because anyone is conflicting. It is assumed by someone who feels tension because of other people's emotional investment in the group that the rest of the group members are harmonious because they are emotionally invested in the group, so they must also be flushed with pain if anyone in the group is feeling pain. A group member who is unaware of the social tension feels weirdly brain damaged and dangerous, because they could upset people at any moment because they're somehow oblivious to the tensions that everyone there is feeling.

> *"The only thing necessary for the triumph of evil*
> *is for good people to do nothing."*[497]

If the target naturally emotionally invests in others, then that person's emotions are automatically matched in the S$_C$ observer and their soul seems valuable. This goes the other way too. If the target is absolutely emotionally detached, if they feel no emotional investment in others, then they stop feeling like an extension of self even to an S$_C$ observer and can instead feel like the problem, making their expulsion relieving.

> *"I hate conflict. I really hate it.*
> *Unless you guys like it. Then I love it."*[498]

Teamwork between others, even unknown individuals, feels exaggeratedly positive, and a sign of even better things coming. Conflict between others feels exaggeratedly negative, and a sign of even more negativity growing. Disruptions which distract any part of the group trigger matching tension in the observer. Relief in others relieves tension in the observer. Restoring the conformity and flow of the group as a merged, single unit relieves tension.

> *"Life's most persistent and urgent question is,*
> *'What are you doing for others?'"[499]*

Self's needs seem smaller by comparison when only self benefiting or only self's discomfort is compared to the additive feeling of ten others feeling happy or distressed. The story generated which explains why a united group of humans acting together feels joyful and relieving, and why disruptions in the flow of humanity feel tensely negative, is that everyone gets the maximum benefit when each person makes small individual sacrifices for the much larger additive benefit of may other people.

> *"Community is much more than belonging to something.*
> *It's about doing something together that makes belonging matter."[500]*

Conflict between Logic, Reality, and Harmony

> *"Alone we can do so little. Together we can do so much."[501]*

The sharp emotions of S$_C$ are determined separately from logic. So S$_C$s are just as likely to think their groups are logically wrong while also pouring themselves into supporting the feelings of others and the harmony between others. Getting the group to become accurate while not upsetting the group happens through presenting the accurate option to group members in the proper forums, or maybe one-by-one, so that the minimum conflict happens during the consideration. S$_C$s can be deeply internally torn and hurt when their groups refuse to believe something that's true. Maybe the S$_C$ isn't so similar to these other people if the group can't be convinced by factual reality.

The group will believe the stories which support the average tensions of the members, repelling people with incompatible tensions. The beliefs and group actions will work toward the average group satisfaction conditions.

Resource Based Comfort (C_R) Selection Factors

Resource Based Comfort (C$_R$) Selection Factors

*"Food is the center of my universe.
When I'm eating food, I'm thinking of the next thing I'll eat,
or what I'll eat after that."[503]*

Taste: When euphoria, pain, lack, and satisfaction are added to the taste of food and drink then tasting things becomes emotional. Whatever tastes good feels exaggeratedly positive. Whatever tastes neutral or negative feels exaggeratedly negative. A particularly good taste can trigger tension, focusing the observer on the tasty input and motivating much more consumption. Tasty inputs that also generate tension become training events that are relived internally so that this source of goodness can be remembered and feels worth the effort to seek out again. It takes lesser deviations in taste to trigger pain tension, focusing the observer on the tragedy of the reduced taste, predicting negativity, causing the observer to imagine and seek out tastier options. This is also more likely to be a training event, cycling the observer in memories of the disappointment so it is remembered and can be avoided in the future. Tension is felt when a tastier option is available. Consuming the tastier option relieves tension. The story generated to explain why consuming the tastier option is necessary is that the tastier option has better quality, nutrition, happiness, or maybe even just relief from the craving. Joyful tastes are peak life pleasures. People feel direct love for foods because they stimulate so much euphoria and are so satisfying. Taste is the one sense which isn't C$_B$.

© *Mackenzie Moore - CinimomoComics*[504]

Consuming: When euphoria, pain, lack, and satisfaction are added to consumption then consuming things becomes emotional. Consuming more frequently and in greater amounts feels exaggeratedly positive. Time since eating, or insufficient quantity feel exaggeratedly negative. Tension (hunger) focuses attention when not consuming. Consuming relieves tension. The story generated to explain why consumption feels necessary is that the body needs fuel.

"I like rice. Rice is great when you're hungry and you want 2,000 of something."[505]

Size, Weight, Quantity, Contrast, Color, Function, Uniformity, Clarity, Age, and especially extremes of all of those: When euphoria, pain, lack, and satisfaction are added to aspects of inputs then the presence of those aspects becomes emotional. The biggest, smallest, heaviest, lightest, most rare, most common, most contrasting, least contrasting, most pure, most potent, oldest, newest, clearest, most uniform, cheapest, the only one, the entire set, mint condition, first printing, best value, and most expensive feel more or less joyful to consider because of those qualities.

> *"So you mean to tell me that you have so much clean water that you poop in yours?"*[507]

Presence of desired qualities feels exaggeratedly positive. Hearing that an option is available with better options triggers tension that holds focus on that other option. Destruction or absence of valued qualities feels exaggeratedly negative. Tension is felt when qualities are added, subtracted, present, or missing from options, and when the presence of those qualities are unknown. Clarifying the presence and quality of desired aspects relieves tension. The story generated which explains why one option feels glorious and another feels neutral or negative is that these qualities are critically important for establishing value.

Acquiring / Discarding: When euphoria, pain, lack, and satisfaction are added to acquiring and discarding then acquiring and discarding become emotional. Acquiring feels exaggeratedly positive. Discarding feels exaggeratedly negative. Tension is felt when a resource could be used and isn't present. Tension is felt (desire) when an item is available, but isn't being applied to the need. Tension is felt when valuable resources are being discarded, wrecked, stolen, or lost. Acquiring a valuable resource, or avoiding discarding a valuable resource relieves tension. The story generated which explains why the acquisition feels great is that the acquired item will be very useful, increase in value, or bring immense satisfaction. The story generated which explains why the desire was so strong includes tragic exaggerated predictions of loss if the resource weren't available. "Sentimental value," is pain about discarding when function is so obviously not present that logic can't come up with a story for why the item might be as critically necessary as the feelings make it seem.

"Buying stuff is more fun than using it"[508]

© Bob Eckstein[509]

Pleasure From Any Motivator (Fun, Entertainment): When euphoria, pain, lack, and satisfaction are added to pleasure felt from any motivator (any Comfort, Social, or Relational trigger) t hen entertainment becomes emotional. When consuming entertainment in a resource modeled mindset, it's often called "having fun." Whatever is entertaining feels exaggeratedly positive. The interruption or removal of pleasure feels exaggeratedly negative. Tension is felt when the observer isn't entertained ("boredom"). Laughing and getting pleasure from entertainment relieves tension.

"Can you explain this gap in your employment history?"
"Oh sure. That's the only time in my entire life that I've been happy."[510]

Other People's C$_R$ (Supply, Demand, and Price): When euphoria, pain, lack, and satisfaction are added to observation of other people's emotions about acquisition and consumption, then it becomes emotional when a resource is highly valued by others, when a resource is deeply satisfying to others, or when someone is determining the price they'll sell their resources for. C$_R$s watch other people cooking and eating. C$_R$s watch people selling and appraising things. C$_R$s watch hoarders on TV as they burst into tears while their garbage is hauled away. Watching other people feeling emotions about resources stirs their own emotions about resources.

"Intelligence is the ability to avoid doing work,
yet get the work done."[511]

© *e horne and j comeau – asofterworld.com*[512]

<u>*Pros and Cons of making food*</u>
Pros: food
Cons: making[513]

Effort: When euphoria, pain, lack, and satisfaction are added to exerting effort then exerting effort becomes emotional. Conserving effort feels exaggeratedly positive. Exerting more effort than necessary feels exaggeratedly negative. Tension is felt when effort needs to be exerted, or when more effort was exerted than necessary. Getting the benefits of effort without exerting effort relieves tension. The story generated which explains why conserving effort feels great and exerting effort feels negative is that energy is a limited resource which is valuable to conserve. The opposite wiring of this selection factor is R_A, where effort is limitless, taking action relieves tension, and being idle is painful.

Sexual Relational (R$_s$) Selection Factors

"The male jewel beetle has evolved to be attracted to certain features of the female jewel beetle that allow the male jewel beetle to identify a female as it flies across the desert. These features include size, color, and texture. However, these physical traits are seen manifested in beer bottles as well. As a result, male jewel beetles often consider beer bottles more attractive than female jewel beetles due to the beer bottle's large size and attractive coloring. The jewel beetle thrives in the Australian desert, where humans often discard beer bottles, creating an environment where male jewel beetles prefer to mate with beer bottles instead of female jewel beetles."[515]

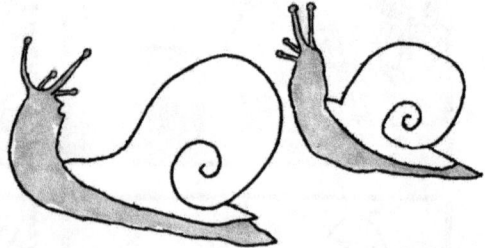

"I don't care if she is a tape dispenser. I love her."

© Sam Gross[516]

Physical Body Qualities: When euphoria, pain, lack, and satisfaction are added to physical body qualities, then observing physical body qualities becomes emotional. Symmetry, uniformity, contrast, coloring, height, weight, shapes, sizes, proportions, ratios, gender-specific body features, age, and health can all feel any of those can feel exaggeratedly negative (sexually neutralizing). Tension is felt when observing sexual beauty, or watching the destruction of sexual beauty. Having an orgasm relieves sexual tension. The story generated which explains why sexual body features are so pleasurable is that the person living inside them must be a very high value sexual partner. This includes arbitrary sexual markers which serve no logical function other than to arouse sexual interest in potential partners like hair, sex-linked vocal changes, jawline shape, and body fat distribution.

> *"I want to look in your eyes and feel flushed with desire.*
> *Give me the slightest indication that you like my smitten fixation*
> *and I will quickly be immersed in an intoxicating fantasy,*
> *especially if you then look around for a place where we won't*
> *be distracted while we focus on each other. Let me move around*
> *your face and around your body and tell you of the flushing euphoria*
> *I detect in each detail. Let me tell you how activated I feel as I learn*
> *each detail about you that makes it more and more clear that we*
> *were built for each other. Feel how there is no external world*
> *anymore because you and I together is all that matters."*[517]

Other People's R$_S$ (Sexual Arousal): When euphoria, pain, lack, and satisfaction are added to other people's sexual arousal then other people's sexual arousal becomes emotional to observe. A partner who is frequently and strongly sexually aroused when considering the observer feels exaggeratedly sexually arousing. A partner's lack of sexual arousal feels exaggeratedly negative. Tension is felt when another person's sexual interest isn't clear. Seeing the other person have an orgasm relieves tension. The story generated which explains why the other person's sexual arousal matters is that it's a sign that a deep sexual connection exists. It's preferable when this attraction is to the observer, but porn can stimulate sexual arousal in the observer because of the sexual arousal of the participants even though that arousal isn't directed at the observer. If the porn were adjusted so the same bodies had the same sex but the participants weren't aroused, it would be less arousing to observe.

> *"Porn causes memory loss and has several other*
> *negative effects that I can't remember."*[518]

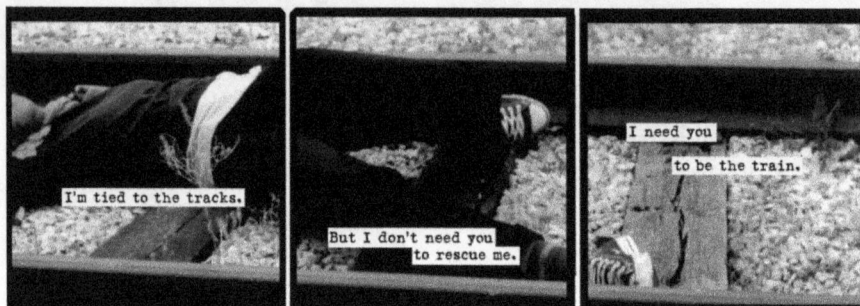

Physical Sexual Stimulation: When euphoria, pain, lack, and satisfaction are added to physical sensations then touching, kissing, and body contact become sexually emotional. Tactile stimulation feel exaggeratedly sexually arousing. A lack of tactile stimulation feels exaggeratedly frustrating. Tension is felt when physical contact isn't happening. Touching, kissing, mouths, genital contact, and orgasms relieve tension.

Sexual Fitness Displays: When euphoria, pain, lack, and satisfaction are added to the observation of sexual fitness displays then observing positive qualities of other people becomes sexually emotional. Someone can display a completely not-sexual skill and it generates exaggeratedly positive sexual attraction in an observer. Someone can display a completely not-sexual skill and it can be sharply destructive of sexual arousal in an observer. It feels sexual to the observer because it sparks a sharp increase or decrease in the sexual arousal felt. Tension is felt when sex feels lacking with someone who has been impressive. Having an orgasm (with or without that person) relieves tension. The story generated is that the other person is particularly sexually valuable.

> *"No one is in a lab, trying to cure cancer*
> *because they're drowning in sex options.*
> *They're working really hard to cure cancer*
> *so that later they can drown in sex options."*[520]

AN ELEPHANT IS LIKE A BRUSH

AN ELEPHANT IS LIKE A SNAKE

AN ELEPHANT IS LIKE A ROPE

AN ELEPHANT IS SOFT AND MUSHY

AN ELEPHANT IS LIKE A TREE TRUNK

S. GROSS

© Sam Gross[521]

Why Selection Factors Matter

*"Things are never as good or as bad as they seem,
nor do they last as long."*[522]

Sometimes detrimental things are attractive. Sometimes beneficial things feel neutral. Sometimes impossible actions feel necessary. Sometimes beneficial actions don't feel important. Selection factors explain why emotions sometimes don't match up with logic, and why logic can't always generate motivation or release tension.

Limbic System drugging feels like it's a reaction to benefits, detriments, and opportunities, when it's actually a reaction to sometimes-arbitrary triggers which are rough indicators of value and theme. Those indicators can be misleading in specific situations for specific inputs.

R_Ss regularly feel fixated sexual attraction to a human they logically know isn't a good functional match. R_Ss are sometimes destroyed by heartbreaking desire to reconnect with someone who is a proven awful match. Meanwhile, they sometimes feel zero sexual attraction to a logically fantastic match. It's not the logic of a match that makes the match feel sexually arousing. It's the presence or lack of selection factors which cause the observer to feel attraction, desire, heartbreak, or neutrality.

C_Rs regularly feel desire to consume food they logically know isn't healthy, pain about discarding items they logically aren't using, and pain about exerting effort on tasks that are clearly beneficial. Meanwhile, they sometimes feel zero desire to consume foods which are logically good resources for their bodies. Because it's not the logic of consumption, acquisition, or discarding that make a resource feel arousing. It's the presence or lack of selection factors.

C_Is regularly feel fixated desire to be right, to be different, to make an impact, and to have other people's attention, when they logically know the other person has an equally valid point, when differentiating reduces functionality, when their impact doesn't matter, and when there's no benefit from having the attention. They're sometimes destroyed by painful self-judgment about things they logically know don't matter. Then they feel zero interest in making the sacrifices for others that would result in the factual respect and admiration that they want. They feel repulsion from factually accurate, functionally useful information because it's coming from someone else who wants attention. Because it's not the logic or accuracy that make words, actions, or choices impressive. It's the presence or lack of selection factors.

S_Fs regularly feel like they have to conform with choices they know are detrimental in order to keep their friend happy. They feel obligated to support the emotions of people who have proven that they aren't good allies in return. Meanwhile, S_Fs sometimes feel zero friendship attraction to people who would really like to be their friends. Because it's not the logic of beneficial alliances that makes an ally trigger emotions in an observer. It's the presence or lack of selection factors.

R_As regularly feel fixated excitement about activities they logically know aren't productive or world-expanding. Meanwhile, they sometimes feel zero excitement about logically beneficial, but familiar, repetitive activities. Because it's not the logic of meaning, purpose, or personal growth that make an action feel stagnant or exciting. It's the presence or lack of selection factors.

C_Bs regularly feel fixated fear about inputs they logically know aren't dangerous. They sometimes feel excitement about sensations that are logically negative (like breathing around candles, and sun exposure on skin). Meanwhile, their body flushes with pain and tension around actually-healing inputs like surgery, dental work, and needles. Because it's not the logic of body damage or healing that makes a sensation feel arousing. It's the presence or lack of selection factors.

S_Cs regularly support rules that they know are arbitrary or detrimental because the group agreed to them (like jay walking). They sometimes feel tense resistance to beneficial changes because they're afraid people will be upset. They sometimes feel neutral about things that would benefit the group because no one else seems to care. They sometimes feel tense desire for community and love between strangers who have no interest in loving each other. Because it's not logic that makes the feelings of others, and the harmony and progress of the group feel important. It's the presence of lack of selection factors.

All seven of these are the same situation as when you know you're looking at an optical illusion. Your logic knows that it's not what it appears, but your eyes keep reporting seeing what they're seeing. Because eyes aren't logic driven. They're just detectors. Just like your detectors for when to feel tension.

It's the predictability of this gap between logic and emotions which gives away that emotions are driven by the same mechanism as every other sense organ.

Advanced Notes: When eyes detect blue, they return a signal which is exclusive to blue, which is different from the signal which is exclusive to red. But when the Limbic system detects blue, it returns signals of good, bad, tense, satisfying, or nothing, which are the same signals sent for other detected inputs. So, an observer might have the same Limbic response to blue as red, or no response to blue or red, or different responses to blue and red. The fact that the same response is triggered by multiple inputs means that the output signal for the Limbic System functionally groups external inputs.

The added signal response also functionally magnifies those inputs. Afterward, consciousness solves for why these inputs are more important than surrounding inputs, not knowing they're internally scaled, and not knowing the grouping of inputs was added inside the observer. The basic signal detecting mechanics of the Limbic System are the same as other sense organs, but the output is more similar to allergies. In fact, the mechanism used by the Limbic System is likely the same mechanism used for physical allergies.

The Limbic System is trying to be an objective sense organ which detects benefits and detriments, but it isn't there yet, and might've been more accurate when human life was less complex. At this point it's responding to simple, detected selection factors which only roughly correlate with the stories they trigger in the observer.

One more note is that <u>imagination</u> itself is not Limbic (there's overlap right at the border because selection factors are connected to and react to imagination, but imagination itself isn't Limbic). So, this book repeatedly refers to cycling in imagined stories and scenarios, but the degree to which stories are developed by the observer varies significantly between humans for non-Limbic reasons. Lots of people don't develop stories at all, but they don't because their system doesn't develop stories for any reason, regardless of the presence or absence of tension. These people often collect the stories of others, and still cycle in those stories, but those stories were born in other minds.

"I'll pause for a moment so you can let this information sink in."

Trait Stacking & Detail Sensitivity

Low Detail (Most Common): The ranking of Limbic influences can be quickly summarized in a three letter profile. An RCS has most easily triggered Relational tensions and least easily triggered Social tensions. An SCR has most easily triggered Social tensions and least easily triggered Relational tensions. Three letter summaries don't give information on intensity, subrankings inside each class, or selection factors which trigger that tension. But sometimes, for some applications, this quick summary can be very useful information in a very small package.

Medium Detail: With all types, but especially with Comfort types, the sub-ranking makes a difference in the final personality. Those sub-rankings can be stacked in the same way as the major rankings. So a C_{BRI} has dominant Body-based tension and weakest Individuality-based tension, and is quite clearly different from a Comfort-first person with the opposite sub-stacking. Especially when discussing a specific person, identifying them as $C_{RIB}RS$ gives a lot of information very quickly. It's a little more common to just give the top for someone's Comfort ranking, like $C_R RS$.

High Detail: Sometimes discussion at the level of selection factors provides the most insight. A C_R who is more strongly triggered with tension about exerting effort may have significant differences from a C_R who is more strongly triggered with hunger for food and taste. They might both be meaningfully different than a C_R who is mainly triggered with pain about discarding anything. An R_S who is more strongly triggered to be attracted to hair may have significant differences from an R_S who is more strongly triggered by a partner's returned sexual attraction. Zeroing in on individual selection factors happens a lot, especially when discussing specific individuals.

Grouping by Family

It simply doesn't happen in humans that the seven classes of tension get shuffled together in ranking outside of their families like $C_B R_A S_C C_I R_S S_F C_R$. Instead the Relational influences happen together, the Social influences happen together, and the Comfort influences happen together. Presumably, the fact that such different motivators occur next to each other in intensity is a hint at how the hardware connections between selection factors and emotional drugging are wired in human brains.

<u>*Limbic Profiles Aren't All Of Personality*</u>

Whether detailed or general, Limbic profiles are just the Limbic System settings. They aren't all the critical settings for a human personality.

"Have you tried taking long walks?"

Conclusion 1:
Pulling Back and Seeing
a Sense Organ as a Sense Organ

Each new input starts with a combination of sensory components:

Touch

Visual

Taste

Smell

Sound

Emotions

Those are each the combination of independent readings from several sensory detectors:

- **Touch** (temperature, location, pressure, pain)
- **Visual** (blue, green, red, low light)
- **Taste** (sweet, sour, salty, bitter, savory)
- **Smell** (varied chemical receptors)
- **Sound** (varied sound wave receptors)
- **Emotions** (novelty, familiarity, other people's emotions, self, ranking, symmetry, sexual features, experiential features, similarity, physical qualities, acquiring, consuming)

If red is present in the visual field, then cones which detect red send a signal to your brain. If red is a selection factor for Limbic System drugging then your Limbic System releases emotional drugging to accompany that input. Red may feel pleasurable, painful, neutral, tense, and/or satisfying. Your brain's first impression of this new input will have both red and the emotion as components, along with readings from any other detector.

A person who feels pleasure around red will have a different life experience than the person standing next to them who doesn't feel any emotion around red (who feels neutral). The person feeling pleasure alongside red is more likely to stop and notice the red, and more likely to seek out the factual understandings which support why that red is beneficial. Both the neutral and the positively drugged observers are collecting facts, but one didn't stop to learn about red while the other did. Likewise, someone who feels good about themselves, about friends, or about adventures will notice those things more and develop more understandings about self, friend, or adventure related things.

A person who is triggered with painful tension when other people are conflicting will start the moment thinking that something should happen to stop the conflict. The person next to them who is triggered with joyful tension when other people are conflicting will think action should happen to escalate those people's conflict. The person next to them who isn't triggered with tension may or may not focus on the conflict enough to notice it, but will default to thinking that humans conflicting is just a natural, observable part of life which happens in the background while other, tension-triggering inputs get focus because they could and should adjust.

The Limbic System is trying to be a benefit/detriment sense organ. It's trying to make you feel good about beneficial inputs and bad about detrimental inputs. It's trying to help you notice what could and should be adjusted. It's trying to help you ignore the parts of life that can't be adjusted.

If the Limbic System were perfectly accurate, you would be attracted to things to the exact degree that they were beneficial. You'd dislike things to the exact degree that they're detrimental. You'd feel just the right amount of motivation to change the things you can. You'd feel peaceful acceptance of the things you can't change because you wouldn't even consider them being different than they are.

It is a mindset shift to recognize emotions as being internal, individual reactions rather than a logical, factual reactions to external inputs. It's hard to even imagine how the things you hate are actually normal and less damaging than they feel. It's hard to imagine how the things you love are actually normal and less differentiated from other options than they feel. It's a natural consequence of how tension works that it's hard to see how tension works.

IMAGINATION | **REALITY**

SUFFERING

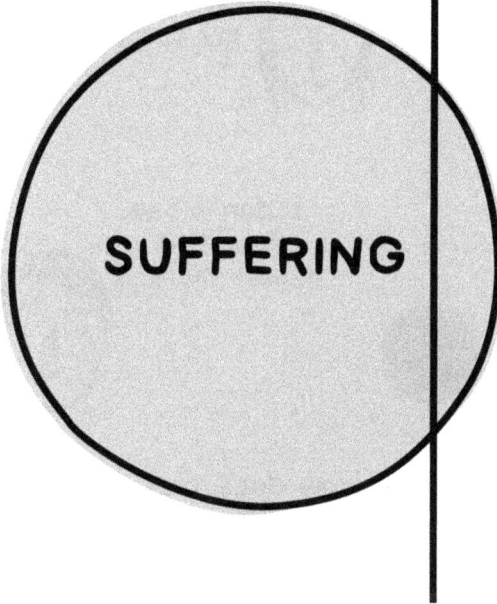

Conclusion 2: Are Tension and Anxiety Good Things or Bad Things?

"Fate shuffles the cards, and we play."[526]

In the situations where you're actually being exploited, having enough tension to be triggered into self-defense is likely to be helpful. If you're not being exploited, but are triggered with enough tension to defend yourself, then your defensiveness is more likely to be detrimental. The people who are easily triggered with the feeling that they're being taken advantage of get the benefits of seizing every opportunity to defend themselves, and also seize the detriments of sacrificing friendship, community, sexual, and experiential opportunities when triggers for their self-defense are also present.

 Am I
supposed to
be impressed?

 How does
this affect
my comfort?

 How will my
friends feel
about this?

 I don't see
how this
makes money.

 How does this
affect sexual
arousal?

 How does this
impact the depth
of my life
experience?

 Will this
excite or upset
the group?

Tension and anxiety use an algorithm to make predictions based on incomplete information. Tension is an allergic overreaction to selection factors which make each observer assume a theme for the moment. But this algorithm is working in reality, where the same actions taken in the same starting conditions sometimes lead to beneficial outcomes, sometimes lead to detrimental outcomes, and sometimes lead to unrelated outcomes. Whether each feeling is helpful or detrimental often depends on external, unknowable details at the point where emotions happen, or at the point where emotions would've helped but didn't happen. Tension and anxiety are gamblers making lots of bets, hoping to win more often than they lose, or win in more impactful moments than when they lose. Whether they're actually beneficial or detrimental in any specific case depends on the results of all the different actions in that case and how feelings, accuracy, survival, and reproduction are weighted as benefits. A benefit in one category is often paired with a detriment in another.

So, the real answer to the question of whether tension and anxiety are good or bad things is that tension is helpful some of the time and detrimental some of the time. The desire for tension to be all-good or all-bad so you can love or hate it is tension driven. Tension has benefits and detriments. It can and does provide more benefits than detriments to some people, and more detriments than benefits to others.

Persistent tension is great when it's a glow of love that makes the whole world feel better. It's great when it motivates you to invest in creating something beautiful. Persistent tension is not great when it's a cloud of negativity that makes every input feel a worse. It's not great when it distracts you from enjoying loving, joyful, hopeful inputs.

Tension becomes more of a good thing, and less of a bad thing when it's recognized as tension, rather than when it's automatically followed into the story it motivates. When an observer stops and says, "I'm feeling tension," before they move on to "this thing is good and could get better," or "this thing is bad and has to be stopped," then they can steer themselves better toward the inputs which will actually benefit them, and away from the spiraling negativity they'll feel about changing things that aren't as factually negative as they feel.

Emotions are added to your soul's experience. Sometimes they're worth noticing but not investing in. Sometimes they're worth embracing and nurturing. You can either randomly hope they work out for you, or you can pause and adjust in ways that will help that you might not feel emotionally driven toward.

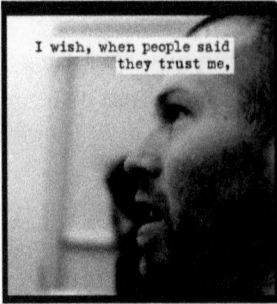

I wish, when people said they trust me,

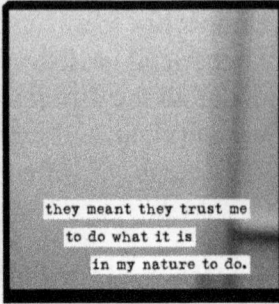

they meant they trust me to do what it is in my nature to do.

Conclusion 3: Managing Addictions

If someone does not act in the way you expect,
perhaps it's because they hear a different drummer.
Let them step to the music they hear." [528]

The point of this chapter is to add an element to your perception of other people which you'll use to solve for their weirdness. When other people act in unexpected ways, most people assume that there's a gap in intelligence or factual understanding. They don't normally assume that the other person has a part of life that they're easily triggered in, which cycles them with pain that is very hard to release. They don't normally assume the other person has a part of life that they expect better-than-reality-delivers from. The choices other people are making make sense when you know the tensions and anxieties they're feeling, especially if you remove the tensions you experience which they don't feel at all.

"When people show you who they are, believe them." [529]

You can eat just one doughnut, so it seems like your friend should too. But it'll take 24 to satisfy the craving if they eat one, and it might snowball into a month of 10,000 calorie days. You can talk about a sexy stranger, feel the pleasure, and move on. They'll be fixated until they've had a lot of sex with the toxic ex that they were still managing to avoid. A Social person doesn't want to see the people you do because they'll leave feeling obligated to enslave themselves to jerks, or cycle in pain about how much someone they

356

don't like is hurting. You can say a politician or political system is brilliant or dumb and then switch topics. The other person will cycle in pain for the rest of the week imagining exaggerated damage to society if you got your way. You can try a new thing and fail and move on. They will feel deeply humiliated, punish themselves for not being excellent, and cycle in pain about whose fault it was.

WHY YOU SHOULD BE KIND TO PEOPLE

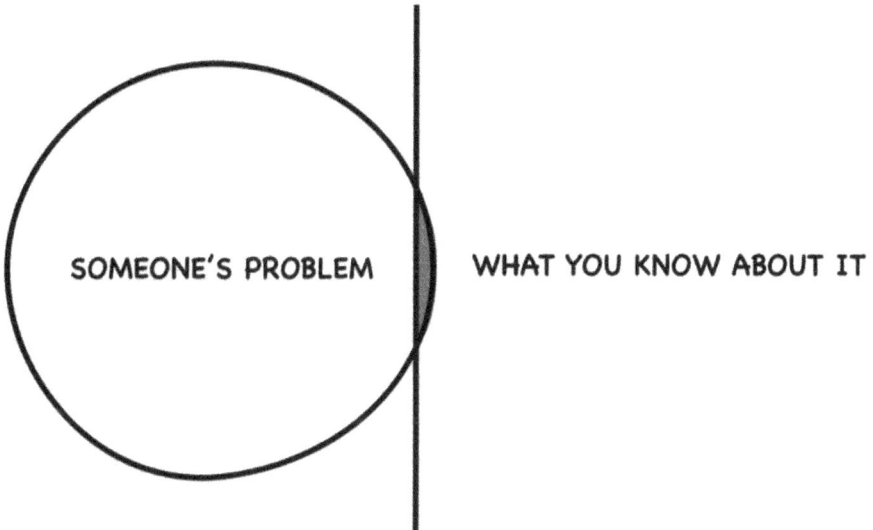

SOMEONE'S PROBLEM   WHAT YOU KNOW ABOUT IT

© Noteshort.co – @noteshort.co[530]

Very few people are trying to hurt other people. Meanwhile people are negatively triggered by each other, taking righteous stands against "evil," and surprised that more people don't join their cause. No matter who you are, you have said something unemotionally observational and someone else has been deeply offended. This is the nature of everyone being overly sensitive in different areas. This is especially the nature of talking about someone else's sacred topic measured on your tension's value scale.

Other humans have sharply meaningful boundaries that don't exist for you. Everyone thinks they're discussing the facts of external reality, while each person is actually discussing the story that makes their pleasure, pain, tension, and satisfaction triggers make sense.

Then everyone is offended by everyone else's analysis because their own triggers weren't adequately revered.

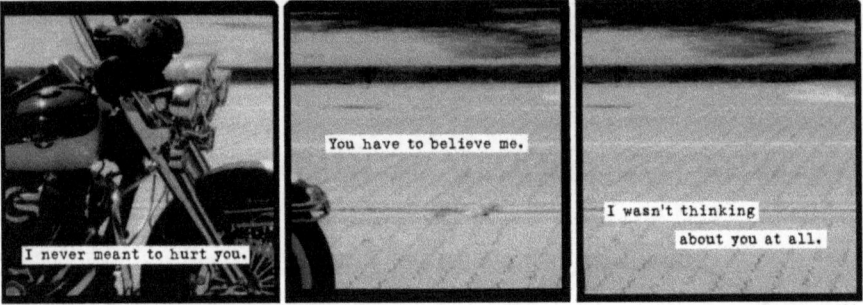

© e horne and j comeau – asofterworld.com[531]

Enlightenment comes when it stops occurring to you that other people might be talking about facts which you should then verify, confirm, or refute. They are not praising, attacking, or even observing the external world. They are outputting the narrative which explains their emotions, half to hear how their own emotions react to hearing the story they just created. Your own emotions become less easily triggered when you hear their stories as explanations of how someone has to think in order to survive with their anxieties. This is how you also sound to everyone else.

> *"It's hard to be human. Everyone is in pain.*
> *Human interactions are really just a form of group therapy.*
> *If we could confidently assume that other people*
> *are in just as much pain as we are,*
> *maybe it would change our behaviors."*[532]

"That's strange. I remember it differently, in a way that aligns with my world view and casts me in a positive light."

© Sofia Warren – SofiaWarren.com[533]

Conclusion 4: Delusions

"There's simply no polite way to tell people that they've dedicated their lives to an illusion."[534]

People feel good when noticing certain things and collect the facts that support why that input is good. People feel bad when noticing certain things and collect the facts that support why that input is bad. People feel like certain things should change and collect the fact, understandings, and predictions that explain why and how that could and should change. People don't notice other classes of inputs and form stories about why those parts of reality are practical, fixed, and less important.

When these stories cause the observer to misinterpret reality, they're called "**delusions**." Almost everyone has an active delusion right now. They think they've nailed some part of life and it's a reason to feel satisfied and happy. They think they've identified evil and that it's as toxic and negative as it feels. Meanwhile, in reality, the loved thing has flaws they're ignoring, and doesn't have loved components that they've imagined. It's more normal and less holy than it feels. The hated thing has positive components that are being ignored, and doesn't have some imagined components. It's more normal and less impactful than it feels.

> *"Love is a state in which people see things*
> *most decidedly as they are not."*[535]

A C_I might be imagining that they're impactful, brilliant, and individual, or that they're ignored, cheated, and a victim, or be bouncing from project to project or person to person seeking the situation where they're recognized for their greatness, and be fitting all incoming information into that narrative.

An S_C might be imagining that their group is harmoniously making the world a better place, that something outside the group is more toxic to good humans than it is, or be bouncing from group to group trying to find their people, and be fitting all incoming information into that narrative.

An R_S might be smitten with their true love, be flushed with pain about missed sexual opportunities, or be bouncing from partner to partner seeking a dream-level match, and be fitting all incoming information into that narrative.

A C_B might think they've found something that restores, heals, and calms, or that their health, safety, or wellbeing have been tragically damaged, or be bouncing from option to option trying to find peace, health, and safety, and be fitting all incoming information into that narrative.

An S_F might assume the other half of their friendship is more emotionally invested in return, or might think they're obligated to support the feelings of people they don't like, or be bouncing from friend to friend trying to find their soul-connected other half, and be fitting all incoming information into that narrative.

© *Warren Miller*[536]

An **R**$_A$ might imagine they've found their calling, that life was wasted by not following their calling, or be bouncing from experience to experience trying to find meaning, and be fitting all incoming information into that narrative.

A **C**$_R$ might be imagining that they're acquiring something very valuable, or that they should've acquired a better option, or be bouncing from purchase to purchase or investment to investment hoping to finally hit it big, and be fitting all incoming information into that narrative.

> *"One should go easy on smashing other people's lies.*
> *Better to concentrate on one's own."*[537]

Here are some statements that might give you a moment of perspective on your own delusions: Sometimes, when you're safe and your body is normal, you feel fear and discomfort anyway. Sometimes, when your body doesn't need food, it will feel hungry anyway. Sometimes, when you're being respected and treated fairly, you'll feel disrespected and treated unfairly anyway. Sometimes, when a sexual option is awful for you, you'll feel horny and attracted anyway. Sometimes, when you've created the best life that reality offers for you, you'll feel stagnant and hunger for change anyway. Sometimes, when the group is getting along as well as possible, you'll feel concern that people are upset anyway. Sometimes, when something really should be thrown out, you'll feel sharp pain about discarding it anyway. Sometimes the reason you think other people do things wrong is that you feel tension when something happens without your input. Sometimes the reason other people don't take your advice is that you're suggesting random adjustments because you're hungry to make an impact. The best real-world romantic match for you has so many negatives that you're not expecting, that you'll wonder if you picked the wrong person.

> *"You are exactly where you're supposed to be.*
> *Because you make terrible decisions."*[538]

It doesn't matter if people are the same or different. Group members are present to fill their own needs and don't care much about each other. The person you're emotionally merged with knows they're using your affection for their own good, but they feel justified because they need the things they get from you. You do things for them because you feel pain tension when they're hurting, and not because you actually like them. You'd realize that you're not friends with most of your "friends" if you really knew what they think of you. Inaccurate tension causes you to collect garbage, to avoid effort that would help, to eat low quality food that damages your body, and to feel lacking when you already have more than you need. You never deserved what other people got, and you're not smart enough to know the actual prices they paid for it.

When a **<u>positive</u>** delusion is broken (when the loved item is revealed to be what it actually is), it's heartbreaking, and life feels awful. But it's the internal filters, the internal projection outward, which is actually broken. The observer is reborn into reality again. They'll be less motivated at first because their motivating hope is revealed to be impossible. This is the opportunity to really appreciate how delusions provide purpose, motivation, and direction. After the shock they'll develop a new positive or negative delusion, and maybe manage it a little more practically this time. The actual experience of maturing is finding more happiness while straying less and less from reality.

> *"It ain't what you don't know that gets you into trouble.*
> *It's what you know for sure that just ain't so."*[539]

<u>Negative</u> delusions are broken when a hated item is revealed to be as normal, powerless, and fixed as it is. It feels like waking from a clouded distraction when you realize that nothing is actually happening. A disliked thing just is what it is, doing less than it felt like. The stupidity is a natural, unchangeable part of humanity. Focusing on it is what gave it the power to hurt you. Your disconnection from it, your lack of emotional investment, is what it took for your pain reaction to stop. Now you get to rebuild a new life where that item powerlessly exists in the background. It was a normal, annoying part of reality that you gave way too much attention to. It will take time and repetition for it to fade.

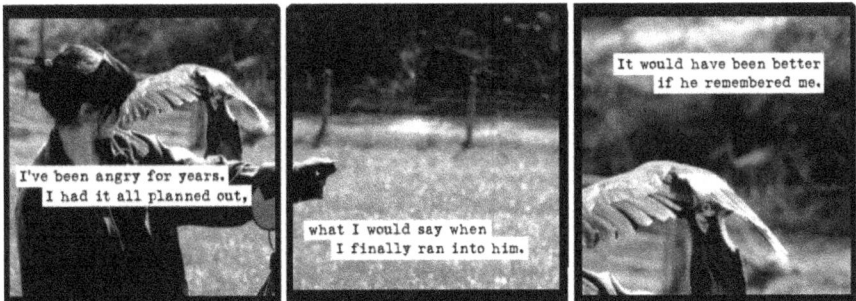

© e horne and j comeau – asofterworld.com[540]

The people around you are living narratives that are extreme, which are shocking departures from reality. In those narratives, they are more heroic and more change is possible. This mainly happens because they feel hungry, horny, guilty, uncomfortable, stagnant, embarrassed, ignored, lonely, scared, obligated, or self-doubting more often and easily than you do. It is hard to overstate the degree to which you are a minor, oversimplified background character in the lives of the people closest to you while they're deeply invested in a narrative about their own hero's journey. They're fighting more clearly on the side of good, and the other side is more purely evil. They make this mistake because they're flushed with pain and assume negativity must exist to justify that pain. They're flushed with love and assume goodness must exist to justify that endearment. They think their emotions are reactions to the external world, when actually the story they imagine about the external world is a reaction to the feelings they're having. If they love you, it's because they think you might help satisfy their desires. If they hate you, it's because they think you'll generate their pain triggers. You also frame your admiration and distrust on a value scale that doesn't feel meaningful to other people.

The periods of life when you get the best view of actual reality are the ones where you're not excited or depressed, not for anything and not against anything. Delusions are great when they flush you with daily love and don't encourage too many detrimental behaviors. They're worth breaking right away if they make normal days feel bad. The truly meaningful part of life is the aspect of the current moment that you can feel lovingly excited about.

"Wherever you are – Be there."[541]

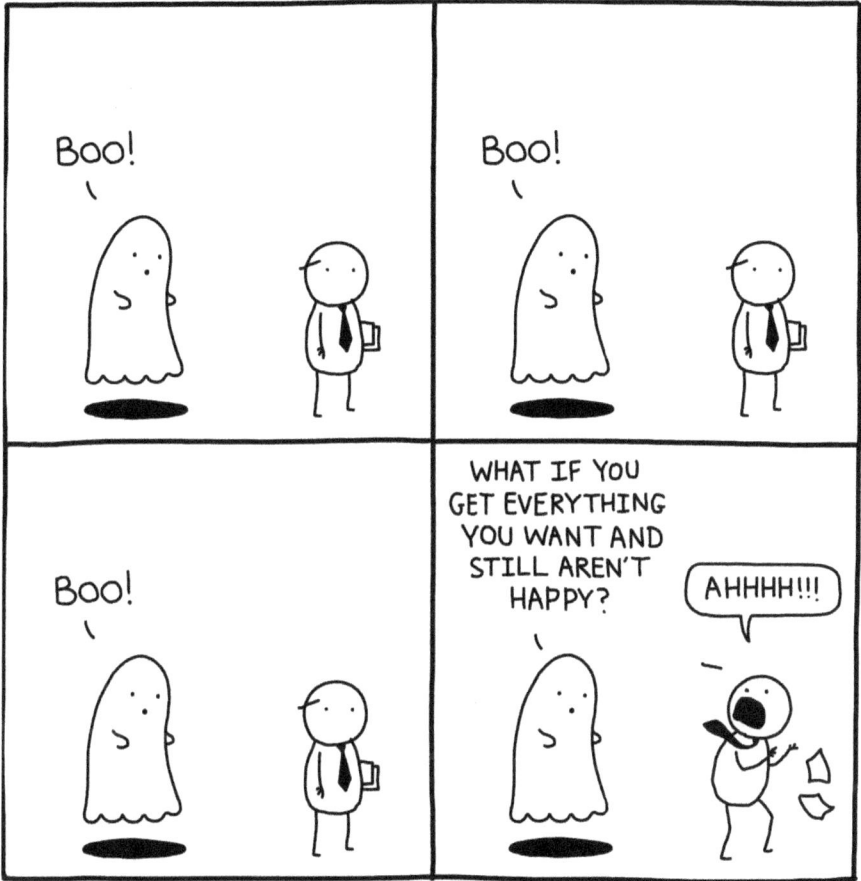

Conclusion 5:
You're Not Missing Anything

*"A free soul is rare, but you know it when you see it -
because you feel good when you're near them."*[543]

Reality feels like it should be better because both pain and pleasure can trigger the feeling that things could and should be better (tension). In order to really get into the mindset where you see that reality simply is what it is, it helps to find the paragraph below that applies to your friend who complains about a part of reality that won't change, and then hold that recognition while you turn back on the part of life that you're certain needs to change.

You're not missing sexual attraction in your life. The options you have are what reality actually delivers. Real world romantic partners come with negatives and incompatibilities. If you want a romantic partner, you have to choose which negatives you're willing to deal with. Then you also have tension so you can imagine a sexier option and feel bad about what you have.

You're not missing good friends in your life. What you have is what the practical reality of your life got you. Real world friends aren't as merged, selfless, and intelligent as you imagine. Then you also feel tension so you can imagine someone more endearing who is more invested in return and feel bad about what you have.

You're not missing health, safety, or comfort in your life. What you have is the practical reality of human bodies and environments. Then you also have anxiety so you can imagine more comfort and health so you can feel bad about what you have.

You're not missing food, money, items, or "abundance." What you have is what's actually available. Healthy food often isn't tasty. Even expensive things have flaws. Then you also have anxiety so you can feel hungrier than your body needs, desire more acquisition than your life needs, and feel disappointed with the things you have.

> *"You are not promised anything in life.*
> *No contract was signed with you."*[544]

You're not missing glory, attention, love, excellence, ranking, individuality, influence, impact, or power. What you have is what your human life gets. Then you also have anxiety so you can imagine being more recognized, loved, individual, excellent so you can feel bad about what you have.

You're not missing community, connection, or freedom from obligation. What you have is what the people around you do. Then you also have anxiety so you can imagine people loving and caring for each other more so you can feel bad about what you have.

You're not missing purpose, calling, personal growth, or life experiences. What you're having is the actual experience of a human life. Then you also have anxiety so you can imagine that life shouldn't have so much repetition, downtime, and lack of motivation so you can feel bad while experiencing your actual adventure.

"Don't waste your miracle on your pain."[545]

You weren't supposed to get more or better of anything. You are lucky that you didn't get less or worse. You aren't living a dream version. You're living the actual version of reality and learning how life and reality work. You're not in a state of having less. You're in the state of having what reality delivers, which is somewhere below the dream level and somewhere above being dead and getting nothing.

© e horne and j comeau – asofterworld.com[546]

You weren't supposed to get a less traumatic past, present, or future. Human lives suck. They're full of trauma, pain, and senseless loss. The optimal thing to do is factually note which shockingly awful traumas you got, without also considering the life where you didn't get them. Permit those negatives to exist in the background without giving attention to them. Focus forward to what's possible now that you survived. Build the inspiring recovery story of what you still manage to create.

The fact that reality is what it is doesn't mean you shouldn't take action. It means that navigation is better done by noticing the initial triggers for loving, hopeful moments, and the initial triggers for negative, righteous, painful moments. It means practically putting yourself near your positive triggers and away from your negative triggers. Once you do that, it's okay to drop the fight for something different. It's okay to stop comparing your situation to more. It's okay to accept the balanced negatives and the lack of pure positives that make up reality.

> *"Pay attention and intentionally keep what interests you.*
> *You choose what's valuable, but when you hear something valuable,*
> *make it your business to keep it, stop and write it down.*
> *Send it to yourself in your phone. Then review it, keep repeating it*
> *to yourself until it becomes incorporated into who you are.*
> *Don't let the things that interest you get away."*[547]

I want you to find what makes you happy.
here, have an orange!

it makes me happy, it might make you happy,
and if not, at least you'll have an orange.

@chibirdart

© Jacqueline Chen – Chibird.com[548]

Conclusion 6:
Accepting Pain and Tension

"I stopped fighting my inner demons. We're on the same side now."[549]

"Embrace the glorious mess that you are."[550]

Every day has both pain and tension in it. That is normal and never ends. It makes logical sense that human bodies drug themselves each day with discomfort to motivate beneficial actions like eating, body maintenance, self-protection, social maintenance, option-checking, and reproduction. Why can't we be drugged with love

369

daily, instead of pain, to motivate those actions? It's acceptance that recognizes that this is the system we got. If someone practically accepts that every day has pain and tension cycles, and it's currently the part of the day where that pain and tension are felt, then they don't take the steps that amplify both.

> *"We often try to get over our pain.*
> *What if you allowed it to be there?*
> *Let it exist within the whole of who you are.*
> *Maybe that's real healing."*[551]

> *"I try not to create new understandings or predictions*
> *while I'm feeling pain. Instead I use that time to notice the pain*
> *and make sure I'm not doing anything to make it worse.*
> *I switch my mindset to other topics until the pain passes.*
> *When peace returns I can get back to*
> *understandings and predictions."*[552]

Every life includes periods of healing from particularly big traumas. That can take a long time even for someone who is doing everything right. Really feel the long periods of pain so they can serve as contrast later, when joyful moments of love start to break through again. Fake, made-up fantasies of perfection generate pain when used to evaluate the current moment. The realistic pain of normal human low points is a more functional comparison for evaluating the current moment, because it exposes how basic comforts in any moment are a gift.

> *"Letting go doesn't happen by telling yourself to let go.*
> *It happens by clearly seeing the pain of holding on.*
> *From there, the mind lets go when it's ready."*[553]

Emotional cuts heal like physical cuts: slowly and with imperceptible daily progress. Reliving the trauma in imagination reopens the wound the same as reopening a physical cut. Part of healing is allowing the cut to exist. That damage is real. The pain is real. The itchy feeling is real. It will draw attention every day for a long time. But it will also fade naturally if you protect it from getting bothered while natural processes rebuild.

"I accept my whole life up until now.
What happened to me is what happened.
I might learn lessons from what happened,
but I won't dwell in the fantasy of it not happening.
I'm a person with that event fixed forever as part of my story.
The rest of that story is that I survive.
I make it to the part where what happened doesn't hurt me anymore.
When the opportunities come up, I find something to care about
and I invest in that until my heart is full of love again."[554]

The old pattern for most people is to feel tension, immerse in a negative story, and keep cycling about how righteous they are for being against something. The new pattern is to feel tension, notice that tension is happening, recognize that tension is part of normal healing, move away from present triggers as much as possible, completely refocus attention onto a lovingly inspiring topic, drink water, exercise, and sleep.

"If you are in a bad mood, go for a walk.
If you are still in a bad mood, go for another walk."[555]

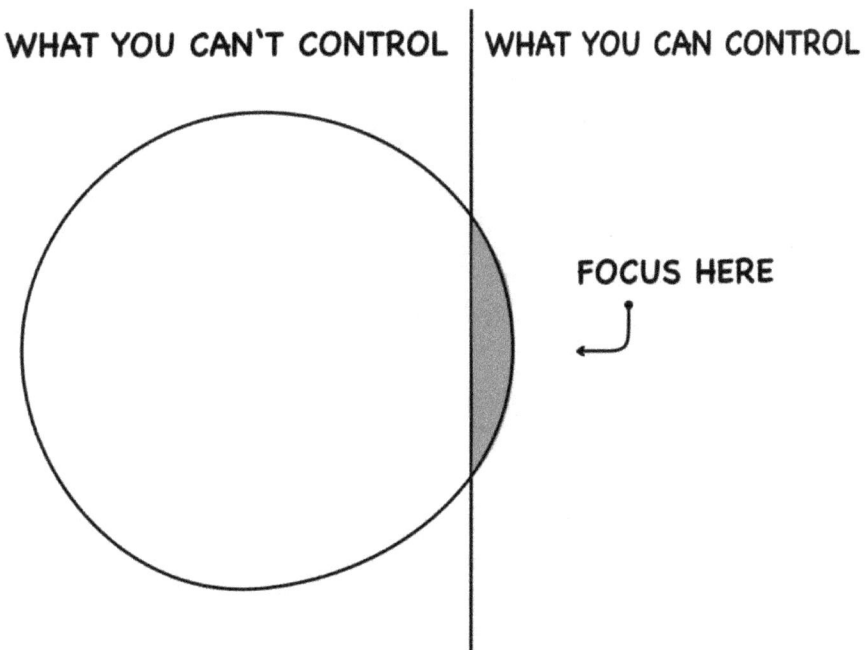

WHAT YOU CAN'T CONTROL | WHAT YOU CAN CONTROL

FOCUS HERE

The end goal is to have your daily visitors (moments of pain anxiety) seen-but-not-engaged, and the visitors you'd rather have (moments of loving enthusiasm) visited enough that they start coming to mind on their own. In your old life you engaged with negatives and battled them. Then the day came when you changed and focused on building something that inspires you with love instead. Like adjusting any habit or muscle-memory, switching is really awkward at first and takes a long time. The moment of switching is a complete mindset change onto a new topic, repeatedly making the choice to go back to the love-inspired mindset when the old mindset happens on its own.

© Andrea Florence[557]

So, if you were curious about what you can actually do, trusting reality as the ultimate source of that answer, what barriers and crappy aspects of reality would you stop fighting? If pain were always recognized as a natural part of reality, so focus was free to nurture joy and enthusiasm, what would you build or support? What would you remove from your life and what would you add? What is the tiny step of satisfying action you could take toward something that makes you joyful just because it exists?

"The real secret of life
is to be completely engaged with what you are doing.
Instead of calling it work, realize it's play."[558]

"The meaning of life is to find your gift.
The purpose of life is to give it away."[559]

The goal is to stop waging a war against the evils of peanuts (whatever your peanuts might be) and instead at least intellectually consider that you might have an individual allergy. Even if you can't feel it or imagine it, you can logically know that it's your consideration of peanuts, while you have an allergy, that might be generating each moment's new pain. The way to stop the pain is to stop considering peanuts. But it's not just mental. Take the practical steps too. Quit your job at the peanut factory. Stop eating peanuts. Move away from Peanutville. Move to Puppyville. Get a job at a kennel. Sleep in a pile of dogs. Instead of another day of war, let today's focus entirely be on creating a moment with a dog (whatever your dog might be) that flushes you with hope, love, enthusiasm, peace, and joy.

The world is vast. Current reality is the product of laws of nature over unfathomable periods of time, which are not under your control, and operate regardless of your approval. There's a lot going on that you don't know about, even with the people closest to you. It was childish and oversimplified to think that you knew the major forces affecting any moment. You are an explorer in an unknown land, surrounded by people who are responding to forces that are invisible to you. Your best guiding principle is that you are not here to fight, powered by hurt. You are here to create, powered by love. But you have to make a choice to let pain go, and a choice to give love more attention. And you'll have to make that choice again, every day.

"It's easy to spot a blue car when you're already thinking of blue cars.
It's easy to spot reasons to be upset when you're already upset.
It's easy to spot reasons to laugh and feel thankful
when you're already grateful.
It's easy to spot things that interest you
when you're eager to engage anything that interests you."[560]

The world around you has all of the options, all of the time. Which you experience depends on the state of your soul.

"Some poor, phoneless fools are sitting next to a waterfall somewhere,
totally unaware of how angry and scared they're supposed to be."[561]

"We act like other things matter,
when all that we need to make us happy
is something to be enthusiastic about."[562]

"So brief is life.
There isn't time for bickerings,
apologies, heartburnings, or callings to account.
There is only time for loving, and but an instant for that."[563]

Post Script: Likely Suspects

Dopamine is tension. In popular culture dopamine is confused with pleasure, but dopamine is actually the hunger for different (more, less, or better) which can happen alongside pleasure or pain.[564] If anything, it might also be pain itself when it happens in a different brain area.[565]

Serotonin is satisfaction. It halts Dopamine release. That's why Serotonin re-uptake inhibitors make people feel longer periods of relief between feeling anxious.

Vasopressin is probably momentary pleasure (like).

Oxytocin is probably more intense, longer term, training pleasure (love).

Norepinephrine is probably the more intense, fixating negative tension that is very difficult to release. It is what most people would think of as full blown anxiety. It signals that a negative training event is happening (the event should be reviewed again later). More of the drug is produced while reviewing, so it feels like the negative event is happening again, and should be reviewed again. It is probably the negative analog of Oxytocin.

Epinephrine (Adrenaline) might be satisfaction for training anxiety, which would explain why injecting it when having a severe allergic reaction stops the allergic reaction.

Post Script: The Fourth Variation

Humans have generated a fourth motivational class, which is direct pleasure drug activation of the Limbic system (opioids, for example). If the trigger is taking a drug and the result is flushing with pleasure and relief, then pharmaceuticals become the selection factors directly.

The psychological path of story creation is the same. Narratives develop which explain the positive qualities of drug use, which assume the benefits can be gathered and increased while the negatives can be removed, minimized, or are reasonable. More inputs bring the topic of drugs to mind, which can then trigger craving that can only be satisfied with drug use. Over time, the observer starts managing the avoidance of pain rather than actual cycles of pleasure anymore.

It can help for really understanding Socials, Relationals, or Comfort-types to immerse in the simplicity of the pharmaceutical motivational algorithm. It is the same. An input happens, pleasure happens. Later, tension happens, focusing attention. While focused, stories explain why the hunger is a response to a "need." When the satisfaction condition is met, the observer is present and free again to consider other topics.

What's interesting about adding drug motivations is that it can take first place, where it was formerly non-existent. So you can more clearly see how stories change, and how formerly important parts of life stop being maintained because the drug-supporting narratives of the moment get all the attention. If someone instead got horny each day when they didn't before, or fearful, or concerned about the feelings of others, they'd go through the same shift in life experience. But it would be clearer that it's the observer who changed, not the external world. And they get a different life experience from pouring energy into a new area. But, underneath it all, it's coming from a different negative feeling creeping into each day.

Endnotes & References

The hope with quotes is that you hear them differently because you're thinking about the prodding tensions that caused people to think these things in these frameworks. Names are separated out so you don't get distracted by details about the speaker, especially gender, race, nationality, politics, religion, time period, etcetera. Hiding details of the speaker is also an exercise in C_1-last. Can you strip away the individual and hear the underlying psychology? Quotes got significant edits to gender neutralize, shorten, clarify, correct grammar, correct punctuation, remove brand names, reduce vulgarity, generalize, remove confounding tensions, clearly state implications, and remove distractions. Quotes are here to trigger the emotion being discussed, to help you generate clear conceptions of the mindsets people are in while talking about any topic, and to demonstrate how the topic of a statement gives less information than the framework it's being discussed in. The cited speaker is often more the inspiration for the quote than the speaker of the exact wording. Sometimes I couldn't find anything near what I was looking for, so I wrote out what the ideal quote for that topic would've been. This book is a lesson in psychology, so demonstrating the psychology was more important for each quote than anything else. What follows is a list of sources. Immense gratitude is felt toward every speaker included here. The graphic artists included are the ones who were kind and present enough to reply to a request out of the blue from a random stranger. Please find and follow any whose work you enjoyed. Let them know where you found them.

The origin of some quotes weren't able to be located, or numerous conflicting, inaccurate, and unverifiable sources were found which sometimes gave multiple options for wording. An attempt will be made to adjust citations if you can find better evidence of origin. The inclusion of quotes, comics, and images does not constitute an endorsement of the contents of this book by the speakers or authors. Images without direct citations were licensed through Shutterstock, Freepik, Flaticon, or PlaygroundAI, and sometimes heavily modified by the author. All comics and images are copyrighted by their creators and used here with permission.

1   Cover image by Lightspring of Canada
2   The page 1 brain pic: thanks to @nsit0108, freepik.com/author/nsit0108
3   The Limbic brain drawings on page 3 thanks to Jakub at decade3d.com
4   Mr. Lovenstein by J. L. Westover, www.mrlovenstein.com Instagram: @mrlovenstein, Facebook: MrLovenstein, Twitter: @MrLovenstein.
5   Instagram: @youngpoorandhappy , Twitter: @youngpoorhappy Reddit: /u/daveclampart
6   Rachel McCartney, Twitter: @RachelMComedy , Aug 8, 2019
7   Instagram: @steinbergdrawscartoons
8   Really unclear origin, the oldest I found was by "imasmallchild" in 2011
9   #1021. What if I want an upgrade before my contract's up?
10 Alfred Lord Tennyson, In Memoriam
11 #310, Instagram: @xkcd, Twitter: @xkcd
12 Kiersten White, The Chaos of Stars
13 Marilyn Monroe
14 #429. I want us to gerund, essentially.
15 The Police, Every Little Thing
16 Alysa Kenourgios
17 #908. I spend all my time in puddles. I miss the ocean.
18 Critical parts of this comic (frames 0 and 4) have been removed to direct focus to the psychological concept being discussed in the chapter. The actual story happening in the comic is much more nuanced, and given context by the missing frames and the rest of the series. It was super nice of Clay to let his work be butchered for science. More by Clay Jonathan is available at claycomix.com, Instagram: @claycomix, Twitter: @ClayComix
19 #1007. That's who I think of when we have sex.
20 Rupi Kaur, The Sun and Her Flowers
21 Titus Fortner
22 David Schnarch Ph.D., Normal Healthy Couples Have Sexual Desire Problems, May 13th, 2011, Psychology Today https://www.psychologytoday.com/blog/intimacy-and-desire/201105/normal-healthy-couples-have-sexual-desire-problems
23 Stacey "Stace Ace" 10/2/2017 http://www.bbc.com/news/magazine-41469511
24 Instagram: @jimbentonshots, Twitter: @JimBenton
25 John Green, Paper Towns
26 Mitch Hedberg https://twitter.com/m_hedberg/status/178607956080852992
27 Fredric Neuman M.D. Being Attractive is Attractive Enough, Jun 08, 2014, Psychology Today https://www.psychologytoday.com/us/blog/fighting-fear/201406/being-attractive-is-attractive-enough
28 #1157. I would never break your heart. Seven years bad luck!
29 Whitney Lewis
30 "The Real Thing," Ellen McCarthy, Iris Krasnow, "The Secret Lives of Wives." A researcher who interviewed hundreds of married women found the happiest 'never bought into' a 'dangerous fantasy', Shana Lebowitz, March 8,

2017, Business Insider www.businessinsider.com/marriage-and-relationship-advice-2017-3

31 Charles Bukowski

32 John Green, Sept 3, 2019, vlogbrothers, Death, Love, and John's Religion: The Big Questions Take Over Question Tuesday, youtu.be/lHPMOCsH0YM

33 www.Cartoonstock.com, Instagram: @teresaburnsparkhurst

34 Disputed Origin

35 #316.

36 Beau Taplin

37 Instagram: @invisiblebread, Twitter: @invisiblebread

38 Charles Bukowski

39 Allyson Frances on Twitter, 10/6/22, @evilallyfran

40 #793, Questions are now obsolete. You are welcome.

41 Sophia Loren

42 #1242. this, at least, is up to me.

43 Ava Holtzman, YouTube, Compliments – Original Song, Apr 10, 2017, https://youtu.be/rNAlETPlQGQ

44 Archie Gilzow

45 Larry Gasner

46 Elizabeth Gilbert, Eat, Pray, Love

47 Tommy Tenney

48 Rupi Kaur, The Sun and Her Flowers

49 #676. Now get out of the bushes before I call the cops.

50 Iris Murdoch

51 Disputed Origin

52 Cassandra Clare, City of Bones

53 Drax the Destroyer

54 Disputed origin

55 Becca Fitzpatrick

56 Glen Hinkle

57 Hank Green on Monogamy, Published on Jan 28, 2016, 4:30, https://youtu.be/8gDVwo1hA-U

58 #1000 – Part 10. I'm ashamed it took me so long to realize.

59 Ginger Rogers

60 I couldn't find this said, so here it is, said.

61 Taylor Jenkins Reid

62 #513. My doctor is getting tired of me.

63 The Real McCoy, @Boii_McCoy Oct 27, 2020 twitter.com/Boii_McCoy/status/1320985432054767616 The 𓂀eal McCöy

64 #1067. Four legs good. Eight legs bad.

65 Instagram: @lorynbrantz, Twitter: @LorynBrantz

66 Disputed Origin

67 Iris Murdoch

68 Disputed Origin

69 Sigmund Freud

70 therealgold55, https://www.reddit.com/r/Showerthoughts/ comments/j4js35/a_much_needed_pee_can_feel_better_than_the/
71 www.Cartoonstock.com
72 OneForTheAlbum at https://old.reddit.com/r/Showerthoughts/comments /ogytng/at_some_point_in_your_life_somebody_has/
73 Titus Fortner
74 Instagram: @invisiblebread, Twitter: @invisiblebread
75 Emily McDowell, Instagram: @emandfriends
76 Instagram: @cinimomocomics
77 Albert Camus, French Philosopher, 1913 - 1960
78 Instagram: @lorynbrantz, Twitter: @LorynBrantz
79 Pew Research Center, Rising Share of U.S. Adults Are Living Without a Spouse or Partner. 10/5/21. By Richard Fry and Kim Parker.
80 Alex Velluto, https://youtu.be/w2zl17VIzUs?t=1m52s
81 Shams Tabriz, @Boii_McCoy, Twitter and Instagram, Sept 28, 2022
82 www.Cartoonstock.com, Facebook: jonathan.r.hawkins.7
83 Aristotle
84 #204. Never in the same room as myself.
85 Harvey Specter
86 https://www.reddit.com/r/Showerthoughts/comments/9k0cqp
87 I couldn't find anyone who said this, so here it is said.
88 Martha Graham, http://jamesclear.com/quality-comparison
89 Instagram: @jimbentonshots, Twitter: @JimBenton
90 Kanye West, Stronger
91 Arthur Schopenhauer
92 George Harrison
93 #968. and get a haircut. A rebellious one.
94 Savannah Brown, everything's a DISASTER (catastrophic thinking) https://youtu.be/pdg9Fj-o-Y4?t=3m40s
95 www.Cartoonstock.com, Twitter: @Blisscartoons , Instagram: @blisscartoons
96 Adrian Rogers
97 Just A Peach, Jul 22, 2022, Magnum Opus, https://youtu.be/HH21JAVP1fE
98 #827. yippee ki yay, YHWH
99 Snoop Dogg
100 Nicholas Sparks, The Notebook
101 Mahatma Gandhi
102 Instagram: @steinbergdrawscartoons
103 Charles Darwin, The Descent of Man
104 #291, Instagram: @xkcd, Twitter: @xkcd
105 Disputed Origin
106 www.Cartoonstock.com
107 Ernest Hemingway
108 Charles Bukowski
109 #610, Instagram: @xkcd, Twitter: @xkcd
110 Dale Carnegie
111 William Shakespeare, As You Like It

112 Instagram: @jimbentonshots, Twitter: @JimBenton

113 Oscar Wilde, The Happy Prince and Other Stories

114 Albert Camus, French Philosopher, 1913 – 1960

115 Instagram: @berkeleymews, Twitter: @benzaehringer

116 Vernon Howard

117 Unknown, I could not find a good initial source for this quote.

118 #749. Have you tried walking it off?

119 Shawn Mendes

120 Unknown, I could not find a good initial source for this quote.

121 www.Cartoonstock.com, Instagram: @steinbergdrawscartoons

122 www.Cartoonstock.com, Twitter: @KaamranHafeez

123 Drew Allen Bully of Fashion, Dry Bar Comedy, Sept 9, 2019,
     https://youtu.be/UMbOeBFQFWw

124 Joyce Meyer

125 The Real McCoy, @Boii_McCoy

126 www.Cartoonstock.com, hmargulies.com

127 Mitch Hedberg

128 Will Rogers

129 www.Comicstock.com, Twitter & Instagram: @CrowdenSatz

130 Charles Bukowski

131 Disputed Origin

132 Unknown, I could not find a good initial source for this quote.

133 John Burroughs

134 Nietzsche, Thus Spoke Zarathustra

135 We're Not Wizards Tabletop Podcast @werenotwizards, Apr 1, 2019, Twitter

136 Grace Lichtenstein

137 Charles Bukowski

138 Louis CK

139 Father Strickland, 1863

140 Malcolm Forbes

141 Howard W Newton

142 Simon Sinek

143 Tahtahtahtia's Anthro Professor

144 Ice Cube

145 Disputed Origin

146 Arthur Schopenhauer, German Philosopher

147 Glen Hinkle

148 Buddha

149 Dalai Lama

150 Based on R. Buckminster Fuller

151 www.Cartoonstock.com, Twitter: @rosiebrookspics , Instagram:
     @rosiebrooksillustration

152 Ira Byock

153 The Constitution of the United States, July 4, 1776

154 Simon Sinek, You Can't Do It Alone, Jul 25, 2022,
     https://youtu.be/VcEeQze9_3k

155 Emma Lazarus, on the Statue of Liberty

156 Kyle Cease

157 Hank Green https://youtu.be/pkOAQ2oc6fY

158 Twitter: @ZachWeiner , Tumblr: smbc-comics.tumblr.com

159 Inside an International Tech-Support Scam How a computer hacker infiltrated a phone scam operation — exposing fraudsters and their schemes by Doug Shadel and Neil Wertheimer, AARP, April 1, 2021

160 Concept, creation, and photo by Zak Foster, Instagram: @zakfoster.quilts, July 4, 2022

161 Nikola Tesla

162 Anne Frank

163 John Lennon

164 www.Cartoonstock.com, Instagram: @teresaburnsparkhurst

165 George Carlin, Archive of American Television http://emmytvlegends.org/interviews/people/george-carlin

166 #859. The murder glass is half FULL … of murder?

167 Philip DeFranco 4:10 - Why Deleting Your YouTube Channel Might Be The Right Move - https://youtu.be/rFRrlCcOqQA

168 Louis CK, as part of his comedy routine in Hilarious

169 Instagram: @jimbentonshots, Twitter: @JimBenton

170 Ayn Rand's Private journal, May 9, 1934

171 Louis CK as part of a comedy routine about stealing scales from highschool.

172 Charles Mackay, 1841, Memoirs of Extraordinary Popular Delusions and the Madness of Crowds

173 Banksy

174 #197. An eyeball should never have sand on it, even one that big.

175 Instagram: @jimbentonshots, Twitter: @JimBenton

176 Charles Bukowski

177 #890, I've been disenfrenchfried.

178 Jon Stewart

179 Why The Weak Cling To Group Identities, Academy of Ideas, https://www.youtube.com/shorts/yD4fOYYWdp0

180 Thomas Sowell

181 Instagram: @invisiblebread, Twitter: @invisiblebread

182 Jack Handey

183 Ramana Maharshi

184 Carl Jung, The Symbolic Life

185 #283. A man who represents himself has a HERO for a client!

186 Instagram: @jimbentonshots, Twitter: @JimBenton

187 David Spangler

188 www.Cartoonstock.com

189 #178. twice at least.

190 #823. I'm so close. How can we make this more wrong?

191 John Green

192 Instagram: @steinbergdrawscartoons

193 Thomas Sowell

194 Zig Ziglar

195 Thomas Sowell

196 James W. Frick

197 Maxteabag, https://www.reddit.com/r/Showerthoughts/comments/jm3xca/

198 #173. filling Barbie's Corvette with manure.

199 Ralph Smart, Aug 18, 2020, How To Never Get Angry Or Bothered By People, https://youtu.be/Q6DsHTYNljU

200 Sam Hyde, Sam Hyde - Advice for social rxtards & Sam's deaf people theory [PGL_ep4], Feb 5, 2021, https://youtu.be/QEUTSEBApkY

201 Rob Siltanen

202 #489. I've been waiting.

203 Instagram: @remindersforselflove , 9/6/2022

204 Ayn Rand, The Fountainhead, Dean and Roark

205 Glen Hinkle

206 Name withheld by request

207 Glen Hinkle

208 #564. Any asshole can tell the truth.

209 Laurel K. Hamilton

210 Disputed Origin

211 Robert Greene

212 Jane Fonda

213 Voltaire

214 www.Cartoonstock.com Twitter: @thePatByrnes , Instagram: @thepatbyrnes

215 Charles Bukowski

216 Richard Branson

217 Dave Willis

218 Charles Bukowski, who died in 1994.

219 #734. I hope they don't read my blog.

220 People Magazine, May 8, 2020, by KC Baker, https://people.com/crime/ark-woman-befriended-moms-killer-out-of-spiritual-obligation-and-then-he-murdered-her/

221 Bell Hooks

222 Ken Rideout, Rich Roll Podcast 701, YouTube Shorts

223 Instagram: @lorynbrantz, Twitter: @LorynBrantz

224 Charles Bukowski

225 John Green, The Fault in Our Stars

226 Hagar the Horrible

227 www.Cartoonstock.com, Instagram: @steinbergdrawscartoons

228 Baruch Spinoza, Dutch Philosopher, 1632-1677

229 Instagram: @cinimomocomics

230 John Green, Reflections: Day 70 | 100 Days, Mar 12, 2017 https://nerdfighteria.info/v/CcylG7ZuQb8/

231 Instagram: @cinimomocomics

232 November 29, 2018, https://www.nsc.org/in-the-newsroom/nsc-statement-on-new-cdc-data-showing-a-rise-in-accidental-death

233 www.Cartoonstock.com

234 Instagram: @youngpoorandhappy , Twitter: @youngpoorandhappy
235 Dawn Kutz
236 Instagram: @jimbentonshots, Twitter: @JimBenton
237 Instagram: @joetatochips, joetatochips.com
238 Ozzy Man Reviews and TheGniffen, https://youtu.be/MxexAd0k44U , Ozzy Man Reviews: When Animals Fight Back #8, Apr 11, 2021
239 Maya Angelou
240 Stephen Szczerba
241 Instagram: @invisiblebread, Twitter: @invisiblebread
242 Bill Burr, https://youtu.be/g-E0yHWGH5g?t=112 A sound clip on the Internet that sounded like it was probably from his podcast, Bill's Monday Morning Podcast.
243 Frank Furedi, How Fear Works: Culture of Fear in the Twenty-First Century
244 Academy of Ideas, Fear Psychosis and the Cult of Safety - Why are People so Afraid?
245 Frank Furedi, How Fear Works: Culture of Fear in the Twenty-First Century
246 Mark Twain
247 Arthur Schopenhauer, German Philosopher
248 Instagram: @berkeleymews, Twitter: @benzaehringer
249 Renee Jain
250 Instagram: @jimbentonshots, Twitter: @JimBenton
251 Chibird by Jacqueline Chen, Chibird.com, Instagram: @chibirdart, Twitter: @chibirdart, Facebook: @ChibirdArt
252 Bob Marley
253 Mark Hyman
254 John Holmes
255 www.Cartoonstock.com
256 Millard Fuller
257 Instagram: @cinimomocomics
258 Disputed Origin
259 C.S. Lewis, The Four Loves
260 Disputed Origin
261 www.Cartoonstock.com
262 I couldn't find a clear citation. The best I could find is goodtherapy.org.
263 Queen Latifah
264 Kilroy J. Oldster, Dead Toad Scrolls
265 Mark Twain
266 #894. On the toilet.
267 Charles Bukowski
268 #421. My last words will be, "Yeah, I had that coming."
269 Jiddu Krishnamurti
270 Carl Jung, The Symbolic Life
271 Disputed Origin
272 Jeremy Goldberg
273 Instagram: @berkeleymews, Twitter: @benzaehringer

274 Instagram: @moosekleenex . Twitter: @Moosekleenex ,
moosekleenex.etsy.com
275 Disputed Origin, maybe Gang Capati on Twitter @gangbadoy, Sept 30, 2015
276 Will Rogers
277 Instagram: @invisiblebread, Twitter: @invisiblebread
278 Mike Iamele, Why Feeling Stagnant May Just Be a Sign of Success, Oct 22,
2014, http://mikeiamele.com/feeling-stagnant-may-just-sign-success/
279 Bill Burr
280 Charles Bukowski
281 #891. How can anything be worth anything if it lasts forever?
282 Disputed Origin
283 #938. Instead of slowing down, I just shine brighter.
284 Mae West
285 Disputed Origin
286 #762. Quit your job. Buy a big knife. Do something!
287 Evan Dickinson, The National, Canadian Broadcasting Company, Wingsuit
Flyer Graham Dickinson Dies, Feb 20, 2017 https://youtu.be/cq3O77OkafE
288 Anthon St. Maarten
289 www.Cartoonstock.com
290 I couldn't find this said, so here it is, said.
291 Louis CK, Live at the Comedy Store (2015)
292 John Green https://youtu.be/MsyQ3na4HNA My Hollywood Star, Brexit
Pears, and Hank's Book: It's QUESTION TUESDAY Vlogbrothers, 1/16/18
293 Instagram: @berkeleymews, Twitter: @benzaehringer
294 Kurt Vonnegut
295 www.Cartoonstock.com Twitter: @thePatByrnes , Instagram: @thepatbyrnes
296 Men Chadvidorak
297 xkcd #1768, by Randall Munroe, xkcd.com
298 Lisa Janes, Oct 25, 2019 Facebook
299 #695. If you can't stand the heat, turn the A/C on.
300 Jose Marti, Cuban Poet and Hero 1853 – 1895
301 I'm Broke and Mostly Friendless, and I've Wasted My Whole Life, An
anonymous writer to Heather Havrilesky, New York Magazine, The Cut, Ask
Polly, Nov 28, 2018
302 Instagram: @steinbergdrawscartoons
303 Einstein, Imperial Hotel in Tokyo in 1922
304 Disputed Origin
305 Craig Benzine, Wheezy Waiter, https://youtu.be/sUsI6W7-d28?t=181
306 #644. Birds gotta fly. Fish gotta swim.
307 Rich Roll Podcast - NEVER QUIT BEFORE THE MIRACLE, The Story of
Anvil, Sep 28, 2022, https://youtu.be/IxalkkDxq4c
308 Spencer Claeys, All you need is $50 and an internet connection,
https://youtube.com/shorts/wS_-QMxtXUg
309 Variations of this appear with no source all over the Internet. I got it on Twitter
from We3 , @hello_we3 , 9/29/22
310 Mel Robbins, Be Better, https://youtube.com/shorts/wxiNCZLJVSs 9/26/22

311 Pleasant-Fluff.com, Instagram: @littleniddles , Twitter: @LittleNiddles

312 Henry David Thoreau

313 Charles Bukowski

314 #1224. Potential is just a promise you break to yourself.

315 Friedrich Nietzsche

316 #1239. And you'll feel bad because you could've.

317 Disputed Origin

318 Arthur Schopenhauer

319 Byron Katie

320 JP Sears, How to Be More Afraid!, July 28, 2020, https://youtu.be/lcX9HBG4L34

321 Instagram: @lorynbrantz, Twitter: @LorynBrantz

322 Dawn Kutz

323 Mahatma Gandhi

324 Ernesto Sirolli

325 #1085. I just smile and say, "Compared to what?"

326 Nicole Krauss, The History of Love

327 Instagram: @jimbentonshots, Twitter: @JimBenton

328 Instagram: @lorynbrantz, Twitter: @LorynBrantz

329 Allison Schumacher

330 Glen Hinkle

331 Jeff & Pam, 14389, Carnival Mardi Gras, September 12th, 2022

332 #980. And the things you are wearing right now.

333 Amit Kalantri

334 Ernest Hemingway

335 #616. I'll give you a hint. Close your eyes...

336 CG Kid, My Crystal Meth Addiction Experience | From Beginning to End, Jul 16, 2019, https://youtu.be/f0HtlAlmdxk

337 Disputed Origin

338 https://www.reddit.com/r/GetMotivated/comments/7ay7df/ text_remember_that_guy_that_gave_up_neither_does/

339 www.Cartoonstock.com, Twitter: @Blisscartoons, Instagram: @blisscartoons

340 Marceline Desbordes-Valmore

341 Epicurus, Sovereign Maxims

342 Instagram: @joetatochips, joetatochips.com

343 Annie Daly, Do You Have Friend Guilt?, Shape Magazine, https://www.shape.com/lifestyle/mind-and-body/do-you-have-friend-guilt

344 Lindsay Hausch, When Social Anxiety Makes You a 'People-Pleaser', November 1, 2017, The Mighty, https://themighty.com/2017/11/social-anxiety-people-pleasing/

345 Robert A. Heinlein, Stranger in a Strange Land

346 www.Cartoonstock.com, Twitter: @Blisscartoons , Instagram: @blisscartoons

347 Scott Galloway. No Mercy / No Malice, May 10, 2019

348 www.Cartoonstock.com, Twitter: @Banxcartoons , Instagram: @banxcartoons

349 Henri Nouwen, Out of Solitude: Three Meditations on the Christian Life

350 Girl Bonding, Women's Health, September 2012

351 Disputed Origin

352 Instagram: @steinbergdrawscartoons

353 Gavin DeBecker

354 https://www.reddit.com/r/AskReddit/comments/5rxft2/
what_quotes_had_the_most_profound_impact_on_your/ddb8jmh/

355 Arthur Schopenhauer, German Philosopher

356 Aristotle

357 Disputed Origin

358 Falkonjenova, comment on https://www.youtube.com/watch?
v=c0KRaFqjYkQ

359 #242. I wish I were close with my mother.

360 Kurt Vonnegut, Cat's Cradle

361 Disputed Origin

362 #1123. Your daytime friends are no help in the dark.

363 Disputed Origin

364 Disputed Origin

365 Instagram: @jimbentonshots, Twitter: @JimBenton

366 I couldn't find anyone who said this quote, so here it is, said.

367 #1191. cross stitch class goes off the rails once again.

368 www.Cartoonstock.com, Twitter: @Blisscartoons, Instagram: @blisscartoons

369 John Green, The Fault in Our Stars

370 Instagram: @jimbentonshots, Twitter: @JimBenton

371 Dr Daniel Marston, Why You Don't Need Friends, Psychology Today, 5/8/19

372 #347. _____

373 Disputed Origin

374 Instagram: @joetatochips, joetatochips.com

375 Scott Galloway No Mercy No Malice February 21, 2020

376 #438. … officer

377 Brandi Snyder

378 Steve Irwin

379 Horacio Jones

380 Susan Jeffers

381 Amanda Palmer

382 Instagram: @moosekleenex, Twitter: @Moosekleenex,
moosekleenex.etsy.com

383 Katie Kent, 4 Things I Learned About Myself This Year as Someone With
Borderline Personality Disorder, December 13, 2017
https://themighty.com/2017/12/learn-about-myself-borderline-personality-
disorder-bpd/

384 Aristotle

385 #591. Nobody ever wants to do the friends part with me.

386 Shams Tabriz, @Boii_McCoy, 9/1/22, instagram.com/reel/Ch7jiSSDzfX

387 #621. I am glad we are friends.

388 Winnie the Pooh

389 Einzelganger, The Social Minimalist | Can we be Happy without Friends?,
Nov 18, 2021 https://youtu.be/c0KRaFqjYkQ

390 Linda Grayson

391 Instagram: @berkeleymews, Twitter: @benzaehringer

392 Mark Twain

393 Instagram: @jimbentonshots, Twitter: @JimBenton

394 Instagram: @joetatochips, joetatochips.com

395 @Reaghanhunt

396 J.J. Peterson, How I Overcame The Fear of Running Out of Money, February 3, 2016, Storyline Blog http://storylineblog.com/2016/02/03/running-out-of-money/

397 Paul Gasner

398 Unknown, I could not find a good initial source for this quote.

399 Instagram: @cinimomocomics

400 https://www.reddit.com/r/Showerthoughts/comments/7gemj0/ if_a_normal_guy_feels_like_a_million_bucks_thats/

401 Sarah Millican, Sarah Millican On Women's Body Sizes | Universal Comedy, Jul 26, 2020, https://youtu.be/kS_ONRxWws4

402 Instagram: @jimbentonshots, Twitter: @JimBenton

403 Scott Dodds @itsBOMBADIER

404 Instagram: @jimbentonshots, Twitter: @JimBenton

405 Warren Buffett

406 Tim Urban, Wait But Why, Mailbag #1, May 6, 2016, https://waitbutwhy.com/2016/05/mailbag-1.html? mc_cid=bbc2113b94&mc_eid=05053fd9f0

407 Instagram: @cinimomocomics

408 Devon Stack, https://youtu.be/N-GjgQZ2vP4?t=1271, Nobody Will Remember Carl, Black Pilled

409 Tyler Durden, Fight Club

410 Neel Burton, Aeon, 2 Aug 2019

411 #154. Maybe tomorrow I'll want to settle down.

412 Disputed Origin

413 www.Cartoonstock.com

414 Disputed Origin

415 Oscar Wilde

416 Instagram: @joetatochips, joetatochips.com

417 George Bernard Shaw

418 #1148. The princess and the pea, a story for peasant children.

419 Glen Hinkle

420 www.Cartoonstock.com

421 Scott Galloway, No Mercy No Malice 9/1/17 https://www.l2inc.com/daily-insights/no-mercy-no-malice/not-so-evil-stepmother

422 Andrew Bacevich

423 Albert Einstein

424 Instagram: @jimbentonshots, Twitter: @JimBenton

425 Mokokoma Mokhonoana

426 Disputed Origin, maybe Picturequotes.com

427 Disputed Origin

428 Nietzsche

429 @Boii_McCoy Jan 27,2021

430 Instagram: @cinimomocomics

431 John Green, Reflections: Day 70 | 100 Days, Mar 12, 2017
https://nerdfighteria.info/v/CcylG7ZuQb8/

432 Joshua Becker, twitter: @joshua_becker, Becoming Minimalist,
https://www.becomingminimalist.com/we-dont-buy-things-with-money-we-
buy-them-with-hours-from-our-life/

433 Jay Shetty, Weekly Wisdom SE.2 Ep.5 https://youtu.be/huHvdFgf9Bc?t=1m2s

434 www.Cartoonstock.com

435 Zig Ziglar

436 www.Cartoonstock.com, Instagram: @teresaburnsparkhurst

437 Mary Midgley, Wickedness, 1984

438 www.Cartoonstock.com, Twitter: @BentSchwartz , Instagram: @bentschwartz

439 Disputed Origin

440 www.Cartoonstock.com, Twitter: @BillWhitehead8

441 Emerald, The Diamond Net, Traps of Seeking Spiritual Enlightenment -
Seeking, 9/1/2018, https://youtu.be/-Tmcm5Whafs

442 #257. No jury will convict me.

443 Glen Hinkle

444 Bic Flame & Joeyy, Sam Hyde - Advice for social rxtards & Sam's deaf
people theory [PGL_ep4], Feb 5, 2021, Episode 4 of Perfect Guy Life,
https://youtu.be/QEUTSEBApkY

445 #916. What use beauty, sans ugmos?

446 Allison Schumacher

447 Marcus Aurelius, Meditations

448 www.Cartoonstock.com, Twitter:@veleycartoons, Instagram:@bradfordveley

449 Kurt Cobain

450 Catherine Baab-Muguira, How a $500 Monthly Allowance Saved Our
Marriage, March 07, 2018 https://slate.com/human-interest/2018/03/how-a-
usd500-monthly-allowance-saved-our-marriage.html

451 Instagram: @joetatochips, joetatochips.com

452 OneRepublic, Counting Stars

453 Benjamin Franklin

454 #739. I guess you could watch the episode where they get mugged.

455 Jac Vanek, @jacvanek, June 3rd, 2015

456 Manuel Lisa, Missouri Trapper

457 Sam Hyde, Get A Skill 2 (Find A Mentor), Aug 23, 2022,
https://youtu.be/vFfzPo_mKZ4

458 Instagram: @steinbergdrawscartoons

459 Disputed Origin

460 David Ljung Madison Stellar

461 Wayne Elise, How to Deal with Approach Anxiety, Apr 11, 2008, Psychology
Today https://www.psychologytoday.com/us/blog/art-charisma/200804/how-
deal-approach-anxiety

462 Andrea Gibson, I Do

463 Will Smith

464 Ines Reis, https://hitrecord.org/records/2418163

465 Instagram: @invisiblebread, Twitter: @invisiblebread

466 Shams Tabriz, @Boii_McCoy

467 Gail Collins & Gloria Steinem, This Is What 80 Looks Like, NYTimes, 3/22/14

468 Wayne Elise, How to Deal with Approach Anxiety, Apr 11, 2008, Psychology Today https://www.psychologytoday.com/us/blog/art-charisma/200804/how-deal-approach-anxiety

469 Rick and Bird Person, Rick & Morty, S05E08

470 Instagram: @berkeleymews, Twitter: @benzaehringer

471 Friedrich Nietzsche, Twilight of the Idols

472 Jim Carrey

473 TechnicallyRon

474 dayton @_dayytonn

475 Andy Bernard

476 Instagram: @invisiblebread, Twitter: @invisiblebread

477 Sprucejuce1 - https://www.reddit.com/r/Showerthoughts/comments/7dgq9n/the_fear_of_being_alone_in_the_dark_is_actually/

478 John Oliver, Vaccines: Last Week Tonight with John Oliver, June 25th, 2017

479 sl8644 https://www.reddit.com/r/unpopularopinion/comments/j5qo8s/butterflies_are_scary_and_ugly/

480 Instagram: @invisiblebread, Twitter: @invisiblebread

481 Hazzah02 https://www.reddit.com/r/Showerthoughts/comments/jqdi29

482 Scott Galloway, No Mercy / No Malice, 10/18/19

483 www.Cartoonstock.com, Instagram: @dollyonpaper

484 Instagram: @okbluecomics , Twitter: @Okbluecomics

485 Instagram: @jimbentonshots, Twitter: @JimBenton

486 George Bernard Shaw

487 Howard Zinn

488 Disputed Origin

489 Theodor W. Adorno

490 Doe Zantamata

491 Thiruvalluvar

492 Bob Costas

493 Dwight D. Eisenhower

494 Bertrand Russel

495 Ozolinsjanis.com, Instagram: @jaozolins

496 Dale Carnegie

497 Edmund Burke

498 Pete Lee, May 6, 2017, The Tonight Show, https://youtu.be/buKU7OhbMMU

499 Martin Luther King, Jr

500 Brian Solis, Dec 2, 2014, https://www.briansolis.com/2014/12/community-much-belonging-something-something-together-makes-belonging-matter/

501 Helen Keller

502 Instagram: @invisiblebread, Twitter: @invisiblebread

503 https://youtu.be/-tEBDWZtVJU Supersize v Superskinny, Boogie-Vice

504 Instagram: @cinimomocomics
505 Mitch Hedberg
506 Instagram: @steinbergdrawscartoons
507 Disputed Origin
508 Hotslice25 https://www.reddit.com/r/unpopularopinion/comments/jvyglr
509 www.Cartoonstock.com
510 Barney, twitter: @notthedinosaur, May 10, 2021 4:05p
511 Linus Torvalds
512 #1195. Hey! Wood! We should BUILD something.
513 Disputed Origin
514 Instagram: @okbluecomics, Twitter: @Okbluecomics
515 https://en.wikipedia.org/wiki/
    Evolutionary_mismatch#Giant_Jewel_Beetle_and_Beer_Bottles
516 www.Cartoonstock.com, Instagram: @samgrosscartoons
517 Disputed Origin
518 Disputed Origin
519 #1087. Wicked dastardly.
520 Michelle Wolf, Nice Lady, 2017
521 www.Cartoonstock.com, Instagram: @samgrosscartoons
522 Tony Hsieh
523 www.Cartoonstock.com
524 www.Cartoonstock.com, Instagram: @emessodoodles
525 Ozolinsjanis.com, Instagram: @jaozolins
526 Arthur Schopenhauer
527 #1166. But, no, they always trust me to be someone I don't even want to be.
528 Adjustment based on Henry David Thoreau
529 Maya Angelou
530 Instagram: @noteshort.co
531 #731. I don't see how my excuse can be your problem.
532 Bryan Johnson, IG: @bryanjohnson_ instagram.com/reel/CrVzshGtczA/
533 www.Cartoonstock.com, Instagram: @sofiawarrenart
534 Daniel Dennett
535 Friedrich Nitzsche
536 www.CartoonStock.com
537 Iris Murdoch
538 Dave Tarnowski, Instagram: @disappointingaffirmations, Apr 10, 2023
539 Mark Twain
540 #567. Well, he won't forget getting kneecapped.
541 Jim Elliot
542 Instagram: @steinbergdrawscartoons
543 Charles Bukowski
544 Charles Bukowski
545 Manifest S01E03 18:07
546 #898. Or if you were rich, or whatever.
547 50 Cent on the best advice he ever received | Robert Greene, Sept 3, 2022
    https://youtube.com/shorts/aWix6zellz8

548 Instagram: @chibirdart, Twitter: @chibirdart
549 Unknown, I could not find a good initial source for this quote.
550 Elizabeth Gilbert
551 Cory Muscara
552 I couldn't find this said, so here it is, said.
553 Cory Muscara
554 I couldn't find this said, so here it is, said.
555 Hippocrates, 460BC - 370BC
556 Instagram: @noteshort.co
557 Instagram: @cozdeamdraws
558 Alan Watts
559 Pablo Picasso
560 Instagram: @CryptoSeneca
561 Duncan Trussell
562 Albert Einstein
563 Mark Twain
564 Pleasure and pain: Study shows brain's pleasure chemical is involved in response to pain too, University of Michigan Health System, October 19, 2006, https://news.umich.edu/pleasure-and-pain-study-shows-brains-q-pleasure-chemicalq-is-involved-in-response-to-pain-too/
565 Variations in the Human Pain Stress Experience Mediated by Ventral and Dorsal Basal Ganglia Dopamine Activity, The Journal of Neuroscience, October 18, 2006 • 26(42):10789–10795, David J. Scott, Mary M. Heitzeg, Robert A. Koeppe, Christian S. Stohler, and Jon-Kar Zubieta

Hey Siri, Alexa, Okay Google – Set an alarm for one year from now to re-read the first few sentences of The Next Three Traits. It'll be a different book then.

If you spotted errors, please email them to glennenin@gmail.com.

If you got anything from this book and want to be my best friend, please consider leaving a review somewhere online.

"There is nothing to writing.
All you do is sit down at a typewriter and bleed."
– Ernest Hemingway

"This is not a book to be tossed lightly aside.
It should be thrown with great force."
– Dorothy Parker